MILTON L. RAKOVE

Don't Make No Waves

An Insider's Analysis of the Daley Machine

Don't Back No Losers

Indiana University Press   Bloomington

Manufactured in the United States of America

Library of Congress Cataloging in Publication Data

Rakove, Milton L.
    Don't make no waves—don't back no losers.

    Bibliography
    1. Chicago-Politics and government—1951– 2. Daley, Richard J., 1902– I. Title.

F548.52.R34   320.9′773′1104   75-1939
ISBN 0-253-11725-9   5 6 7 85 84 83 82 81

For SHIRLEY, *who suggested, encouraged, persuaded, reasoned, rationalized, supported, criticized, argued, fought, typed, retyped, edited, hoped, believed, prayed, doubted, despaired, triumphed, and rejoiced. This is her book, too.*

Contents

PREFACE   ix

INTRODUCTION   1

1. Dick Daley's Town   21
   The City
   The People
   The Role of the Irish

2. The Mayor: The Big Precinct Captain
   in the Sky   43
   Daley the Man
   Daley the Politician
   Daley the Mayor

3. Daley's Politburo   90
   Structure and Dynamics
   Picking the Ticket
   Dealing with Dissidents and Troublemakers

4. The Ward Organizations   106
   The Role of the Committeeman
   The Patronage System
   Working the Precinct
   The Rewards of Politics

5. The Machine and the Democratic Party   132
   The Machine and the Suburban Democrats
   The Machine and the State Democratic Party
   The Machine and the National Democratic Party

6. The Machine and the Political Opposition   163
   The Loyal Opposition: The Republicans in Chicago
   The Independents

7. Government and the Machine   198
   Dealing with Washington
   Dealing with Springfield
   The City Government and the Machine

8. Whither the Machine?   233
   The Machine and the Suburbs
   The Machine and the Blacks
   The Future of the Machine

   BIBLIOGRAPHY   285

   INDEX   290

Preface

❧

The purpose of this book is to describe, dissect, and analyze the dynamics, goals, strategies, behavior patterns, and underlying philosophy of the Daley political machine in the city of Chicago. The book was undertaken in the belief that an analysis of the Chicago machine can contribute to an understanding of the future course of urban politics in America.

I began the research on this book ten years ago. Trained at the University of Chicago under Hans Morgenthau and Leo Strauss, and interested for a number of years primarily in the dynamics of urban politics, I came to realize after years of teaching, studying, and thinking that it is difficult, if not impossible, to understand the nature of urban politics without immersing oneself in political life.

Aware of the opportunities for study and analysis available in Chicago with its political machine, I spent a number of years as a participant-observer of politics as it is practiced in Chicago. I have been an advisor, speechwriter, and campaign strategist for candidates for office ranging from ward committeeman to governor; worked as a precinct captain in a ward organization; attended ward organization meetings and political rallies regularly; marched in the St. Patrick's Day Parade carrying a Daley banner and shouting "We want Daley!" as the ward organization passed by the reviewing stand on which the mayor stood; helped plan campaigns in smoke-filled rooms; been offered the compensations due me as a member in good standing of the organization; and finally ran for public office on the county ticket, and experienced the frustrations and rewards of a candidate for local office in Cook County.

Calling on those experiences, this book is an attempt to describe a functioning political system and to analyze the dynamics of that system. The research method employed was to participate, observe, and cogitate upon the results of that participation and observation. No questionnaires were sent out and collated, no formal interviews were conducted, no mathematical formulas employed, no data bank collected, and no computer programmed. This is not a scientific treatise on the nature of politics and political behavior, not because scientific treatises have no place in understanding some phenomena and actions, but rather because I believe such an approach is of little value in understanding political motivation and political behavior. I agree with most professional politicians that politics is not a science but, rather, an art, that political behavior does not lend itself to analysis by scientific methods, and that the attempt to measure the irrational processes of politics by rational techniques is generally irrelevant to understanding those processes.

I was struck, from the beginning, by the paucity of scholarly research on the contemporary Chicago machine, except for some work by Edward C. Banfield, James Q. Wilson, Martin Meyerson, and a few others. After canvassing the literature in the field, I realized that it was almost thirty-five years since Harold Gosnell had done his study of the then existing Chicago machine, *Machine Politics: Chicago Model*, and that no serious scholar had done an in-depth analysis of the contemporary Chicago machine built by Mayor Richard J. Daley.

It was clear, from the beginning, that participation-observation offered the best means to pursue the research for this book. It was also evident that insights and information could be gained from active members of the machine only after long and mutually beneficial relationships had been established. To establish those relationships I had to work in the machine as an active participant as well as an interested observer. I found the experience both challenging and rewarding. Working a precinct was worth more than a score of formal interviews with suspicious precinct captains. Evenings in Alderman Vito Marzullo's ward headquarters were more useful than dozens of questionnaires sent to unresponsive committeemen. One stint on the campaign trail as a candidate for public office provided more insights than would a half-dozen models of a campaign structure. Days and nights spent in smoke-filled rooms while planning strategy for campaigns laid bare the realities of political behavior and the stakes of the contest. Informal luncheon meetings in the Gavel Room, Toffenetti's, and the Bismarck Inn and the Walnut Room of the Bismarck hotel were invaluable and enlightening.

Because much of the information and insights in the book have been gathered through an unstructured, informal process, I cannot document, by formal citation, the sources of information. I can only assure the reader that all quotations are reasonably accurate, that events described have occurred, and that hypotheses and interpretations of that information and those events were arrived at after long and careful thought and analysis. Many other quotations and background material, however, are drawn from the books, articles, and newspapers cited in the bibliography.

I have tried my utmost to maintain an objective, analytical frame of reference in dealing with the Chicago machine, its members, and its policies. I have made a conscious effort to paint a picture of politics in Chicago as it is, leaving it to others to describe it as it ought to be. I make no value judgments on the morality or immorality of the actions of the machine as an entity, or its members as individuals. Nor do I attempt to measure its successes or failures by evaluating the quality of the governmental process in Chicago and Cook County, or the public policies the machine has pursued in the city and county. This is not to say that both areas of political activity are not legitimate subjects for research and analysis. They are. But those matters are not dealt with in this book, and, indeed, could be the subjects of other books.

Many people have contributed to this book, some unknowingly and others consciously. I am deeply indebted to a number of machine professional politicians who have given me information, insights, guidance, explanation, and, occasionally, encouragement. Unfortunately, I can name none of them here. Without exception, when asked if they would like to be mentioned, they declined, with thanks, preferring to make no waves, and opting for taking no chances and backing no possible losers.

Four of my colleagues read earlier versions of the manuscript and offered criticisms and suggestions for improving the writing or the line of argument. I want to express my appreciation to Professors Melvin Holli, David Leege, and John Gardiner of the University of Illinois at Chicago Circle, and Joseph Small, S.J., of Loyola University, for their help.

Two members of the staff of the Department of Political Science at the University of Illinois at Chicago Circle, Mrs. Anita Worthington and Ms. Beatrice Villar, were invaluable to me in seeing the manuscript through the typing and retyping during its preparation. The field research of a number of students in my urban politics courses contributed to the manuscript. Two students in particular, Ms. Mary Spellman and Mr. Robert

Whitebloom, offered valuable assistance and suggestions during the preparation of the book.

To Mr. John Gallman, Editorial Director of Indiana University Press, I owe my thanks for his enthusiasm, incisive criticism, and help in bringing the book to press. My readers can be grateful, as I am, to Ms. Karen S. Craig for her careful and critical editing of the manuscript for publication.

Four members of my family contributed to the final version of this book. My son Jack and my daughter-in-law Helen read the first draft of the manuscript with critical historians' eyes. My daughter Roberta's youthful but pragmatic insights and comments on the Chicago political scene she knows so well were a valuable addition to the book. Finally, I have tried to express my gratitude to my wife in the dedicatory page. But there is no way to adequately acknowledge her role in the completion of this book. Suffice it to say that without her help this book would never have been conceived or completed.

Don't Make No Waves

An Insider's Analysis of the Daley Machine

Don't Back No Losers

Introduction

The Democratic machine in Chicago is the last of the great big-city machines in the history of modern American politics. Although contemporary observers refer to it as the Daley machine, the machine preceded Daley, and, while it has prospered most under Daley, it will almost certainly survive Daley. The machine has had an unbroken record of rule over the city of Chicago and Cook County for forty years, and while it has occasionally suffered reverses, it has always demonstrated an ability to recoup its losses and retain its power. While other machines in other great cities of this nation have deteriorated, reformed, or disappeared, the Chicago machine has neither deteriorated, nor significantly reformed, and it has certainly not disappeared.

How has this machine survived and prospered in the face of the decline of such machines in almost all other major American cities? How has it survived the great changes which have taken place in contemporary American urban society? How has it dealt with ethnic hostilities, racial tensions, economic crises, and massive population migrations and changes? How has it fought off all attempts to reform the city and the machine? What does the word "politics" mean, not in esoteric theory, or in contrived models of political systems, or in statistical compendiums of political behavior and motivation, or in philosophical treatises of the ideal *polis*, or in make-believe political games, but rather in the real world of practical politics and practical men who make their livings and seek fame and fortune in that real world? How do they deal with their constituents and each other? What rewards do they seek? What do they think of the obligations of the governors toward the governed, of the rights of the governed, of the role of government in society, and of the purpose of society itself?

If one would understand politics, one could find no better place to study it than in the big cities of America. For here, at this level, the real politics in contemporary American society takes place, the bones of political conflict are laid bare, the tensions that exacerbate American society are exposed, the aspirations and desires of contending groups in the body politic are made meaningful, and the time-tested techniques of dealing with the internal tensions and conflicts and the external relationships of a body politic can be best examined and studied.

For these purposes, the city of Chicago provides a classic laboratory. The city has undergone explosive growth, massive industrial development, economic crises, ethnic immigration, massive black and Latin migration into the city, substantial white exodus from the city, political corruption, labor strife, ethnic and racial conflict, blight, pollution, exploitation of natural resources, and every other ill which has plagued American cities in the twentieth century. In such a milieu, the student can come to grips with the reality of political life and political behavior.

With the overpowering growth of the bureaucracy and the decline of the political branch of American government, the Congress, American national politics has become government by an entrenched bureaucracy which is beyond the control of the political process. Since the functions of national government have become almost completely administrative, we have little national politics and a plethora of national administration. The opposite is true, however, at the local levels of government, especially in the major cities. Despite the theoretical assumptions propounded by well-meaning reformers that the functions of local government are essentially administrative and that there is no need for politics at that level, the fact of life in contemporary American society is that it is precisely at that level that the political questions manifest themselves. If politics is, as Harold Lasswell once described it, the process of who gets what, when, where and how, the answer to that question is still being fought out in the big cities of America. For, despite the oft-repeated cliché that local governments need only pick up garbage, provide police and fire protection, clean streets, and maintain schools, the service functions of big-city governments in this country are subordinated to and dominated by political conflict between blacks, Latins, and whites; the poor and the lower middle class; Catholics, Jews, and Protestants; and the other disparate elements that make up American big cities today.

The task of political leadership in our cities today is the control, amelioration, and resolution of those burgeoning conflicts. Should government aid be given to parochial schools? Should public housing in big cities be built on available vacant land in all neighborhoods, or should such projects be placed in the black ghettos? Should public schools be centrally administered or locally controlled by neighborhood groups? Should expressways be built to enable suburbanites to get to the city, or should the funds be used to provide mass public transit for unemployed blacks so that they can get to the suburban areas where the new jobs are being created? Should public funds for recreation, job training, and welfare be funneled through City Hall or through community organizations? Who should control health care in the city? These and numerous other questions cannot be answered by local government bureaucrats. They must be fought out initially in the political arena by those groups in our cities most interested and involved in them, and political solutions must be worked out by those groups before the problems can be turned over to government bureaucrats for implementation.

If the purpose of politics is to provide, not just a battleground for the confrontation of contending forces on such questions, but also a process for dealing with them, then the city of Chicago also provides a classic laboratory and a political system which could serve as a pragmatic model of successful politics in an American city. For whatever criticisms have been leveled at the Chicago machine, even by its most severe critics, the durability of the machine, its efficiency, and its ability to survive and prosper, despite the urban crisis, cannot be challenged.

One could describe the Chicago machine as a complex organism proceeding in simplistic fashion toward preordained goals using time-tested, traditional techniques. The research design of this book is first to dissect the component parts of the organism, second to describe the techniques used by that organism, and third to evaluate the efficacy of the goals pursued by that organism.

As an organism, the Chicago machine is a hydra-headed monster. It encompasses elements of every major political, economic, racial, ethnic, religious, governmental, and paramilitary power group within the city. It recognizes the reality of all forms of power—social, economic, political, and military, and it understands the need to subordinate all other forms of power to the political. It operates on two levels—internal dynamics and external relationships. It is cognizant of the pitfalls of politics, and of the inadequacies of all political techniques and systems. It uses the two tools of politics, compromise and the threat or use of force, to achieve its objectives. Although few, if any, of its leaders have read Machiavelli, the machine operates on the basis of the maxims laid down by the great Florentine over four hundred years ago about the nature of man and political society. The machine believes with Machiavelli that men in politics are greedy, emotional, and passionate, and are not governed by reason, morality, or concern for their fellow man. It believes that men can be co-opted, bought, persuaded, or frightened into subservience to or cooperation with the machine. Every man has his price, according to the machine, and the major problems are to find out what that price is and whether it is worth paying. Those unwilling to be bought must be persuaded or, if necessary, dealt with by force.

The machine is also cognizant of the need for compromise, for tempering of goals, and for retreat. It expands to the outer limits of its power as rapidly as possible, seizing every available opportunity, and raising the ante when necessary to keep the machine and its component parts functioning. But it also reduces its aims, tempers its techniques, and contracts its perimeter when the opposition is too strong, the going is too tough, or the odds are too high. It understands the need to balance resources and objectives, and to set goals which are consonant with the power the machine can bring to bear. It comprehends the dangers of overreaching itself, the disadvantages of operating too far from home in alien territory, the advantages and benefits to be derived from operating on its home grounds, and of limiting its goals by the reality of the power relationships at a particular time in a given situation. This is not to say that the machine has always operated successfully, always employed the right techniques, or always achieved its objectives. But it has operated fairly successfully for forty years in Chicago, it has achieved many of its objectives, and, while it has made mistakes and suffered reverses, it has always survived to fight another day.

While many of the machine's leaders are regular churchgoers and devout practitioners of their religions, they do not allow their religious beliefs to inhibit their practical political lives. Like Machiavelli, they separate morality from politics, rendering unto Caesar what is Caesar's and to God what is God's. Most of them operate within a system of values which enables them to conduct their private lives in accordance with their moral beliefs, and their public lives in accordance with practical political realities. They are, on the whole, practitioners of Rakove's first law of politics: "The individual is influenced by principle in direct proportion to his distance from the political situation."

The machine's leaders have little use for ideology or philosophy in their political lives, and if they hold any ideological or philosophical beliefs, they are always willing to subordinate those beliefs to practical political necessity. The Chicago Democratic machine is essentially nonideological in its orientation. It is dedicated primarily to gaining and retaining office, and to reaping the rewards of office. Its movers and shapers are relatively unconcerned with philosophical terms like liberalism and conservatism. Its primary demands on its members are loyalty and political efficiency. In return, it carries out its obligations by providing its members with jobs, contacts, contracts, and its own "social security" system.

A member of the organization remains in good standing as long as he delivers his ward or precinct. Service to the people is considered one of the prime requisites of good politics. To give that service, a politician should live in his neighborhood; be of the same ethnic, racial, and religious background as his constituents; have the same outlook and aspirations as his people; and reflect and represent that outlook and those aspirations. There is an implicit recognition of the principle of democratic representation, not just on the basis of numbers or territory, but also on the basis of ethnic, religious, racial, social, and cultural aspirations and needs. But obligations to one's constituents must be subordinated to loyalty to the organization. And, while the pursuit of private interests is condoned and recognized, it, too, must be subordinated to the needs of the machine.

The men who run the Chicago machine have many of the basic aspirations, drives, behavior patterns, and values of all politicians in all political systems in all places at all times. Their aspirations and careers would have been the same if the accident of birth had placed them in a place or culture other than the one into which they were born or brought by their forebears. Had Mayor Richard J. Daley been born in Russia, he would probably be the mayor of Kiev and chairman of the central committee of the Communist party of the Kiev region. Had Alderman Tom Keane been born in India, he would probably be chairman of the finance committee of the city council in New Delhi and a district leader in that city. If Alderman Vito Marzullo had remained in Italy instead of emigrating to the United States at age twelve, he would be a district leader in Naples or Genoa, have a small insurance business and an undertaking parlor, and be a godfather to the people of his neighborhood. If City Revenue Director Marshall Korshak's parents had emigrated to Israel rather than to the United States, Korshak would have been a city official in Tel Aviv or Haifa, practicing law on the side, and seizing whatever opportunities came his way. And if William Dawson's ancestors had not been brought to the United States several hundred years ago from Africa as slaves, the late congressman and ward boss would have been a legislator in Ghana or Guinea, and would have been ministering to the needs of his constituents there while amassing a private fortune.

The politicians who run Chicago are not basically different from the Richard Nixons, the Lyndon Johnsons, the Winston Churchills, the Georges Pompidous, the Nelson Rockefellers, the Charles Percys, the Joseph Stalins, the Charles de Gaulles, the George Wallaces, and the John Lindsays. All these men were political animals or precinct workers who reached for the top. But while their techniques, drives, and behavior patterns were similar to those which motivate the men who run the Chicago machine, their aspirations were different.

The Nixons, Johnsons, De Gaulles, Churchills, and Stalins sought power on a larger stage than did their blood brothers in Chicago. They wanted to cast their shadows over national and international scenes. They widened the political scope of their lenses from the precinct to the district to the city to the state to the nation and, finally, to the world. They wanted to walk the corridors of history in full view of millions or hundreds of millions of awed subjects. Like the ancient Pharaohs, they wanted their lives to be inscribed in the book of Clio, the Muse of History, as great conquerors, founders of long-lived dynasties, architects of massive social and political changes, or as rulers or representatives of great masses of their fellow men.

But the men who have controlled the Chicago Democratic political machine and governmental power in the city for the past forty years focused their attention on and directed their power drives to local political and economic power and office. This difference in aspiration distinguishes the generality of Democratic machine politicians in Chicago from their counterparts on the national and international scene. And, more than anything else, this difference in aspiration accounts for the success and longevity of the Chicago machine. The essential ingredient of the machine's success has been its almost single-minded concentration on the retention of power in the city of Chicago. To that end, the machine subordinates power and perquisites at all other levels of the American political and governmental system—county, state, and national—and sacrifices the interests of individuals, groups, governments, the Democratic party, and the electorate at those levels to the machine's interests in the city.

This attitude toward political and governmental power manifests itself most clearly in the way in which influential members of the Chicago machine reverse the normal attitude toward public office which characterizes the behavior of most politically ambitious aspirants. In most political systems, a newcomer begins at the local level and gradually works himself up to the county, state, and national levels. A budding politician runs for an aldermanic seat in the city council, waits for an opening in the state legislature, and, after serving his time at the state level, tries for national office. In the Democratic organization of Chicago and Cook County, however, this process is reversed for influential members of the organization. They are sent to the Illinois General Assembly in Springfield, and possibly even to Congress, to gain experience and are then brought back to the city or county to serve the party. Many of the major local officeholders in the party's inner circle have followed this route.

Why do these men prefer local office to state or national office? The answer lies in the psychology of some professional politicians in their approach to politics and public office. "There are only two reasons to run for public office," a longtime member of the Democratic organization explains. "One is to make a buck. The other is to get in the limelight." In other words, professional politicians seek public office either to advance their economic self-interest, or to gain power, or for a combination of these reasons.

An aspiring politician seeking public office for his economic self-interest finds the local scene a far more fertile field to plow than the state or national political scene. Prerogatives can be dispensed more readily by the party organization, access to the sources of power is easier, and checks by legislative and administrative officials on the disbursement of the perquisites of politics are better controlled. If the objective of an aspiring politician is power, the local political scene usually offers a better opportunity to be a big fish in a small pond than does the interminable process of slowly climbing the ladder of American politics to a position of authority and responsibility at either the state or national level. And for pragmatic, nonideological types, the issue-oriented politics of the national scene has little appeal in contrast to the practical, close-to-home, and potentially more economically rewarding local political scene. Since there is never a dearth of ambitious, liberal, issue-oriented people who are willing to undertake the vicissitudes of political life at the national level, the locally oriented politicians have little trouble in reserving to themselves those offices from which the more fruitful rewards of politics flow, and where they are less subject to the whims of a capricious electorate than those who must compete with each other for state and national offices.

This attitude toward politics and public office is the key to an understanding of the dynamics of the Democratic political organization of Cook County. The men who dominate the organization are practical, pragmatic, parochial, and nonideological. Their primary concern is their own self-interest. This is not to say that they have no concern for the public good, but rather that that concern is secondary to their own interests. In this they are no different from businessmen, doctors, lawyers, or academicians, except that politics is their business. Since they seek and hold public office, however, they are expected by those who put them into office to concern themselves with public problems and the interests of society rather than with their own private interests, and to get into office they must pledge themselves to a pursuit of the common good. However, once in public office, the human, private concerns of the public servant assert themselves. How to pursue his private interests while at the same time convincing the electorate that he is pursuing the public interest is the major task of a politician, particularly in a democracy, where the sovereign voters have the power to arbitrarily bring his career to a sudden end.

When an aspiring politician runs for public office he can promise to do all things for all men. He can offer lower taxes to businessmen, higher wages to labor, lower prices to consumers, state aid to parochial schools for the Catholics, support to Israel for the Jews, dedication to civil rights for the blacks, geriatric care for the aged, equal rights for women, better schools for children, more parks for picnickers, better golf courses for golfers, better beaches for swimmers, lower taxes for homeowners, lower rents for renters, and a vision of the Promised Land for all, if only the sovereign voters will put him into public office. But once he gets there, the realities take hold. How is he to make good on all these conflicting promises to diverse interest groups? A sensible man knows that it cannot be done, especially since most of these interests conflict with each other. Lower taxes for businessmen and homeowners means less money for parks, recreational facilities, schools, and other public facilities. Giving state aid to parochial schools may alienate the Protestants. He can always support Israel safely. That may alienate the Arabs, but how many Arabs vote in the city anyway? But in a city with 1,500,000 whites, 500,000 Latins, and 1,300,000 blacks, support for integration, which might pacify the blacks, might alienate the whites. Similarly, raising taxes to improve the schools might appeal to the parents of school children but will alienate other taxpayers.

In other words, the awful truth is that there is no such thing as the public interest, except on very vague, general matters of public policy. But on the day-to-day gut issues of politics, there is a wide divergence of conflicting private interests, all supported under the rubric of the public good. The recognition of this truth is complicated for an incumbent officeholder by another fact of political life. He knows that all these selfish individuals and groups within the electorate are pursuing their own self-interests. He knows, too, that their support for him in the future will be incumbent upon his support for those private, selfish, self-interests. He knows further that he has obligations as a public official to the public interest. And he knows, finally, that the sovereign voters are ungrateful, that while they will forget the things he has done for them, they will never forget the things he has done to them.

How to resolve this dilemma? Pursue your own private interests primarily, support the private interests of the various groups in the electorate secondarily, and publicly profess an overriding concern for the common good. Do as little as you can about emotional political issues. For every time you make a political decision on such issues, somebody wins, somebody loses. Those who win are forgetful. On election day they are out of town, they forget to vote, or they have acquired new concerns about which you have done nothing as yet. But those who lose will remember you. They will mush through five feet of snow to get to the polling place, they will get an absentee ballot to vote against you, if they have to leave town, and they will publicize your dereliction of duty to all who will listen.

Above all, do not raise issues of ideology or philosophy if you want to remain in public office for very long. Those are the things which excite and incite the electorate the most. Instead, concern yourself with materialistic matters. Trim the trees, repair the curbs, get the children a summer job, lower the taxes on the property, and avoid broad social issues and questions, for while the sovereign voters will demand that you take public positions on such issues, they will not vote for you or against you on

election day on the basis of your stand. Instead, they will return you to
public office or reject you for public office on the basis of how well you
have served their private interests.

These elemental political facts govern the attitude and political
behavior of the men who dominate politics in Chicago and Cook County.
Since their primary concerns are getting into office, staying there as long as
possible, and reaping the rewards of office, issue-oriented state and
national politics has no appeal to them. They have no desire to become
president of the United States, United States senator, United States
representative in Congress, governor of the state of Illinois, or representative in the General Assembly. They would rather serve on the Cook
County Board of Commissioners, the Sanitary District Board, the Circuit
Court of Cook County, or in a local bureaucracy, where they are safe from
retribution by the electorate.

This parochialism governs not only the political attitudes but also the
life-styles of the locally oriented politicians. With some exceptions, they
are not world travelers, art connoisseurs, opera buffs, or big spenders. The
accumulation of money is an end in itself, not a means for achieving social
status and prestige. With some exceptions they do not buy mansions on the
Chicago Gold Coast, attend the socially prestigious affairs in the community, or get their names in the gossip columns or the society pages of the
newspapers. Indeed, most of them have an aversion to seeing their names
in print. There is a built-in belief that, when their names appear in the
press, it can only mean trouble. They have an underlying suspicion that
newspaper stories chronicling their careers or their activities would be
unfavorable at best and call the attention of their constituents to their new
status in life at worst. It is better to remain anonymous, avoid publicity,
and keep one's relationships with one's constituents on a private, personal
basis.

With some exceptions, most of them live in the neighborhoods in
which they were born, possibly in a bigger house than most of their
constituents live in, but nothing too fancy or ostentatious. There are men
like 1st Ward Committeeman John D'Arco, who moved from the Taylor
Street district in his 1st Ward to the 400 East Randolph Building on the
lakefront, and 29th Ward Committeeman Bernard Neistein, who lives in
the prestigious Carlyle Building on Lake Shore Drive, but they are the
exceptions rather than the rule. They do not normally leave their wards
except to go to Chicago's Loop or to other ward meetings in the city for
political purposes. Nor do they frequent the gourmet restaurants of the

city or the night spots along Rush Street on the Near North Side. Even when they are in the Loop on political or governmental business, they do not wander far afield from the safety and familiarity of City Hall. They park their Cadillacs across the street, disappear into the labyrinthic structure, and emerge only to walk back across the street to the car.

The innate conservatism of the local Democratic leaders manifests itself even more strikingly in their attitude toward using political and governmental power to resolve the problems of society. They have little concept of broad social problems and social movements. They deal with each other, and with the problems of the community, on a person-to-person, individual basis. They shrink from striking out in new directions, have no interest in blazing new trails, abhor radical solutions to problems, and, in general, resist activism of any sort about anything. "I got two rules," 29th Ward Committeeman Bernard Neistein confided when asked how he had operated so successfully in politics in Chicago for most of his adult life. "The first one is 'Don't make no waves.' The second one is 'Don't back no losers.' "

In those two brief sentences, Committeeman Neistein capsuled the political philosophy of the men who dominate the Democratic organization of Cook County. Behind those principles is a profound understanding of the relationship between those who hold political power in a society and who operate on a professional level, and those for whom politics is an avocation and a means to a different end. James Madison's analysis in *The Federalist Papers* of the divergent interests of the two groups in a society, those who hold property and those who do not, is even more valid for those who hold political power and those who abhor politics and politicians.

According to Madison, those who hold property in a society are primarily interested in protecting that property from those who would take it from them, and those who do not possess property are primarily interested in getting some, taking it if necessary from those who hold it. In a sense, the same thing is true of politics in a society. Those who hold political power are primarily interested in keeping it, while those professionals who are out of office and interested in office are primarily concerned with taking power from those who hold it. Outside these two groups of activists stands the great mass of the population, which has neither the interest, the ability, nor the intestinal fortitude to engage in what Frank Kent called "the great game of politics." But in a democracy they must be wooed by those who seek political power.

The two groups of activists, those who hold power and those who seek it, traditionally employ different tactics in dealing with the electorate. Those who seek power must make waves, must raise issues, and must arouse the electorate in order to remove from office those who hold political power. Those in office must keep the electorate quiescent, passive, and disinterested, since an aroused, interested electorate will usually react unfavorably toward those in office. How to keep the electorate quiet? "Don't make no waves."

This philosophy characterizes the attitudes and behavior patterns of the professional politicians in the Cook County Democratic organization who either hold office or control those who hold office. And it distinguishes them from the wavemakers and the nonprofessionals who would use the political process to solve broad social problems. There is an inherent conflict and dichotomy between these two groups which traditionally participate in the political process at the local level in this country. That conflict can never be resolved. For when wavemakers and nonprofessionals become officeholders, they soon discover the elemental truth that the best and surest way to stay in office is to adopt the behavior patterns and philosophies of the nonwavemakers and professionals. For they, too, soon discover the truth that the professionals and nonwavemakers always knew—that there is no such thing as the public interest insofar as the electorate is concerned; that the private, self-interests of the various groups that compose the electorate must be appeased; and that this can best be done by appealing to those groups on a personal basis and by concerning oneself with those private interests rather than with broad social problems.

They also discover, after assuming office, that there is no such thing as "new politics" or "old politics," that if they want to stay in office there is something called "politics," a game that has been played since time immemorial by men called "politicians," and that it behooves them to join the ranks and play the game if they wish to survive.

I believe that a study of the political motivations, techniques, and aspirations of Chicago's machine politicians can contribute to an under-standing of what many people call "the urban crisis" in America today. While the city of Chicago shares many of the problems of all American big cities, it is unique in its extant political system. Alone of all the big cities, Chicago has resisted reform of its political machine, rejected merit-system employment in its governmental bureaucracy, retained the time-tested political relationships of political bosses to needy constituents, maintained and strengthened centralized political power instead of diffusing that power to the bureaucracy and local community organizations, and been controlled by men whose ambitions have differed significantly from their counterparts in most of the other big cities of America.

The urban crisis in America has its roots in the great population movements of the past twenty-five years, in the deterioration of the quality of life in our major cities, and in the inability of city governments to deal with the problems of the cities since the Second World War. The massive shift of large numbers of southern blacks, some southern whites, and substantial numbers of Spanish-speaking people into the cities, and the exodus of middle-class whites from the cities to the suburbs have significantly altered the character of most American cities. The deterioration of schools, the spread of blight, the debilitation of housing, the erosion of the tax base, the rise in crime, the increase in the percentage of the population in need of welfare, the breakdown of services, and the decline in economic opportunities have made our cities less attractive as places to live, work, raise families, and expand social and cultural horizons.

These trends have been exacerbated by a significant change in the relationships of the governed and the governors of our big cities, of those in need of public services and those who are charged with providing those services. Those who once accepted inequality, poverty, and travail as a normal concomitant of their economic and social status now demand redress of these ills by government as a right and prerogative of citizenship. Their governors, who formerly were expected to exert minimal effort to alleviate societal problems, and who are now expected to do all things for all people, have become increasingly disillusioned with their roles and increasingly pessimistic about the possibility of coping with the problems of twentieth-century urban society. And, in most cities, the political system, the indispensable link between the community and the government, has broken down and no longer fulfills two of the primary functions of politics in a democratic society, those of transmitting the will of the populace to the government and of explaining and buttressing the policies and actions of government to the community.

The difference between the city of Chicago and most of the other big cities of America is that in Chicago the machine politics which once prevailed in American big cities in the period in which they underwent their most explosive growth and development, and provided the best opportunities for their immigrant populations, still exists. Chicago is as well governed as, and probably better governed than, any other big city in

America today. This is not to say, however, that Chicago is well governed. No American big city is well governed today, and it is unlikely that any big city could be, given the kinds of problems confronting our cities, the demands being made on their political and governmental systems, and the inability of those systems to cope with those demands. But the machine has governed the city, retained power, and pacified the citizenry by striking a balance between providing good technical services for the majority of the citizenry; making concessions to every powerful, organized interest group on matters of concern to each group; resisting reform; and providing for the political and economic interests of the machine's leaders.

The mass of the citizenry, whose aspirations and expectations are limited and personal, are pacified by the maintenance of good city services, often at a higher cost than seems necessary but of a fairly good quality. Chicago has a first-class police department, one of the best fire departments in the country, excellent public transportation facilities, a network of high-speed expressways for motorists, good street lighting, adequate sewers, good curb repairs, satisfactory tree trimming and removal, a fairly effective rodent control program, and some urban renewal. The crime rate is no worse than in most other big cities, automobile traffic is fairly well handled, and traffic fatalities have been reduced. Job opportunities are usually the best of any big city in the country, an adequate welfare program has been maintained, the tax rate is kept at a bearable level, and the financial status of the city is fairly sound. Access to governmental agencies for redress of individual grievances is always available to the citizenry through the machine's precinct captains, who can guide the inexperienced and uninitiated through the maze of governmental bureaucracy. An unfortunate miscreant who runs afoul of the law for a misdemeanor or traffic offense can usually get considerate treatment from the police, the corporation counsel's office, and a magistrate.

Since the great mass of the city's citizenry are welfare poor, working class, or, at best, lower-middle class, they do not concern themselves politically with momentous philosophical and ideological issues such as Vietnam, strategic arms limitations talks, recognition of Peking, balanced governmental budgets, and reform. Their horizons are generally limited by their physical, social, and economic needs—their jobs, taxes, dwelling places, local recreational facilities, and neighborhood activities. As long as the machine and the government it controls provides a decent level of services to satisfy those concerns, the machine can work its will and wend its way toward its objectives without interference. And who is to say that

that citizenry is not more realistic, sensible, and aware of its interests than are those who exhort them to concern themselves with and involve themselves in matters of a higher civic virtue?

It is on this crucial point of the needs, interests, and aspirations of the urban masses that the machine differs from those who believe that the type of politics the machine practices with regard to its urban constituency is passé and that the politics of American cities has progressed from the era of Tammany Hall, Boss Tweed, I Am the Law Hague, Tom Pendergast, and James Curley's Last Hurrah. According to the catechism of the urban reformers and sundry other true believers in the inevitability of progress in politics, machine politics in American cities was doomed when the economic, social, and political revolutions of the twentieth century came to fruition in the cities of America. When the immigrant masses who peopled the cities were educated to the mores and values of old America, when their economic progress to middle-class status, and the welfare programs of the New Deal, freed them from dependence on the political machine and its minions, and when they were able to raise their aspirations to a higher plane than sheer physical and economic survival, then the politics of "clout," favors, vote selling, and machine domination of the cities would end, and urban problems could be dealt with by an administrative bureaucracy freed from political influence.

What the urban reformers have never come to terms with is the fact that American cities are still peopled heavily by the immigrants of the 1950s and '60s—blacks from the South, whites from Appalachia, and Spanish speaking from Puerto Rico and Mexico, who are as much in need of guidance and favors as were the ethnic immigrants who came between 1870 and 1920. The ethnic immigrants, who are now second and third generations in the cities, have gained political and economic power, are wedded to the status quo in a political system of which they are major beneficiaries, and are resistant to attempts by the urban reformers to alter that status quo to benefit the new immigrants. And the sons and daughters of the ethnic immigrants who aspired to and have achieved middle-class social and economic respectability have fled the city for the suburbs, where they can either abjure politics altogether or participate in politics in a suburban, Anglo-Saxon-Protestant milieu, divorced from any association with the city machine and its ethnic and racial politics.

In the cities, the black and Spanish-speaking newcomers are beginning to feel their oats as citizens, are organizing politically, and are challenging the second- and third-generation ethnics for a larger slice of the pie which was normally divided between the ethnic politicians and the Anglo-Saxon-Protestant economic overlords of most American cities. The major issue is not the reform of the city's political and governmental institutions sought by upper-middle-class, Anglo-Saxon-Protestant–oriented reformers who live in fringe areas of the cities or in the suburbs. The issue being posed by the ethnics, the blacks, and the Spanish speaking is the control of political power, and the political, social, and economic prerogatives which are the rewards of political power and influence.

The machine in Chicago deals with the "revolution of rising expectations" and the demands of the new immigrant blacks and Spanish speaking by giving ground slowly in those areas of public policy which are important to the blacks and the Spanish speaking, but refuses to make major concessions on matters of significance to the machine's power base in the established urban-ethnic constituency. The machine co-opts those emerging leaders in the black and Spanish-speaking communities who are willing to cooperate; reallocates perquisites and prerogatives to the blacks and the Spanish speaking, taking them from ethnic groups such as the Jews and Germans, who do not support the machine as loyally as their fathers did; and ostracizes or punishes those aspiring black politicians who will not cooperate.

The machine also lives tolerantly with the activities and demands of the urban reformers, who are mainly white Anglo-Saxon Protestant and Jewish, who have no substantial power base in either the ethnic or black communities which make up the bulk of the population of the city, and who cannot match the political, economic, and social perquisites the machine can offer to the emerging, politically ambitious black and Spanish-speaking leadership.

The machine offers welfare to the poor, jobs to those in need of them, status to the socially ambitious, and power to the demonstrably capable and cooperative in the black and Spanish-speaking communities. But it will not integrate the city, put public housing projects in white neighborhoods, concern itself very much with the quality of public education, or interfere with the practices and prerogatives of the economic and political rulers of the city. Above all, the machine will not concern itself with the broad social issues and programs which are so dear to the hearts of the urban reformers. As one of Chicago's leading liberal reformers, radio personality and author Studs Terkel, described the policies of the machine's dominant figure, Mayor Richard J. Daley, "He's marvelous when it comes to building things like highways, parking lots, and industrial complexes. But when it comes to healing the aches and hurts of human beings, Daley comes up short."

"The question, however, arises," as *Commentary* magazine reviewer Joseph Epstein, analyzing *Chicago Daily News* columnist Mike Royko's polemical study of Daley, *Boss*, puts it, "When it comes to healing the aches and hurts of human beings, who comes up long? John Lindsay? Sam Yorty of Los Angeles? Carl Stokes of Cleveland? But then since when have mayors been charged with 'healing' to begin with? Since, one can only imagine, the time within recent years that political language becomes so inflated as to leave the ground or reality altogether, and aldermen were required to have 'charisma,' water commissioners were sounded out on Vietnam, and Chicago became 'a totalitarian state within America,' " according to "a particularly feverish review of [Royko's] book in the *New Yorker*."

Since the black, Spanish-speaking, and southern white immigrants in Chicago, like the older ethnic settlers, are not concerned with "healing the aches and hurts of human beings" other than themselves, the machine does not waste its time or its efforts on such irrelevant matters. Instead, it maintains a tight hold on the political loyalties of the vast majority of the blacks and of the Spanish-speaking population, as it always did with the ethnics, by ministering to their personal needs and private passions, and exacting a pound of flesh in return in the form of the vote on election day.

With the great mass of the populace pacified with adequate technical services and good liaison with the lower levels of the city's bureaucracy for redress of grievances, the machine is free to pursue its primary interests and objectives—the economic and political emoluments which accrue to those who manipulate the levers of political power, and the allocation of significant social and economic rewards to the powerful interest groups in the city whose support is necessary for the machine's survival. Thus, in Chicago, the State Street merchants support the machine in return for first-rate city services for the Loop—good street lighting, snow removal, street cleaning, police protection, parking facilities for automobiles, expressways to bring the cars into the Loop, and fast, efficient public transportation for those who need it to get downtown to work and shop. The North Michigan Avenue merchants, real estate developers, newspaper publishers, and wealthy residents also get first-rate city services, excellent police protection, and tax concessions on their property. The public utilities get lenient treatment from the city council and regulatory agencies. The major financial institutions get substantial deposits of public funds and private real estate tax payments on mortgages in noninterest-bearing accounts, which can be loaned out by the banks and the savings and loan associations at high rates of interest, as well as the right to handle the city's municipal bond transactions. The construction industry tycoons get profitable contracts to build the public and private commercial and residential developments which have characterized a major building boom in the city. The labor unions get high wages and year-round work for their membership, social and economic prerogatives for their leadership, and protection from too much infiltration of the best unions by the blacks and the Spanish-speaking immigrants. Religious leaders are consulted and assisted on matters of interest to their congregations and themselves. Major educational institutions are given good city services, lucrative incomes from tax-exempt property holdings, and socially prestigious appointments for their leading officials. Ethnic associations are given representation on party and governmental bodies, and public recognition of national holidays and national contributions to the city and the country.

With the mass of the citizenry pacified with adequate city services, welfare, and easy access to the governmental bureaucracy for redress of grievances through the machinery of the political system, and with all major potential sources of opposition and reform co-opted or neutralized by adequate concessions or the application of political and governmental power, the machine's leaders are then free to pursue their own primary political and economic interests and ambitions—the acquisition and retention of power and money.

The thesis of this book is that a study of the dynamics, techniques, and relationships of the Chicago machine can provide some insights into the realities of what the politics of American big cities may be like in the decades to come. It may well be true that another of the favorite shibboleths of American urban reformers, the belief that the era of machine politics in American big cities has run its course and will be replaced by nonpartisan, reform, public-regarding, problem-oriented urban political systems is as fallacious as the assumption that the rise of the urban masses to middle-class respectability and outlook would character-ize the evolution of American cities in the second half of the twentieth century.

What is a far more likely development in American cities is a revival of machine politics as the black and Spanish-speaking immigrants gain political power. As the white, middle-class, second- and third-generation ethnic Catholics, and what remains of the liberal Jewish and Anglo-Saxon-Protestant reform-oriented elements of the population of the cities, give up the ghost and flee to the suburbs, black and Spanish-speaking political control of our cities will become a reality.

If, as is likely, the inheritors of political power in the cities will be the pragmatic, power-seeking political types in the emerging black and Spanish-speaking leadership, they will more likely emulate their ethnic forebears and teachers than they will the white, middle-class, public-regarding, issue-oriented reformers who seek their support in our cities today. They will more likely have the same aspirations, employ the same techniques, and pursue the same objectives as did the ethnic machine bosses of an earlier period of American urban history. Carl Stokes, Richard Hatcher, Jesse Jackson, Percy Sutton, and others yet to come are the first harvest of the newly planted crop in the political fields of the contemporary American urban political scene.

It may well be true that the Chicago machine is not only the last of the great ethnic political machines of America but will probably be the first of the new black and Spanish-speaking machines which will develop in the years to come. As the aging Irish political aristocracy and its court of sycophants, court jesters, and hangers on are forced to give up the reins of power, those black and Spanish-speaking political leaders who learned their lessons well, who played the game successfully, and who are cognizant of the rewards and prerogatives to be gained, will take over the machine. They, too, will have to pacify the masses with largesse and services, broker the diverse interest groups in the city, become the handmaiden as well as partner of the economic overlords of the city, and employ the political techniques of their ethnic predecessors in Chicago. If that happens, the machine will survive in Chicago, changed in its internal constituency but unchanging in its goals, tactics, and dynamics. As such, it may well be a model of things to come in America, rather than a vestigial curiosity of things past.

❧ *1* ❧

Dick Daley's Town

Chicago is the great American city. New York is one of the capitals of the world and Los Angeles is a constellation of plastic, San Francisco is a lady, Boston has become Urban Renewal, Philadelphia and Baltimore and Washington wink like dull diamonds in the smog of Eastern Megalopolis, and New Orleans is unremarkable past the French Quarter, Detroit is a one-trade town, Pittsburgh has lost its golden triangle, St. Louis has become the golden arch of the corporation, and nights in Kansas City close early. The oil depletion allowance makes Houston and Dallas naught but checkerboards for this sort of game. But Chicago is a great American city. Perhaps it is the last of the great American cities.

NORMAN MAILER
Miami and the Siege of Chicago

The City

No one has ever described the city of Chicago better than the late poet and writer, Carl Sandburg, who once called it "the city of the big shoulders." Chicago has never been a genteel town. It has always been, and still is today, a lusty, brawling, sprawling city.

The city is physically ugly and depressing, except for its magnificent front yard, its lakefront area, stretching from the northern boundary of the city to the far South Side. A scenic eight-lane, high-speed expressway, the Outer Drive, spans the length of the city on its eastern edge from north to south, bordered on one side by Lake Michigan and on the other side by miles of parks and modern high-rise apartment buildings. But inward from the lakefront are miles upon miles of deteriorating neighborhoods, interspersed with industrial developments, before one reaches the newer, cleaner, middle-class residential areas of the city on the far south, southwest, north, and northwest sides. The *New Yorker* magazine's A. J. Liebling once described Chicago as "a boundless agglutination of streets, dramshops, and low buildings without urban character. The Loop," Chicago's central business and entertainment district, said Liebling, "is like Times Square and Radio City set down in the middle of a vast Canarsie. . . . The stranger arrives by car from the airport, approaching the Loop across a tundra of industrial suburbs unchanged in character by the city line, or else comes in on one of the railroads that run through slums of their own making."

Other visitors to the city have been similarly unimpressed by its physical character. In 1889, Rudyard Kipling wrote of Chicago, "Having seen it, I urgently desire never to see it again. It is inhabited by savages. Its water is the water of the Hooghly, and its air is dirt."

Lincoln Steffens, at the turn of the twentieth century, found Chicago, "First in violence, deepest in dirt, unlovely, ill-smelling, irreverent, new, an overgrown gawk of a village, the 'tough' among cities, a spectacle for the nation." In Chicago's downtown area, according to another contemporary observer, "the manufactories vomit dense clouds of bituminous coal smoke, which settle in a black mass in this part of town, so that one can scarcely see across the streets on a damp day, and the huge buildings loom up in the black sky in a ghostly dimness."

Sixty-nine years later, not much had changed in the quality of the air that Chicago's citizens breathe. A local television station entitled a special program in January 1969, "Chicago's Sewer in the Sky." A disk jockey, lured to Chicago from San Francisco in midwinter 1956 by an increase in salary, fled the city for his native California after three days without even halting to notify his new employers that he was leaving. "The sky was gray, the snow was gray, the people were gray," he told a press conference in San Francisco, upon debarking from his plane, vowing never to return again.

Indeed, the climate would deter any but the most hardy souls. Assaulted by blasts of Arctic-Canadian air in the winter, frequently immobilized by blizzards roaring in out of the great plains to the

Dedication of the Sears Tower Building. *Left to right:* George Dunne, President of the Cook County Board of Commissioners; Mayor Richard J. Daley; Arthur Wood, Chairman of the Board of Directors of Sears Roebuck and Co. (Courtesy George Dunne)

Mayor Daley speaking at the dedication of a city incinerator. (Courtesy Vito Marzullo)

Political rally at 25th Ward headquarters. *Left to right:* Charles Bonk, County Commissioner; State Representative Matt Ropa; Alderman Vito Marzullo; State Senator Sam Romano; Judge Thomas Janczy; Congressman Frank Annunzio. (Marshall Marker)

Celebrating 1000 years of Christianity in Poland. *Left to right:* Francis Lorenz, Judge of the Appellate Court; Bernard J. Korzen, Cook County Treasurer; Bishop Aloycius Wyceslo; Mayor Daley. (*Chicago Tribune*)

Columbus Day delegation from Italy visiting Alderman Marzullo. *Left,* standing, Marzullo; *right,* seated, Sam Romano. (Courtesy Vito Marzullo)

Clean-up Parade sponsored by the Heart of Chicago Community Council and Alderman Marzullo. (Paris Studios)

Veterans Day Parade in Chicago. *Second from left,* Robert F. Kennedy. Senator Everett McKinley Dirksen is partially hidden behind Daley's left. (Arthur Schimmel)

The Mayor and Mrs. Daley with Queen Elizabeth II of Great Britain at a formal dinner honoring the Queen during her July 1959 visit to Chicago. (Courtesy Vito Marzullo)

Mayor Daley greets President and Mrs. Lyndon B. Johnson at the airport in Chicago. (Chicago Police Department)

Mayor Daley greets President and Mrs. Richard M. Nixon at the airport in Chicago. (Courtesy Vito Marzullo)

Mayor Daley drives the first spike into the Chicago Transit Authority tracks being laid in the center of the Eisenhower Expressway, 1955. *Right*, Alderman Marzullo looks on. (Courtesy Vito Marzullo)

Greeting each other at an Irish Fellowship Club dinner are, *left*, William G. Clark, State Attorney General; and Bernard J. Korzen, Cook County Treasurer.

Entertaining residents of the Villa Scallabrini Italian Home for Senior Citizens are, *left to right,* Anthony Girolami, former 28th Ward committeeman; Congressman Frank Annunzio; Louis Prima; Alderman Marzullo; and Robert Massey, Judge of the Circuit Court of Cook County. (Al Chiefari)

Opening Day of the season for the Chicago Cubs at Wrigley Field. *Left to right:* Fire Commissioner Robert Quinn; Alderman Michael Bilandic, 11th Ward; former Alderman Thomas Keane; Mayor Daley; Federal District Judge Abraham Lincoln Marowitz; George Dunne. (Barney A. Sterling)

Political rally in the Sherman House for some of the Democratic candidates in the 1970 election. *Left foreground,* John Touhy, Chairman of the State Central Committee of the Democratic Party of Illinois. *(Chicago Tribune)*

In his office at City Hall, Alderman Vito Marzullo holds a seminar for a class in urban politics from Barat College. *Left to right:* Marzullo; Bob Crawford, City Hall correspondent for radio station WBBM; Mary Witte, student; Jay McMullen, City Hall correspondent for the *Chicago Daily News*; Allison Edmonds, student. (Lisa Ebright)

west, and enveloped in the summer by masses of hot, moist air
flowing up out of the Texas Panhandle, the city alternates between
shivering in the winter and steaming in the summer. Spring brings
no relief, since there is no spring. A local joke about the weather is
that Chicago has three seasons—July, August, and winter. An
English visitor, passing through the city during the summer,
remarked to a friend, "My God! These people live in a tropical
climate and don't even know it." "The inhabitants of the city,"
wrote Liebling, "cannot (even) use the weather as a common topic
of conversation . . . since the waters of the Lake retain warmth on
into the fall and intense cold through June, with the result that
there is sometimes a difference of as much as twenty degrees in
temperature between the Lake Shore and the interior."

Chicago's citizens are generally much like the city's climate and
physical appearance—uncultured, tough, but friendly and parochial. They are inured to adversity and corruption. A few years ago,
when a black alderman named Ben Lewis was shot down in cold
blood, the correspondent for an Eastern magazine was immediately
cabled by his New York office for a piece which would include,
among other things, the outraged reaction of the good people of
Chicago. There was no outrage at all, he cabled back. "The feeling
is that if he's an alderman, he's a crook, and if he's a crook, then
that's their business."

Chicagoans have neither the sophistication of New Yorkers or
Berliners, nor the courtliness of San Franciscans or Londoners, nor
the gregarious warmth of Munichers or Romans, nor the cultured
assurance of Bostonians or Parisians. Scandals that would rock
another city to its foundations are accepted as part of a normal way
of life endemic to their city. Gangland assassinations (over one
thousand in the past five decades, practically all of them unsolved),
and corruption among local officials make headlines for a day, but
are soon forgotten as the life of the city moves on. "Chicago is
unique," one-time reform Alderman Robert Merriam of the University of Chicago's 5th Ward, told A. J. Liebling. "It is the only
completely corrupt city in America."

Not only do the citizens tolerate a high degree of crime and
corruption, but they have a sort of perverse pride in their city's
reputation, even when it is not always deserved. When Liebling
challenged Merriam's statement by citing other corrupt American

cities, the native son of Chicago responded defensively, "But they aren't nearly as big." Many Chicagoans quote, with undisguised chauvinism, former 43rd Ward Alderman Mathias ("Paddy") Bauler's succinct and pungent prognostication of his city's civic character. "Chicago," declared Bauler in 1955, "ain't ready for reform." Fifty years earlier, crusading journalist William Stead, author of *If Christ Came to Chicago*, declared, "When I first visited Chicago" (a decade before in 1894), "I thought there was one in a thousand chances of reform succeeding here. Now I think the chances are one in two thousand."

However, despite Bauler's pessimism, there has been some reform in some areas of Chicago's public life. On December 14, 1968, as the birthday of the Prince of Peace drew near at year's end, the *Chicago Daily News* proudly announced that 1968 had been "a no-hit year for Chicago mobsters. For the first time since 1919," wrote reporter Edmund J. Rooney, "there have been no gangland murders." The year 1919 was the year that the Chicago Crime Commission, in a flush of civic pride, began counting such things. In fact, in December 1968 it had actually been almost eighteen months since the last gangland "hit," loan shark Arthur (Boodie) Cowan, who was gangland victim number 1004, was found shot in the head and stuffed into the trunk of his car. This record was a far cry from the two biggest hit years of Chicago's modern history—1926, when 76 gangland slayings were chalked up, and 1928, when 72 victims bit the dust.

In recent years, according to Rooney, the number had drastically decreased before the record-breaking year 1968. "A search of back alleys, car trunks, and other unnatural resting places had turned up only six victims in 1963, four in 1964, seven in 1965, six in 1966, and five in 1967." In fact, so far had reform progressed that, when one of Chicago's best-known police captains, who had accumulated a fortune on a salary of $8,000 a year, was accused by newspapers of being a known associate of syndicate hoodlums, he told me plaintively in 1961, "How can they say that about me? Why, I shot eight of those guys myself!"

Periodically, in Chicago's murky past and, occasionally, in its unrepentant present, high-ranking police officers have turned up in company with some of the Mafia's alleged leading lights such as the police lieutenant who, a few years ago, traveled around the world as the boon companion of Tony ("Big Tuna") Accardo, and the chief investigator for a recent sheriff of Cook County, who acted as chauffeur for Sam ("Momo") Giancana in Mexico and who was sentenced to prison for abetting a robbery. (The former investigator, Richard Cain, was murdered in a typical gangland assassination late in 1973. Giancana was murdered in 1975.)

But, like the decline in gang murders, the contemporary record is pallid pink in comparison with Chicago's scarlet past. During the reign (1915–23, 1927–31) of Mayor William Hale ("Big Bill the Builder") Thompson, according to a contemporary observer, "In four years 215 gangsters were killed and no one punished. The police, however, took a toll of 160 gangsters during the same period. In one instance policemen cruising about the streets in ostensible pursuit of evil doers, but in reality with an eye on incoming trucks laden with liquor, fell afoul of each other and opened fire as if upon the high seas in time of war. The ranking nobility find it necessary to wear steel vests, to ride in cars with bullet proof glass, to cultivate sitting with the back to the wall, to go abroad attended by faithful servitors with assiduous attendance such as a potentate might receive in old Russia."

While occasional instances of payoffs to police officials appear in the current and recent press, the city is clean in comparison to the era of the 1920s. In a single year, during Thompson's mayoralty, gang boss Johnny Torrio, who preceded Al Capone, Chicago's most famous gangster, grossed $4,000,000 from his Chicago beer peddling, $3,000,000 from gambling, $2,000,000 from prostitution, and another $4,000,000 from similar enterprises in the suburbs. Payoffs to police officials and politicians were high and frequent, but Torrio had no objections as long as he could carry on without too much harassment. Chicago alone had more than 12,000 speakeasies, beer flats and brothels that sold illegal liquor. In 1870, Mayor Roswell B. Mason told the city council that there were 2300 licensed saloons to service a population of 306,000. "If one-fifth of the population are men over twenty-one years of age," said the mayor, "we have one saloon for every twenty-six men in the city." During Carter H. Harrison's term in office at the turn of the twentieth century, Chicago had 6400 saloons, 2000 gambling houses, 900 brothels, and only 3325 policemen for the 1,700,000 inhabitants. A score of years later, in the early days of the Thompson era, things had not improved significantly. "Such places as Colosimo's, the infamous Bucket of Blood, the Ansonia, the Athenia, and Freiberg's dance hall, where young whores posed as dancing teachers, were besieged nightly by prospective vice customers. Girls picked them up there and took them to 'call flats.' Major M. C. L. Funkhouser, head of the Morals Division, estimated that the city had nearly 30,000 such rooms. 'Why, in some of them,' said the horrified major, 'it costs five dollars just to sit down and talk for three minutes.' "

Those days are gone forever from the city. It is true that streetwalkers solicit business on Wilson Avenue and 63rd Street, that "B" girls cadge drinks and entice customers in the bars on North Clark Street and South State Street, that the unwary and overeager small town conventioneer could get jackrolled on West Madison Street, and that a few bookies still operate behind cigar store fronts, where the interested observer can note a stream of customers going in while nobody ever comes out. But most of these activities have been reduced to a minimum, if not eliminated, and are totally irrelevant to the life-style of the vast majority of the city's citizenry.

That citizenry, uncultured, tough, and parochial, has been primarily responsible for the city's rapid growth from a frontier village to one of the great cities of the world. The city's population always has been, and still is today, an unmelted melting pot of diverse national, religious, and racial groups who lived side by side within the city's boundaries, but not together. "The French found Chicago," according to political scientist Charles E. Merriam, "the native Americans settled it, the Germans and Irish and Scandinavians were its main strength in the mid-century and for a generation thereafter, the Italians, Poles, Russians, and Bohemians were the second line of defense from the '90's on to the Great War. Since that time the colored man has capped the climax."

Why did they come to this brawling frontier city with its unfriendly climate, unattractive living conditions, and corrupt politics? They came, according to Lloyd Wendt and Herman Kogan, because "Chicago was a city of opportunity, no place for the weak, the docile or the squeamish. Its workers slaughtered more pork and beef, loaded more grain, made more soup, tanned more hides, poured more steel, built more plows and railroad cars than any other place in the land. Most of these workers had not journeyed to the city to create a political utopia. They came to make homes and to make money. They created what was needed for the vast commerce that grew up in the wilderness they had opened: houses and bridges and streets, factories, hotels and skyscrapers. They dispatched buyers and sellers, promoters and schemers. They sent out mail-order catalogues and to produce them they set up massive printing plants. When their tasks were done they were weary, most of them, and they left the chores of politics and politicking to those who hungered for power and prestige."

Primarily because of the attraction of its economic opportunities for the underprivileged masses, Chicago underwent a rapid expansion of its population in the last years of the nineteenth century and early years of the twentieth century. Beginning with a population of 350, Chicago grew rapidly. By 1860 the population had reached 100,000. After the great fire of 1871, which destroyed the central core of the city, the population exploded. By 1890 Chicago was the second largest city in the United States with a population of over 1,000,000, and by 1930 the city had 3,376,438 residents. Since 1930 the population has leveled off, rising slightly to 3,620,962 in 1950, declining to 3,550,404 in 1960, and then down to 3,369,359 in 1970. In area the city has grown from 10.186 square miles in 1840 to its present 224.2 square miles.

Within the Chicago metropolitan area, significant changes are taking place in the character of the population. Chicago and its suburbs are in the midst of the two great population movements which characterize contemporary American society—a massive migration of blacks from the South into the cities of the North, and an exodus of whites from the cities to the suburbs. The black population of Chicago has increased from 227,000 in 1940 to 509,000 in 1950, to 838,000 in 1960, to 1,102,620 in 1970, and is expected to reach 1,540,000 by 1980 out of a projected population of 3,774,000. At the same time, the black population of the suburban ring of the city increased by only 37,000 between 1950 and 1960, and is expected to reach a total of about 347,000 out of 4,800,000 persons by 1980. Chicago, like many North American big cities, is becoming a largely black core-city, with a rapidly expanding Spanish-speaking population, surrounded by a heavily white fringe area and almost completely white suburban ring.

The primary reason for the rapid growth of the city and its

surrounding area is a fortuitous geographic location. Chicago is in the heart of the rich farmlands of the Middle West, with access to one of the great bodies of fresh water in the world, Lake Michigan, astride the main routes of almost all the major railroads and main highway arteries of the United States, and close to the iron ore and coal of the Great Lakes region. Iron ore brought by barge cheaply from Minnesota and Michigan, and coal from the rich fields to the south and east have made the Chicago area the center of a great iron and steel industry. On a normal day, approximately 35,000 railroad freight cars, with an average capacity of 50 short tons, are handled in the Chicago freight yards. Even before the opening of the St. Lawrence Seaway, which made Chicago an ocean port, the port of Chicago had the largest volume of traffic of any inland port in America. With the opening of the seaway, Chicago's water-borne commerce will be exceeded only by the port of New York. Iron, coal, steel, chemicals, petroleum products, wheat, corn, sulfur, limestone, sand, gravel, manufactured goods, machinery, and even sugar, molasses, and coffee from Latin America are brought into and transshipped out of Chicago. Chicago's continued growth as a center of commerce, manufacturing, and transportation is assured for the foreseeable future.

The People

Chicago, with 3,300,000 people, about one-third of the population of the state of Illinois, is nationality-ethnic, Latin, black, and Catholic. It developed as a city of nationality, religious, and racial neighborhoods and has remained so until this very day. The ethnic, religious, and racial divisions among the polyglot population of the city have remained fairly rigid and have perpetuated themselves into the second and third generations of the children of the original immigrants. Chicagoans do not identify themselves with their city as an ancient Athenian would with his *polis*, an imperial Roman with his world capital, or even a modern Parisian, Londoner, Florentine, or Berliner with his city. Chicagoans think socially, culturally, economically, and, as a consequence, politically, in terms of their neighborhoods or their ethnic, religious, or racial groups.

The Germans, the Swedes, the Irish, the Poles, the Bohemians, the Lithuanians, the Italians and the Jews inundated the city in successive waves. By 1920, Chicago had more Poles than any city in Poland except Warsaw, more Bohemians than any city in Czechoslovakia except Prague, and more Lithuanians than any city in Lithuania except Vilna. New immigrants almost always moved into old neighborhoods, usually close to the terminus of whatever form of transportation they used to get to the city, the bus or train station. Since those terminal points were usually located in or near the central core of the city, those were the areas in which the new immigrants settled.

The reasons for the tendency of new immigrants to settle near the terminals were quite simple. A new immigrant arriving in a strange environment was not likely to take a taxi or even public transportation with which he was unfamiliar into the distant reaches of the city. His natural inclination was to take his suitcase (if he had one) or his bag or box of belongings, walk around the corner from the terminal, and find a room. His next step was to find a job, preferably as close as possible to where he lived. Once firmly rooted economically, he sent for his family (if he had one) and looked for a larger flat, possibly two or three rooms.

Then the brothers, sisters, cousins, aunts, uncles and grandparents began to arrive. They almost automatically went to the area where the enterprising pioneer immigrants were living and moved in with the relatives until they could afford a room or a couple of rooms of their own. Within a short period of time, shops stocking native foods appeared, restaurants serving native delicacies opened, taverns or wine houses dispensing native alcoholic spirits blossomed, recreational facilities endemic to the native culture were built, and churches or temples serving the religious needs of the local population were established. Thus, island oases of native culture were created in the heart of the city.

The process repeated itself with each ethnic group moving into the city. Chicago became a city of ethnic neighborhoods with almost fixed boundary lines dividing the various nationality groups. Thus, the Germans settled on the Near North Side (at one time known as *Die Nord Zeit*), the Irish on the near South Side, the Jews on the near west side around Maxwell Street, the Italians on the near west side north of the Jews along Taylor Street, the Via Veneto

of Chicago, the Bohemians and Poles on the near southwest side
and the near northwest side around Division and Ashland streets,
the heart of Polonia in Chicago.°

After the restrictive immigration law of 1924 was passed, these
communities began to jell as centers of ethnic culture. The people
in them slowly assimilated somewhat to the life of the city as a
whole, although still retaining strong feelings of identification with
their own ethnic groups. As economic opportunities opened up they
began to search for better living conditions in newer neighborhoods.

However, the old ethnic clannishness and sense of identification
with their cultural groups was still strong. As they moved from the
older neighborhoods into newer communities farther out from the
center of the city, they literally moved *en masse*. Thus, the Jews
moved from the near west side to North Lawndale, the Italians
moved steadily west up the center of the city, the Poles and
Bohemians moved west along the near southern streets of the city,
the Irish and Lithuanians went south, and the Germans and
Scandinavians went northwest.

Within each of these ethnic groups, fissures began to appear
between the more successful *nouveau riche* and those immigrants
who had not done so well in the new world. Wealthier German
Jews settled in Hyde Park and South Shore, close to the intellectual
and cultural stimulation of the University of Chicago, while
successful merchant Jews moved north to Albany Park and Rogers
Park. Bohemian skilled workers went west to Berwyn. German
machinists went to the far northwest reaches of the city. Polish
middle-income workers moved to Cicero. Successful Irish politicians, civil servants, tavern owners and lawyers headed southeast
and southwest. Italian and Greek doctors, accountants, restaurant
owners, and undertakers moved to Austin, Oak Park, River Forest,
Elmwood Park and Westchester. Within each of the areas of the
city and its suburbs new ethnic neighborhoods and enclaves were

---

° The story is told of a Chinese immigrant who came to Chicago and opened a hand
laundry in the heart of Polonia on Chicago's northwest side. After a five-year career in
business, working eighteen hours a day, seven days a week, servicing his Polish customers, the
laundryman left his establishment one day to venture forth into the city at large. Confident of
his ability to communicate with the natives of the city because of his mastery of the language
spoken in his neighborhood, he was horrified to discover that nobody could understand his
English. It took him a little while to discover that he was fluent in Polish.

created. They were now middle class instead of working class, but they were still Irish, Polish, Bohemian, Lithuanian, Greek, German, Italian, and Jewish communities.

The more than 1,000,000 blacks from the South who have emigrated to Chicago, and approximately 350,000–500,000 Mexicans and Puerto Ricans, are the last of the great wave of immigrants, and are following the traditional patterns of movement which characterize the behavior of immigrant groups moving into a new environment. Like the ethnic immigrants before them, southern blacks and Spanish-speaking Latins moving into Chicago settled in the old neighborhoods. As is traditional in such situations, the ethnic old settlers in these communities began to flee from the new immigrants. Most of the South Side, much of the west side, and some of the Near North Side have lost their Irish, Jewish, Italian, Polish, Bohemian, and German populations and have become black and Latin ghettos. Only on the near southwest and northwest sides are the Poles and Bohemians making a stand. The Poles, in particular, remain intransigent and resistant to the black and Latin pressure in the inner areas of the city. The older Polish settlers do not retreat easily from their hard-won homes and six-flat buildings. However, even in these neighborhoods, the relentless pressure of the bursting black and Latin ghettos is slowly breaking down the barriers.

The influx of 1,000,000 blacks and 350,000 Latins into the city has fragmented the population even more deeply than the ethnic divisions. The division between ethnic whites, and the Latins and blacks has added another dimension to the ethnically separated city. In one sense, it has unified the ethnic whites on a single issue—blocking the movement of the blacks and Latins into white neighborhoods. But, at another level, the rapid growth of the black and Latin populations and the steady spread of the black and Latin ghettos have opened a wide chasm within the city's body politic between the black and Latin, and the white populations of the city. In the early 1970s race had replaced nationality as the major cultural and political factor in the life of the city, and the ethnic neighborhoods are changing into racial areas of blacks, browns, and whites.

A third factor in Chicago's life is religion. In the largest Roman Catholic archdiocese in North America, containing approximately

1,750,000 of the faithful, no decision can be made without due consideration for the feelings and aspirations of the majority Catholic population of the city. It is with good reason that the state of Illinois annually awarded license plate number one, not to the governor, but to the Roman Catholic cardinal of Chicago. The influence of the hierarchy and the many parishioners of the Church of Rome is always present in decision making in the politics, law, educational policy, and cultural life of the city.

This is not to say that that influence is necessarily bad or necessarily good—merely that it is so. Roman Catholic power in Chicago has contributed mightily to the growth and development of the city, and to the problems of the city. If, as Christ told his people, his Father's house has many rooms, so does his Roman Catholic church in Chicago have many factions. Some of the most liberal, as well as some of the most conservative, proposals and pressures in the life of Chicago have emanated from the many-splendored, broad-based, variegated Roman Catholic clergy and laity of the city.

In contrast to the dominant Catholic religious community, the Protestant and Jewish communities, with the exception of powerful business leaders, are weak. They are not ignored, they are consulted, but their influence is nowhere near so great as that of the Roman Catholic community. Since most of the Protestants in the city are now the blacks, they can be dealt with on the basis of race rather than religion. And since most of the Jews have fled the city for the suburbs, except for those residing in a few fringe areas, they can be easily ignored, although recognized and tolerated in decision making in the city.

The Role of the Irish

The predominant role of members of the Roman Catholic church in the life of the city is closely related to and buttressed by another cultural fact in Chicago—the control of the city's political life by the Irish.

There is an old cliché about the city of Chicago that the Jews own it, the Irish run it, and the blacks live in it. The cliché is only about half true. The Jews do not own Chicago. White Anglo-Saxon-Protestant businessmen, who live in suburban communities like Lake Forest and Kenilworth, control the economic life of the city.

And the blacks still number less than half the population of the city. But the Irish do run the city.

Irish Catholic dominance of the political and governmental systems of the city is a fact of life in present day Chicago and has been so for many years. The first two major ethnic groups who came into the city from Europe were the Irish and the Germans. While the Germans were an important segment of the city's body politic, the Irish had several advantages which they parlayed into a dominant political role. They spoke and understood English. They were familiar with the English local political and governmental institutions on which the American system was based. They were neutral outsiders in the traditional ethnic antipathies and hostilities which the Central and East European ethnic groups brought to America from their homelands. ("A Lithuanian won't vote for a Pole, and a Pole won't vote for a Lithuanian," according to a Chicago politician. "A German won't vote for either of them—but all three will vote for a 'Turkey,' an Irishman.") And, finally, the Irish became the saloonkeepers in cities like Chicago, and the Irish-owned and -run saloons became the centers of social and political activity not only for the Irish but also for the Polish, Lithuanian, Bohemian, and Italian immigrants who poured into the city after the Irish and Germans. For where would an ethnic laborer go for recreation at night after his twelve-hour stint in the steel mills or the stockyards but to the local saloon?

As a consequence of their control of these recreational centers of the neighborhoods, the Irish saloonkeepers and bartenders became the political counselors of their customers, and the political bosses of the wards and, eventually, of the city. Names like Mike McDonald, Johnny Powers, Bathhouse John Coughlin, and Hinky Dink Kenna illuminated local political life, if not the city's top offices, around the turn of the twentieth century. Their replacements were men like Roger Sullivan, Roger Brennan, Botchy Connors, Dorsey Crowe, Dan Ryan, John Duffy, Pat Nash, Ed Kelly, and John Touhy, Sr. That group was replaced by the Daleys, Cullertons, Keanes, Burkes, Barretts, Dunnes, Gills, and sundry other contemporary Irishmen.

As early as the 1890s, Irish dominance in the city council manifested itself. Of 28 of the most influential aldermen during that decade, 24 were Irish. Of 104 aldermen in the council from 1908 to

1910, nearly one-third were Irish. In 1926, although they were outnumbered by all the other major ethnic groups in the city, 33 of the Democratic city ward committeemen on the party's governing central committee were Irish, and the Irish held a similarly disproportionate share of the patronage jobs. By the beginning of Mayor Daley's term of office in 1955, the Irish still held one-third of the seats in the city council, despite the fact that they constituted only about 10 percent of the city's population (about 350,000), and were far outnumbered by the Poles (about 600,000) and the blacks (about 750,000).

The Irish captured the mayor's office in 1933 with Edward Kelly and have held it ever since. Despite a slow and steady decline in their numerical strength in the city council and the Democratic party's county central committee due to the rapidly increasing number of blacks, and a movement of Irish to the suburbs, the Irish have retreated into the inner sanctums of party and government at the local level and maintained a tight control of both by holding on to the key positions and passing them on to other Irishmen. According to a somewhat bitter Democratic ward committeeman who is not of Irish origin, the "in group" in the Democratic party in Cook County today consists of an "Irish Mafia" of South Side Irishmen of the Roman Catholic faith who frequent the same social activities as the mayor and who are alumni of Daley's high school, De LaSalle.° "Daley takes 50 percent of the quality patronage jobs and gives them out to his friends in the 11th Ward," according to the frustrated politician. "The other 50 percent is distributed to the rest of the wards with Keane and his 'North Side Irish' coming out ahead." †

° Some Democratic politicians have attempted to infiltrate the ranks of the Irish Mafia by assuming Irish names. For example, the Democratic committeeman and alderman of Daley's neighboring 12th Ward, a Polish father and son named Theodore and Donald Swinarski, also use the name of Sweeney. Having an Irish-sounding name helps too. The Democratic committeeman and alderman of the South Side 17th Ward is a black man named Shannon, as was the late committeeman and former congressman from the all-black 24th Ward on Chicago's west side, a man named Collins.

† Tom Keane, former Democratic alderman and current committeeman from the 31st Ward, is the most powerful Democratic politician in Chicago, next to Mayor Daley. He was chairman of the Finance Committee of the Chicago City Council, and probably would have been mayor if Daley had not succeeded in consolidating his power so successfully or if he had faltered in office. In 1975, according to a precinct captain in Keane's ward organization, Keane controls about 450 "good" patronage jobs. The lowest-paying patronage job for any of

In 1962, seven years after Daley assumed office as mayor of Chicago, twelve of the fifty aldermen in the city council were Irish, as were twenty-one of the fifty ward committeemen on the Cook County Democratic Central Committee. In 1970, eight years later, eight of the aldermen and seventeen of the ward committeemen were Irish. (The Irish percentage of the city's population is declining, while the black population is exploding. The Irish have had to give some ground to the blacks in the organization, and anti-organization black aldermen have been moderately successful in winning aldermanic seats in the city council.)

The disparity of Irish power vis-à-vis all the other ethnic groups in the Democratic party manifests itself at the highest levels of city and county government, but not at the state and federal levels of government. The Irish are primarily interested in local office, not in state or federal office. They reverse the normal trend in politics from local to state and national office. For the Irish, the route is more likely to be from Congress and the state legislature to city and county positions.

In 1970, the Irish held the following positions in city and county government: mayor of Chicago (since 1933); president of the Cook County Board of Commissioners (control of approximately 6,000 patronage jobs);* county clerk (patronage and control of election machinery); county assessor (establishes assessment valuation for all property in the county); † member of the board of appeals (appellate court for tax assessments); state's attorney (chief law enforcement officer for the county in charge of prosecutions); clerk of the circuit court (control over 1500 patronage jobs); president of the Chicago Park District (powerful patronage position); ‡ corpora-

---

Keane's 52 precinct captains is in the $8,000–$10,000-per-year bracket, and all the approximately 400 assistant precinct captains have patronage jobs. Keane was also floor leader of the city council. He and Daley maintained absolute control over all legislative matters and procedures in the council. Other Finance Committee chairmen before Alderman Keane were P. J. Cullerton, Dan Ryan, John Duffy, John S. Clark, and James Bowler (all Irish). In 1974 Keane was convicted of mail fraud and had to resign his aldermanic seat. His wife, Adeline, was slated for alderman in his place.

* Previous Irish county board presidents who served before incumbent George Dunne were two Dan Ryans (father and son) and John Duffy.

† One Irish former county assessor who left the Democratic party and became a Republican was subsequently indicted and sent to prison for income tax evasion by the Democratic United States Attorney for Northern Illinois.

‡ The vice-president, the secretary, the attorney general, the acting general superintendent, and one of the other three commissioners were also Irish.

tion counsel of the city of Chicago (chief law enforcement officer of
the city); superintendent of police (of thirty-five police commissioners and superintendents since 1861, twenty-one were Irish; in 1964,
forty-one of the seventy-two top administrative positions in the
police department were held by Irish); fire commissioner (two of the
three first deputy fire marshals and seven of the nine second deputy
fire marshals were Irish);* superintendent of public schools; president of the board of education (control over massive patronage in
the nonteaching personnel of the school system);†president of the
Metropolitan Sanitary District Board of Trustees (at one time
massive patronage, and still in control of important leases and
contracts); purchasing agent of the city of Chicago; president of the
Chicago Civil Service Commission; president of the Chicago Plan
Commission; city collector; Cook County civil defense director; and
the commissioners of the departments of sanitation and streets,
water and sewers, buildings, and consumer sales and weights and
measures (all these are assisted by a plethora of Irish deputies,
assistant commissioners, and superintendents).

An interesting phenomenon is that of nine Daley appointees to
the board of directors of the Chicago Public Library, only one was
Irish (this is an unsalaried post); but of four of the mayor's
appointees to the board of the Chicago Transit Authority, three

* Commissioner Robert Quinn, an old boyhood friend of Daley, became famous (or
infamous) among Chicagoans who had never heard of him before when he ordered the air
raid sirens in the city turned on in September 1959, at about 11:30 P.M. when the mayor's
beloved Chicago White Sox clinched the American League pennant by winning a night
baseball game in Comiskey Park, a few blocks from the mayor's home. The siren created
something of a panic in some parts of the city, with some people going out into the streets,
others inundating police, fire, radio, television, and newspaper switchboards with inquiring
calls. A goodly number of people, however, paid no attention to the siren, either because of
the native fatalism characteristic of much of Chicago's population, or else because they had
no idea of what the air raid sirens meant, because of the state of the city's civil defense efforts.
Those efforts seem to consist mainly of providing literature to citizens who are able to find the
Office of Civil Defense in the labyrinthic depths of the Museum of Science and Industry in
Chicago's Hyde Park area.

† Most Irish parents send their children to the city's Catholic parochial schools, but the
Irish maintain control of the public school system, probably more for patronage purposes than
for educational reasons. A significant percentage of the nonteaching personnel in the public
school system is Irish. Years ago, only graduates of Chicago Teachers College could teach in
the Chicago public schools. Irish Catholic graduates of Catholic parochial high schools were
given preference in getting admitted to Chicago Teachers College, and the administrative
staff of the board of education is still heavily dominated by Irish Catholics, partly because of
this situation.

were Irish (this post pays $15,000 annually). Of fifty ward superin-
tendents, fourteen were Irish, matching the number of Italians (the
Irish seem willing to divide the spoils equally here), and doubling
the Poles, who number only seven, although the Poles far outnum-
ber the Irish and the Italians together in the city's population.

In the judiciary, too, Chicago's Irish lawyer-politicians seek
political rewards at the local levels of government and politics
rather than at the state or national level. This could be for a number
of reasons—the parochial political outlook of local Irish lawyer-politicians; the protection the local organization can give a sitting local
judge in contrast to the possible scrutiny of judicial conduct by
federal officials in Washington; the fact that the Democratic
organization's legal needs are more deeply involved in matters
coming under local, rather than federal, jurisdiction; the fact that
the Democratic organization can control and discipline local and
state judges who must be slated for office for an elective term; the
practice of nominating local and state judges by judicial nominating
conventions and electing them by confirmation of an uninformed
and disinterested electorate, rather than nomination by the president of the United States, investigation by the Federal Bureau of
Investigation and confirmation by the United States Senate, which
can probe deeply into backgrounds and qualifications and which
can remove by impeachment; and, finally, the loss of control over a
federal judge once he has taken office with a life term and is subject
only to removal by the United States Congress.

A check of the number of Irish in the judiciary in Cook County
and the state of Illinois for 1970 revealed that of sixty-six Cook
County circuit court judges, at least twenty-five were Irish. Of
twelve appellate court judges in the state of Illinois' First Judicial
District (encompassing Cook County), six were Irish. Of the three
Illinois state supreme court justices in the First District of Illinois,
one was Irish. At the federal judicial level in Cook County, just
three out of ten members of the United States Court of Appeals for
the Seventh Circuit were Irish, and of eleven judges on the United
States District Court for Northern Illinois, only one, Daley's former
law partner, William Lynch, was Irish. (The United States Attorney
for Northern Illinois is also usually Irish whenever a Democratic
president sits in the White House.)

The chief judge of the Circuit Court of Cook County in 1970, who assigned cases to all the judges on the circuit court, was John Boyle (Irish), a former state's attorney of Cook County, who completely dominated the executive committee of the circuit court divisions. The executive committee was responsible for the selection of magistrates and the renewal of their appointments (magistrates earned $23,500 annually, while maintaining their private law practices); the presiding judge of the chancery division of the circuit court, who appointed masters in chancery and trustees for receiverships (the annual fees for this work often surpassed the annual salaries of circuit and superior court judges); the presiding judge of the law division of the circuit court; the head of the probate court; and the presiding judge of the criminal division of the circuit court (another former law partner of Mayor Daley) were all Irish.

Few Irish go to Congress, to either the United States Senate or the House of Representatives. Former Senator Paul Douglas and newly elected Senator Adlai Stevenson III are Anglo-Saxon Protestants. The Illinois Democratic delegation, which has seven city Democrats in the House of Representatives, is headed by Dan Rostenkowski, a Pole, who replaced Sidney Yates, a Jew. Poles, Jews, Italians, and only one black, William Dawson (before 1970), made up the congressional delegation, except for an Irish congressman from Daley's district, Morgan Murphy, Jr., son of Daley's old friend, Morgan Murphy, Sr. Murphy, Jr., replaced William Murphy, who retired in 1970. Two other Irish city congressmen, Daniel Ronan and Thomas O'Brien, both of whom died, were replaced by two black men.°

In the state legislature, in both the senate and house, the number of Irish representatives from Chicago in the Democratic party was comparable to their numbers in the Congress. In 1970, of sixteen Democratic state senators from Chicago, only three were Irish, and of thirty-seven Democratic state representatives in the house, only seven were Irish. But the two major power positions of Democratic floor leader in both houses were held by Irish stalwarts

° The Democratic organization exacted retribution on the Polish, Bohemian, and Italian citizens of the suburbs of Cicero and Berwyn, which are in the late Ronan's district. These towns have turned Republican and are violently antiblack. The new Democratic congressman chosen in 1970 to represent them was a black man, George Collins from the west side's black 24th Ward. When Collins was killed in a plane crash in 1973, his wife was chosen to fill his seat.

McGloon and Touhy. They were the link between the mayor of Chicago and the Illinois General Assembly leadership in Springfield.

In the executive branch of state government, Bohemians like Otto Kerner, Jews like Sam Shapiro and Henry Horner, and Anglo-Saxon Protestants like the late Adlai Stevenson and Sherwood Dixon can be run for governor. The rest of the state ticket can be made up of other ethnic Catholics, downstate Anglo-Saxon Protestants, and an occasional Jewish candidate. Names like Donald Prince, Alan Dixon, and Adlai Stevenson III (Anglo-Saxon Protestants), Michael Bakalis (Greek), Joseph Lohman (Jewish), and Francis Lorenz (Polish Catholic), with an occasional Irishman named Clark or Howlett suffice to fill out the state ticket. The Irish have little interest in the state offices. If the alien ethnics or non-Catholics win, fine and dandy. If the result is otherwise, there is no great loss. And the same applies to the state legislature as long as the Irish retain the Democratic leadership posts in the two houses.

As for Cook County, the ethnics and the blacks are given fair representation on the county board, except for the powerful presidency of the board, and the chairmanship of the finance committee of the board, which usually remains in Irish hands. Presidents Dunne, Duffy, and Ryan all held the finance chairmanship before succeeding to the county board presidency. Of the ten Democratic county commissioners from the city who are automatically elected (six Republicans from the suburbs make up the remainder of the sixteen-man board), only three Irish held seats, George Dunne, John Touhy, and Ruby Ryan (Dan Ryan's widow). Three Poles, two blacks, one Italian, and one Luxemburger held the other seven seats. The Luxemburger, Commissioner Jerome Huppert, Democratic committeeman of the 50th Ward, is, at present, finance chairman.

Insofar as the other county offices are concerned, two or three moderately important offices such as county treasurer, sheriff, and one member of the board of appeals were allocated to a Pole, a Jew, and a German-Pole. While there is significant patronage in the first two offices, most of the patronage jobs are low level, are not too lucrative in salary, and can be used to keep the Poles, blacks, and other ethnics quiet, if not happy. And the sheriff's law-enforcement powers are outside the city. Offices like sheriff and the Board of Election Commissioners of the City of Chicago are offices which, in the vernacular, take a lot of heat from the press and reform groups. Those can be allocated to Poles, Jews, and others. The coroner, the clerk of the appellate court and the county recorder of deeds can be a Scandinavian, a German, a Bohemian, or a Lithuanian. The other citywide offices (there are only two) need not be Irish either. A Pole can be city clerk; a Jew, a Bohemian, or a black can be city treasurer. These offices, too, are not important from either a patronage or power standpoint.

The primary objective is to retain control for the Irish of those offices in the city which have policy-making powers, which have significant patronage, which deal with law enforcement or with the control of the election machinery. With that accomplished, the Irish faithful can wield the power and exercise the prerogatives while pacifying the other ethnics, Catholics, blacks, and Jews with some part of the action. For is it not true, by the dogma, that the Irish are by nature best qualified to govern and politically manipulate the levers of power in the cities of this country after being denied those opportunities for so long in the land of their birth by their Anglo-Saxon oppressors?

An objective appraisal of the performance of the majority of the members of Chicago's political Irish Mafia would, in most cases, attest to the validity of the dogma. With some exceptions, Irish politicians and administrators have generally, if not universally, proved to be hardworking, capable, and efficient in running wards and administering city and county offices. Of course that recognition must be tempered by the fact that many of the most efficient of the politicians have also used their offices and powers to further enhance their pecuniary ambitions. A significant number of the most successful Irish politicians have become wealthy during their terms in public office. But so have the other ethnic and racial politicians. It was ever thus in Chicago, and the Irish do deliver goods and services to the rest of the citizenry, even if it often costs somewhat more than it should.

The Irish are not only the manipulators of the key power positions in the city and county political and governmental offices. They are also the arbiters of the racial conflict, the dispensers of perquisites to the other ethnic and religious groups and the blacks, and also serve as the go-between, if not the handmaiden, of the

Protestant businessmen who own the city's major industries and financial institutions, and the other ethnics and blacks.

The Irish succeeded, at least to date, in pacifying the poor blacks in the city with welfare and jobs, in buying off the most politically able among the blacks with public office and patronage, and in fending off the militant civil rights activists by adding enough police and political power to the other techniques to keep a modicum of order, if not peace, in the black ghettos.

They pacified the predominantly Catholic, strongly conservative, white ethnics by refusing to use governmental and political power to push integration in the city, especially in the area of housing. Public housing units, in particular, are highly segregated and were always placed in black neighborhoods. As long as the policy worked, the white ethnics were willing to tolerate, if not support, massive welfare programs which help to keep the black community quiescent, if not happy, although the blacks are becoming increasingly restive and militant over their role in the life of the city.

This policy also helps to satisfy the needs of the financial and business overlords of the city who need a good labor supply, a low tax rate, a decent level of order in the city, good city services, and a political and governmental climate which enables them to pursue their economic interests and the city's well-being, since, in the eyes of most of the city's leading businessmen, there is no conflict between their interests and Chicago's prosperity and future prospects.

Chicago is Dick Daley's town. Uncultured and parochial, tough albeit friendly, conservative yet tolerant, self-deprecating but proud. A Babylon to the rural Rubes, a Mecca to anyone in search of a job, a Sodom or Gomorrah to conventioneers seeking a little illicit excitement, a Jerusalem to all those who worship at the altar of the fast buck. But not an Athens, neither a Rome, nor a London, and never a Paris.

The city has experienced great fires, economic depressions, financial crises, nationality differences, religious tensions, racial conflicts, spreading blight, gang wars, political corruption, and all the other problems common to urban life in America. But it has survived them all, eliminated some, reduced others, learned to live with others, and progressed steadily far beyond the hopes of the city's founders.

It took Chicago thirty years to wipe out the stigma of the era of Al Capone. It has taken a few years to recover from the shambles of the Democratic convention of 1968. But those who knew Chicago knew that the Cassandras who predicted the city's decline would be wrong, that the *auslanders* who had sampled the city's attractions would still come, and that the outraged liberals and reformers who had vowed eternal hostility because of the events of August 1968, would, in time, forgive and forget.

On September 12, 1969, one year after the Democratic National Convention, John Pekkanen, chief of the Chicago bureau of *Life* magazine, described his feelings about Chicago in the pages of his magazine:

On the plaza that overlooks the Chicago River, with a view of some of Chicago's most stunning architecture, I chatted the other day with a friend. He told me that last September he and his wife, both sickened by Convention Week, had decided to leave the city. They're still here. And we both know other people who felt the same way and are still here too. We agreed that Chicago, despite its flaws, its corruption, its occasional insensitivity, is a city that has a way of drawing you into it. For all its sprawl and size it remains an intimate city with a strong feeling of neighborhood. Chicago forces you, almost against your will, to like it and finally to love it. It happened to him and it has happened to me.

The Mayor: The Big Precinct Captain in the Sky

What Charles de Gaulle was to France and Winston Churchill was to England; what Joseph Stalin was to Russia and Francisco Franco was to Spain; what James Curley was to Boston and Frank Hague was to Jersey City; and what Robert Moses and Fiorello La Guardia were to New York; Richard Joseph Daley, mayor of Chicago since 1955, and chairman of the Cook County Democratic Central Committee for the past twenty-two years, has been to Chicago. For over two decades Daley has stood astride the city like a colossus.

Daley operates from a broad-based power structure encompassing the business, labor, religious, and ethnic leaders in the community, and is also the unchallenged head of the most efficient and disciplined political organization in the country. The stocky, impeccably dressed, Front-of-the-Yards Irish Catholic politician has proved to be one of the most capable municipal administrators in the country, as well as the most effective political leader in Chicago's turbulent history. He uses his political power to get what he wants for his city, and his administrative power to strengthen the effectiveness of the political organization in which he has spent his life. He gives service and loyalty to both masters impartially and sees no contradiction in his dual responsibilities. His favorite, often-uttered maxim that "Good government is good politics and good politics is good government" is, for him, not a cliché but a *modus operandi* and a guiding principle of both political and administrative behavior. Daley understands power and uses it both as mayor and political leader. Bureaucrats and ward committeemen alike are held to a standard of excellence in performance of their respective tasks and are unceremoniously dumped when they fail to meet their responsibilities to his satisfaction.

Daley has come to personify the Democratic machine in Chicago. No analysis of the machine's dynamics, tactics, objectives, and future prospects can be meaningful except within the context of his impact on his city and its politics. Referred to as the "last of the old-time bosses—or the first of the new breed," he has made a lasting imprint on the physical, political, economic, and cultural life of the city of Chicago, and on its worldwide image for decades to come. For hundreds of millions of people all over the world, for whom the word "Chicago" once conjured up a vision of Al Capone, gangsters, and gunplay, "Chicago" often triggers a kaleidoscope of Mayor Daley shouting down a righteous Senator Abraham Ribicoff, drawing his finger across his throat to silence opposition at the 1968 convention, ordering his police into action against defenseless teenagers, or commanding the persecution and even shooting of poor, exploited blacks who had the temerity to challenge his authority.

How true is the generally accepted, international picture of Chicago's mayor? What is Daley really like? What forces move this man? How did he build and maintain his power both locally and nationally? How will history judge him after he has finally left the scene?

To answer these questions adequately, it is necessary to look at Daley the man, Daley the politician, and Daley the mayor. While it is not possible to separate these three Richard J. Daleys into watertight compartments, the composite Daley, the whole man, is the sum of these three parts. For Daley the politician has been strongly influenced by Daley the man and Daley the mayor. Daley the mayor has been influenced by Daley the man and Daley the politician. And Daley the man has lived his life in the shadows of Daley the politician and Daley the mayor.

All three Daleys, and the composite Daley, have their roots in six wellsprings from which Daley has drawn his philosophy, his inspiration, his sustenance, and his objectives in life as man, politician, and mayor. Those six wellsprings are his faith, his family, his ethnicity, his neighborhood, his party, and his city. He is a devout Roman Catholic. He is the only child of hardworking, God-fearing, unassuming parents, who has raised his own family in the same traditions. He is Irish to the core. He was born, grew up, and has lived all his life in Bridgeport, one of Chicago's authentic Back-of-the-Yards neighborhoods. He has always been a Democrat. And he is a life-long resident of Chicago, a city he has always believed to be the greatest metropolis in the world.

Daley the Man

Daley's physical appearance, especially on television, does not conjure up a picture of either dynamism or ability, and certainly not of charisma. "He would be doomed in the cosmetology of today's politics," said David Halberstam in *Harper's* magazine in August 1968. "Those jowls, that heavyset look. He doesn't look like a modern municipal leader, a cost-accounting specialist; he looks, yes, exactly like a big city boss, right out of the smoke-filled room." William Bowen, in *Fortune* magazine in January 1965, described Daley as "a squat and somewhat jowly politician whose public utterances largely consist of platitudes sprinkled with malapropisms." Columnist Mike Royko of the *Chicago Daily News*, one of Daley's most severe critics, once described the mayor's oratorical prowess. "Until he became mayor," wrote Royko, "Daley was known as a quiet, behind-the-scenes politician. When he started making speeches, it was clear why he has been quiet. He has since developed two much improved styles of oratory: a controlled mumble for TV and an excited gabble for political rallies."

Indeed, the mayor has often committed offenses against the proper use of the English language in some of his public utterances. Among his most famous malapropisms are gems such as, "That is unreasonable reasoning." "I resent the insinuendos." "That isn't true enough to answer." "Together we must rise to ever higher and higher platitudes." "It is amazing what they will be able to do once they get the atom harassed." "For the enlightenment and edification and hallucination of the alderman from the 50th Ward." "They have vilified me, they have crucified, yes, they have even criticized

me." "Ladies and gentlemen of the League of Women Voters."
"Gentlemen, get the thing straight, once and for all, the policeman
isn't there to create disorder, the policeman is there to preserve
disorder." At a political rally during the 1970 election campaign, the
mayor introduced as incumbent president of the Cook County
Board of Commissioners and Democratic candidate for the office,
Dan Ryan, who had once served in the office but who had been
dead for over ten years, while George Dunne, the incumbent
occupant of the office and Democratic candidate sat dumbfounded.
A week later, at another rally, the mayor introduced as candidate
for county treasurer one Herbert Paschen, who had been out of the
office for fourteen years.

"He has simple tastes," said Royko. "Nobody catches him
chatting about literature, music or French cooking. He likes White
Sox games, fishing and parades. He has led more parades than
anyone since Rome fell apart. Hardly a Saturday passes when the
mayor isn't hoofing down the middle of State Street with thousands
of city workers behind him. It has been estimated that he has
paraded the distance from Chicago to Minsk."

All these things about Daley's appearance, his histrionic ability,
and the Daley style are true, but they do not really convey an
accurate picture of the man. Seated behind his desk in his office on
the fifth floor of City Hall; seated at the table in front of the Cook
County Democratic Central Committee's inner circle of powerful
slatemakers; chairing a negotiating session in a conference room
with the most important businessmen and labor leaders in the city;
welcoming the Queen of England and the president of France or of
his own country; walking from the door of City Hall to his limousine
on LaSalle Street; entering a hall filled with the Who's Who of his
city; or pouring it on oratorically from the podium at a conclave of
precinct captains and party workers, Daley radiates a sense of
power, purpose, and confidence.

Daley wears well-made but conservative clothes (he has his suits
made at Duro Brothers, an exclusive tailor on North Michigan
Avenue in Chicago) and was named one of the ten best-dressed men
in America in 1964, having come a long way from his early
Bridgeport days of "fat Max ties, baggy suits and broad brimmed
hats." He retains something of an Irish brogue (he often drops his *t*'s
and *th*'s for *d*'s, greeting people on the street with "Hi, dere. How

are ya?"). He has an Irish temper which he once lost frequently, but has learned to control most of the time, and a good Irish sense of humor, despite his somewhat dour appearance. His conversations are generally monosyllabic and his public speeches are usually models of brevity. In person he looks ten years younger than his seventy-three years, not at all as jowly as he appears on television, and comes across as a short, well-built, well-dressed, sincere, confident, and unassuming man.

Despite the occasional malapropism, Daley projects an image at public gatherings of an effective, well-organized speaker who knows where he is going. "His style comes through," according to one observer, "not as inept but as unpretentious." County board president George Dunne, Daley's possible heir apparent as mayor, recounts Daley's advice to budding candidates for office: "Prepare your talks carefully, and don't go over five minutes. Don't tell off-color stories. If you've had something to drink, stay home." Daley, in public gatherings, is rather taciturn, conservative, and reserved. "How do you approach the mayor? the machine guys ask laughingly. On tiptoe," says newspaperman D. J. R. Bruckner. "And when he speaks to the people, most of the time, he uses few and careful words. Sloppy listening habits are very dangerous around this man."

Daley is a very private man.* "Nobody has ever really known Daley," says Benjamin Adamowski, a renegade Democratic Polish politician, who has known him politically for thirty-five years and who became his bitter enemy. Daley has few close friends. Most of those are old cronies he grew up with in Bridgeport and has known all his life such as his former law partner and now federal judge, William Lynch; the late Steve Bailey, head of the plumbers' union; Chicago Fire Commissioner Robert Quinn; and Morgan Murphy, a Commonwealth Edison Company executive. He has never crossed the line of mixing business and political relationships with social

---

* After having written above that "Daley was an only child of God-fearing, hardworking, unassuming parents," it occurred to me that I was not sure that Daley was an only child. I checked with two people, one a Democratic politician who has known Daley for twenty-five years, and the other, a man who had worked in Daley's office closely with him for a number of years and who had been invited to the weddings of Daley's children. When asked whether Daley was an only child or whether there were any brothers or sisters, both men responded that they thought so but were not sure.

relationships. While he mingles officially as mayor with blueblood Protestant tycoons and captains of industry from Lake Forest and Lakeview Avenue, he has no interest in climbing the social ladder, as so many who came from his background have tried to do.°

"Part of Daley's great influence over other politicians," according to Bruckner, in an unusually penetrating analysis of the mayor's character, "springs from his deep and systematic morality. . . . Daley is powerful. But he is also decent and kind; indulgent he is not, or soft. He has real guts, but he also has courtesy and deep values. He fights clean and hard, and there is simply nothing little, dirty or petty about the man."

Daley drinks only an occasional cocktail in public, or beer at home, does not like off-color stories, and does not swear (despite the allegations about what he shouted at Senator Abraham Ribicoff at the Democratic convention in 1968). "I never used that language in my life," he told a reporter at a press conference after the incident with Ribicoff, "and you say that or anything else and you lie, you're a liar." He does not like excessive drinking by other people, even at Democratic political shindigs where the liquor flows fairly freely. According to a story told by a Chicago newspaperman, "One of Daley's administrators was sitting in a bar one night, drinking too much, when he received a phone call. On the other end came a curt voice, 'This is Mayor Daley. Your wife is rather upset. I think you'd better get home.' 'I don't know how he knew where I was but, of course, I went home right away.' "

Daley is unquestionably personally honest and has not accumulated a large fortune through graft and bribery, as a number of mayors in Chicago's past and some of the powerful contemporary figures in the Democratic organization have done.† The only people

---

° At a banquet held several years ago at the Conrad Hilton hotel, Daley arrived late, looked around the room, and said from the podium, "There certainly is an elegant group here tonight, the most prosperous Irish in Chicago. I can't help but think of your mothers and fathers and grandparents who would never have been allowed in this hotel." There was an uproar of laughter; then Daley said, "I want to offer a prayer for those departed souls who could never get into the Conrad Hilton."

† Of Daley's four predecessors as mayor of Chicago, three had been involved in major corruption. When Mayor William Hale ("Big Bill the Builder") Thompson died, one safe-deposit box in the American Bank and Trust Company yielded a hoard of $1,466,250 in cash when it was opened by probate court examiners. Another box in the First National Bank contained $112,000 in stocks and bonds. Two boxes in the Boulevard National Bank held

who accuse Daley of being dishonest are people who do not know him. Among his bitterest critics—newspapermen, politicians, and civic figures—his personal honesty and integrity with regard to graft are almost universally accepted. Daley is not interested in money so much as in power (as Alderman Tom Keane, the second most powerful man in the Cook County Democratic organization, remarked in 1972, "Daley wanted power, and I wanted money, and we both got what we wanted"). Daley's major interest in money seems to be to make sure that there is enough to take care of his family decently and to provide against adversity and old age. This is not to say that Daley may not have made some money in the kind of law business that might come to the law firm of a rising politician with some political power or clout (Daley once had a law firm with William Lynch, who is now a federal judge), or that a man with his connections in the business and financial worlds may not have been the beneficiary of tips on stocks or investments that bankers and business tycoons might want to pass on to a circle of friends and associates. (Daley's three sons are all in law, insurance, and real estate, and have been the beneficiaries of a considerable amount of city and county business. In 1974, a *Chicago Sun-Times* investigation exposed the fact that Daley secretly owned a small real estate firm in his neighborhood.) But speculation as to Daley's personal finances could, at the most, be only undocumented guesswork. One can say, however, that in a lifetime in public office and politics in a city in which opportunities for graft abound, in which corruption is

---

$220,000 in securities in one, and $22,000 cash in $50, $100, and $500 bills. Thompson's total estate, including real estate holdings, was $2,103,024. Thompson in turn had accused his successor, Mayor Anton J. ("Tony") Cermak, who had served as president of the Cook County Board of Commissioners, of being corrupt. " 'Saving Tony,' " charged Thompson during the 1931 mayoralty campaign, "saved six million out of a $10,000 salary . . . built the County Jail without a boiler . . . and grafts on coal and paving." Ed Kelly, mayor from 1933 to 1947, was indicted along with several other politicians for defrauding the Chicago Metropolitan Sanitary District of five million dollars while he was serving as the district's chief engineer. The indictment was quashed a year later. While Kelly was president of the South Park board, Soldier Field was built on park district land at a cost of eight million dollars. A comparable stadium, built in Los Angeles in the same period, cost $1,700,000. Kelly had been forced to pay $110,000 in back taxes on his income of $450,000 for the years 1927 through 1928. Pat Nash, Kelly's cohort in building the Kelly-Nash machine, was listed as having one of the ten highest incomes among Chicagoans for the year 1925 by the federal government. Nash was Democratic county chairman and was in the sewer contracting business. His firm did more sewer work than any other firm in Chicago.

accepted as a way of life by the citizenry, and as a public figure always exposed to attack by avowed opponents and enemies, no documented accusation of bribery, malfeasance, or corruption has ever been leveled against Daley. Whatever the allegations about the private status of Daley's finances by those who do not know him, the public record and the testimony of those who should and would know stands.

Daley has tremendous physical stamina and works incredibly long hours. According to Ray Simon, who served as his corporation counsel from 1965 to 1969, "Six hours of sleep and he's like a man coming home from a vacation." His work habits go back to his early years, when he worked during the day, went to school at night for eleven long years, and then went home to study. "I always went out dancing every night," said the late Steve Bailey, a Daley boyhood friend, "but Dick went home to study his law books. He would never stop in the saloon and have a drink." Daley did the same thing when he served in the state legislature. While other politicians were out carousing in the St. Nicholas hotel in Springfield, he spent his evenings in his hotel room studying the pending bills. Neil Hartigan, a rising young Irish politician, who in 1972 was elected lieutenant-governor of Illinois, and who served as Daley's administrative assistant for five years (1963–68) says that the mayor often took home a briefcase filled with papers at night after a long day at his desk. "When he came in the next morning," says Hartigan, "he had always done 60 to 100 percent of the work he took home." "He is at early Mass when his enemies are still sleeping," wrote David Halberstam, "and he is still working on city problems at night when they've all gone to bed or are out drinking."

Daley's family life is kept private and separate from his public life. "His private life is really his public life," according to Earl Bush, his former press aide (1955–74). "His whole life is being mayor." He spends as much time at home as his public life as mayor and county chairman allows. He goes home for lunch and dinner as often as possible. At most political dinners Daley shows up after the festivities have begun, makes a grand entrance to a standing ovation, says a few words in praise of the candidate being honored and the Democratic ticket, and then, without staying to eat, exits quietly when the master of ceremonies takes over the podium. An inveterate wake attender, he enters a chapel at a wake quietly, without fanfare, moves through the line with the other mourners as a friend or acquaintance, exchanges a few words with the relatives of the deceased, shakes a few hands on the way out, and departs as unobtrusively as he can.

Daley has been almost unbelievably influenced by his mother and father, whom he worshipped and still refers to as his "Mom and Dad, God love them." His public speeches at political gatherings almost invariably contain a reference to his parents and to the principles they taught him, by which he has lived all his life. Daley's father was a sheet-metal worker who participated in politics as an avocation and who counseled Daley until his death. "I have never seen Richard hit so hard by anything as by his father's death," says a Democratic politician who has known Daley for twenty-five years and who attended his father's wake. The senior Daleys were, according to those who knew them, devout Irish Roman Catholics in the best sense of the term.

Daley has raised his own family of seven children, Patricia, Mary, Eleanor, Richard, Michael, John, and William, according to the precepts he was taught by his own parents. The children attended Nativity Church on 37th Street, two blocks from the Daley home, went to Catholic parochial schools, to Catholic subway universities such as Loyola and DePaul, and lived at home until they married. In 1936, the year he was first elected to the state legislature, Daley married the only girl he had ever seriously courted, Eleanor ("Sis") Guilfoyle from St. Bridget's Parish on Archer Avenue in the neighborhood. Mrs. Daley is a quiet, modest, unassuming woman of great charm and grace who also looks considerably younger than her age. She is equally at home with old neighbors over coffee in her kitchen or in the basement recreation room in her bungalow home, at a state dinner for the Queen of England at the Ambassador East hotel in Chicago, as the guest of the president of the United States and the first lady in the White House, and at a political rally for 2000 Democratic women precinct captains and party workers.

Like many Chicago politicians, businessmen, and lawyers, Daley practices his own brand of nepotism. His family loyalty manifests itself in seeing to it that all deserving members of his family serve their family needs, their communities, and their political party by getting on a government payroll. Of course, since he is mayor of

Chicago and chairman of the Democratic party of Cook County, he has more success than most politicians do in securing public employment for the deserving. Daley's nepotism seems to be an admixture of taking care of relatives, a genuine concern for encouraging people to go into politics and public service, and a stubborn resistance and hostility to critics of his own personal social security system.

According to some unverified rumors, over one hundred of Daley's relatives hold government jobs. On the public payrolls—city, county and state—have been found such names as former Chicago corporation counsel Richard Curry, a cousin, who is now a judge; James O'Donohue, a son of an old Daley friend and one-time 11th Ward alderman, who also served in the corporation counsel's office and who is married to Mrs. Daley's niece; an uncle, Martin Daley, who served as assistant superintendent of maintenance and operation for Cook County; State Representative John M. Daley, a cousin of the mayor; police captain George A. Green, who is married to one of Mrs. Daley's sisters; a brother of Mrs. Daley, Tom Guilfoyle, who served as an engineer for the board of education; and State Representative John J. Houlihan, whose wife is the mayor's cousin. When Daley's daughter married a young man whose father was a physician, the good doctor was appointed to two part-time positions with the city and the county.

Daley's own oldest son, Richard Michael Daley, is clearly being groomed by his father for a career in politics, law, and public service. Young Daley is a graduate of his father's elementary school, Nativity; his high school, Catholic De LaSalle; and law school, DePaul; and began his government service in the city corporation counsel's office. In 1969, young Daley was slated for and elected to the 1970 state constitutional convention as a delegate from Daley's district, getting 89.6 percent of the vote (the best percentage of all of the 116 delegates elected in the state of Illinois). On election night, in the 11th Ward headquarters, the mayor betrayed his filial attachment and deep feelings about his oldest son's auspicious beginning of a political career by breaking down in the middle of a congratulatory speech to the crowd of friends, neighbors, and partyworkers gathered in the backroom of the headquarters. "I hope and pray to God," said the father, "when he's on the floor of the convention he'll always remember the people from whence he

comes, and that he'll always fight for the people." At that point the
mayor's voice broke and he had to wipe the tears from his eyes. Two
years later, the Democratic state senator from Daley's district,
Edward Nihill, stepped down, and young Daley was elected to his
seat in the legislature.

Daley's personal social security system extends also to friends,
sons of old friends, neighbors, and, indeed (rumor has it), to most of
the community of Bridgeport. While it is impossible to find out
exactly how many patronage jobs have been awarded to Daley's
11th Ward Democratic organization by the Democratic party of
Cook County, educated guesses place the number at somewhere
between 1500 and 2000 jobs, three or four times the number
awarded to some of the other top wards in Chicago, and possibly
ten times the number given to many of the wards. Rumor has it,
also, that the six precincts immediately adjacent to the mayor's
home, "Daley's pocket precincts," average 90 patronage jobs per
precinct, an almost unbelievable figure. According to Royko, "In
the East, some families register a new born son at Harvard or Yale.
In Bridgeport they sign him on with the City Water Department." *

Daley's largesse in the matter of keeping his neighbors gainfully
employed extends to private industry too. The 11th Ward Democratic organization patronage dispensers can place people in jobs
ranging from hospital orderlies or apprenticeships in the construc
tion trade unions to positions with Commonwealth Edison and
other major industrial concerns. The mayor habitually keeps a
fatherly eye on any promising young talent in the neighborhood.
When a young Bridgeporter graduates from college, he is likely to
receive a telephone call from the mayor asking him to come down
to his office for a chat. Daley uses these visits to persuade the young
man to take a position with the city, thus to help his career, his city,
and the Bridgeport community.

The key to advancement, however, even if one is from

* According to a "reliable source," 60 to 70 percent of the bridge tenders in Chicago
come from Bridgeport. The Chicago River, which flows west from Lake Michigan and then
branches off north and south, meandering through the city, has a number of bridges which
may have to be raised once or twice a year when a boat with a tall smokestack passes under
them. At such bridges, bridge tenders sit in enclosed towers, whiling the time away, scanning
the horizon, waiting for such a boat to appear. These are most desirable patronage positions,
which are only matched by the custodians of the water purification stations out in Lake
Michigan.

Bridgeport, is combining efficiency on the job with a willingness and ability to participate actively in the political life of the community. As a policeman, seated in a patrol car in front of the police station on the corner of 35th and Lowe, down the street from the mayor's house, described the realities of life in Bridgeport to a young researcher seeking information about the community, "Lady, if I knew anything about politics, I'd be a captain by now."

Daley's life-long residence in the community of Bridgeport has helped shape his character and outlook on life. He was born in Bridgeport, went to Nativity Parochial School, Catholic De LaSalle High School for two years, attended Nativity Church on 37th Street, where he served as an altar boy, and has lived for more than thirty years in a bungalow at 3536 S. Lowe Avenue. The house is distinguished from the other houses on the block only by the one policeman standing watch at the front and by the little-noticed addition to the original bungalow at the back of the house toward the alley. The alley is unpaved and contains a number of potholes. The neighbors on the block have good Irish, Polish, and Lithuanian names like Danaher, Finley, Molloy, Walsh, McGuiness, O'Brien, Rastutis, Rekas, Kroulaidis, Mestrovic, and Zilinski. Kitty-corner, across the street, at the corner of 35th and Lowe, is the Deering Police Station, strategically located to provide quick reinforcements to the policeman on guard at the mayor's home, if necessary.

Daley's street, Lowe Avenue, is typical of many of the other streets in the area and of the neighborhood itself. Bridgeport is a community of about 40,000 people, in the process of a slow erosion of population, down about 20,000 from its high point of 60,000 in 1920. Bridgeporters are predominantly working class and lower-middle class, with an average income of approximately $7,000 per year. About 12 percent of the people earn less than $3,000 per year and about 20 percent earn over $10,000 annually. (Daley, with his mayor's salary of $35,000 per year is considerably above the local income standards). White-collar workers constitute approximately 25 percent of the employed population, compared to a citywide average of 37 percent, and blue-collar workers make up approximately 37 percent of the area's population. About 7 percent of the employable population are jobless.

Few Bridgeporters go to college. According to the 1970 census figures, about 2.3 percent are college graduates, a figure which is matched by black slum communities like North Lawndale and the lower west side of Chicago. The median amount of formal education in the neighborhood is 8.8 years.

Taverns and churches provide the major recreational and social facilities in the neighborhood. "A typical day, well spent in the eyes of the 11th Ward resident," according to a long-time member of the community, "consists of watching nine innings of baseball at Sox Park, a family dinner at one of the church halls, or perhaps playing some sport using the McGuane Park facilities [McGuane Park, which was formerly named after a dead war hero, had its name changed in 1960, to honor a newly deceased 11th Ward Democratic precinct captain]. Other than that, the residents are a stay-at-home lot, content with watching TV. Most residents simply concern themselves with their jobs and identify with blue-collar interests. We can say that, in general, the residents are culturally limited."

According to the 1970 census figures, of a total of 67,160 people in the whole 11th Ward, about 13 percent are foreign born, and 30 percent are first-generation Americans with at least one foreign-born parent. In other words, only a little over half the people of the ward (57 percent) are second-generation Americans. Broken down by nationality, the Irish are outnumbered by the Poles, Latins, Italians, Lithuanians, and Germans. There are about 7500 blacks in the 11th Ward, practically all of them concentrated east of Wentworth Avenue in Armour Square. The black population is the fastest-growing group of the ward's population.

In 1963, when a black family moved into Bridgeport, they found their furniture and belongings piled up on the sidewalk by their newly found unfriendly neighbors. They left and have not come back. In 1965 black comedian Dick Gregory led a group of black picketers past Daley's house for several nights, nearly precipitating a race riot. They, too, left, and have not come back. But the specter of penetration and inundation by the surrounding black community still hangs over beleaguered and encircled Bridgeport, as well as over the nearby communities of New City and McKinley Park. As long as the Democratic political organization in the 11th Ward can keep the white residents in the neighborhood by providing patronage jobs in government and other jobs in industry, the community can remain stable. But given the stagnant character of local industry, if Bridgeporters had to travel far afield to seek employment, they might have to move and the walls would be down.

It is this fact of life, as well as local pride, which makes Mayor Daley the most popular and best loved local folk hero in the community, although he is not the first Bridgeporter to be mayor of Chicago. If Virginia was the mother of presidents in the early days of the Republic, Bridgeport is the mother of mayors in recent Chicago history. The last three mayors of Chicago have been from Bridgeport; beginning in 1933, their rule has lasted over forty years—Edward Kelly (1933–1947), Martin Kennelly (1947–1955), and Richard Daley since 1955. But Daley has been far more concerned about the community and efficient in ministering to its needs than were his two Bridgeport predecessors.° It is with good reason that his Irish, Polish, Lithuanian, German and Italian neighbors support him, that they display his likeness like ikons in their homes and windows, that the neighborhood churches and business establishments contribute to the Democratic organization and receive reciprocal favors, that the *Bridgeport News* supports the mayor and his policies, and that Bridgeporters will pack the galleries at the International Amphitheater in their neighborhood, displaying "We Love Mayor Daley" signs during the Democratic National Convention. Whatever Daley does for the city at large, Bridgeport's needs loom large in the mayor's thoughts, policies, and actions.†

But the specter still remains. How long can Daley continue to hold the line for the community? What happens after he leaves the mayoralty? Nobody knows. The community already has a substan-

---

° Kennelly, a successful businessman and bachelor, moved to the Edgewater Beach hotel on Sheridan Road on Chicago's North Side, and Kelly moved to a brick colonial mansion at 4821 S. Ellis Avenue, in Chicago's exclusive (in the 1930s and 1940s) South Side Kenwood neighborhood.

† An 11th Ward program for the annual circus at the International Amphitheater had a picture of Lyndon B. Johnson with the caption "Our President" over it, a picture of Democratic governor of Illinois Otto Kerner with the caption "Our Governor," and a picture of Mayor Richard J. Daley with the caption "Our Great Mayor." (Neither Johnson, a Protestant from Texas, nor Kerner, a Bohemian from South Lawndale in Chicago, were from Bridgeport.) On 35th Street, as one drives east a couple of blocks from the mayor's house, a huge sign over the Lee Towing Service and Garage proclaims, "We have the greatest Mayor and police force in the world. Support them." At election time, every window on Lowe Avenue bears a Democratic campaign poster.

tial crime rate, significant teen-age delinquency, and some pockets of poverty. Although there has been industrial development and new small plant construction in the area, there has been virtually no residential construction since 1920. Only 2 percent of the 1970 housing units were in structures built since 1940. Beneath the stability, the local pride, and the optimistic face to the future, the shadow lurks. As an influential community leader, when asked about the percentage of blacks in Bridgeport, told an interviewer in 1970, "You have just made your first mistake. We don't mention Negroes in this town."

Paramount among the factors that have governed Daley's life-style is his Irish heritage. Chicago's mayor is fiercely Irish, Gaelic in temperament, and Hibernian in behavior. Practically all his close friends are Irish. Most of the people he surrounds himself with in politics and government are Irish. The telephone on the desk of his office on the fifth floor of City Hall is green. And, while the population of the 11th Ward may be only 4.3 percent Irish, the sons of Erin dominate the ward politically. Visitors to 11th Ward headquarters will find bundles of free copies of the *Irish News* available for distribution.

According to a young researcher, who had grown up in Bridgeport and who was gathering information on the 11th Ward in 1971, "The stories of Irish dominance of the 11th Ward are true. The 11th Ward Democratic organization is an Irish form of the Mafia. When I arrived early at the ward office at 37th and Halsted streets, I found over fifty of the precinct 'helpers' waiting for Richard M. Daley to arrive. In a short time the office was packed with precinct captains and workers—all Irish. Outside of one Italian and myself, I saw nothing but red hair, freckles, and green eyes. I met an old high school chum who is now a helper in a precinct and who works at City Hall. I asked him how one can get into the organization. He smiled and said, 'The first thing you have to do is be Irish!' "

The proudest day of the year for Chicago's mayor is St. Patrick's Day. On that day the Chicago River's murky brown waters are dyed green and the grand parade of the year takes place. Led by the Shannon Rovers, the mayor, carrying his shillelagh, flanked by his immediate entourage of genuine Irish, and surrounded by a coterie of court jesters of pseudo-Irish for a day, steps off from the river bank at the corner of Wacker Drive and State Street. Following him down the middle of State Street (the Broadway of the Second City) is a long procession of marching high school bands; military honor guards; the union floats of janitors, plumbers, iron workers, and pipe fitters; and ward organizations affirming their fealty to the mayor. At the corner of State and Madison streets, the mayor and his court of powerhouses of the Democratic organization assume their places on the podium and take the salute from the faithful parading by the stand. The scene is always somewhat reminiscent of the pictures of the broad-faced members of the Politburo reviewing the troops in Red Square on May Day in Moscow.

In 1955, when he first ran for mayor, Daley described himself as a "Son of a Chicago working man . . . reared in a working man's community . . . played on the sand lots in the great stockyards . . . worked in the stockyards and dreamed." When a rumor spread through Bridgeport that Daley was moving from the neighborhood after being elected mayor, the reaction among his Irish neighbors was "Well, of all the nerve!" There is no evidence that Daley has ever contemplated such a move, considering his feelings about his neighborhood. "The people who live here love their neighborhoods," Daley told a national television audience during the 1968 Democratic National Convention. "I was born in this neighborhood. I still live in it. It is a stockyard area but they're good, honest people, they're hardworking, they've large families with small incomes."

In his undistinguished bungalow on Lowe Avenue, Daley lives a Bridgeport social life at home. His name or the names of members of his family almost never appear in gossip columns or on the society pages of Chicago's newspapers. Although he holds press conferences regularly, with television cameras grinding away, practically all the publicity about him concerns governmental or political matters, not his personal life or his family. He almost never makes a formal speech on television to the people of his city. (One of these rare occasions was when he decided to seek a court injunction restricting Dr. Martin Luther King's civil rights marches in Chicago in 1966, when the marches and the reactions of the outraged ethnic whites threatened to create a major race riot in the city.) He rarely submits to television interviewers for a lengthy conversation. He gave in, at the behest of his wife, and agreed to be interviewed by a woman television personality on WTTW, Chicago's educational channel, after refusing the station's importunities for months. He also consented to be interviewed in 1969 by Fahey Flynn, a local Irish television newscaster, and in 1973 by University of Chicago professor Pastora San Juan Cafferty, who is also a Daley appointee to the board of the Regional Transit Authority. (He was treated with great deference on all three occasions.) In 1968, after the police confrontation with the demonstrators in Grant Park during the Democratic convention, smarting at the criticism of the press and television newsmen, Daley requested an interview with Walter Cronkite, the most respected television newsman in America, and head of CBS's news team covering the convention. Daley was vigorously on the offensive and uncompromisingly righteous in defending his police and his city in the interview. Cronkite, in turn, was generally circumspect and defensive in the colloquy. "How is it," the mayor said to Cronkite, "that you never show on television, Walter, the crowd marching down the street to confront the police. Would you like to be called a pig, would you like to be called—with a four-letter word? Well, that's what happened." The following exchange also took place during the interview:

CRONKITE: Now, here's a question I want to ask you. Who is "they?" Your police—Frank Sullivan, who is in charge of public relations for the police—said today, "Communists." Now is this—

DALEY: There isn't any doubt about it. You know who they are.

CRONKITE: No, I don't actually.

DALEY: Well, you know Hayden? . . . [He's] the head of the Mobilization. Surely you know Dellinger, who went to Hanoi. Why isn't anything said about those people? They're the people who even now see their cues and pick them up in Grant Park. Rennie Davis. What's Rennie Davis?

CRONKITE: Well, I don't know that they're Communists.

DALEY: Well, certainly, neither do I.

This is the man who has dominated Chicago's political and governmental system for two decades. A devout Roman Catholic, strongly influenced by his faith; a true son of Erin, transplanted to the New World; a staunch family man, who clings to the precepts of his working-class, hardworking parents; a neighborhood boy who made good but who never left his environment. Daley is all these things—a complex yet a simple man, molded by his variegated antecedents, and governed by a deep-rooted, unchanging sense of values. These two factors, his heterogeneous makeup and his single-minded purpose in life-style, have created and governed his careers as politician and mayor.

Daley the Politician

According to Professor Edward M. Levine, in his study *The Irish and Irish Politicians*, the social characteristics that most deeply affect the Irish political style are, "A deep and abiding interest in people as distinct individuals; a political morality with distinctive attitudes toward both political means and ends; a near clannish definition of and concern about political loyalty (especially *vis-à-vis* other Irish politicians); and a predominate interest in political power."

Irish politicians, says Levine, remain "of the people"; are interested in power at least as much as in money; decry ostentatious living or overly stylish clothes, maintaining "an inconspicuous residence, social style, style of dress, and a common manner of speech"; abjure gossip-column publicity; "studiously avoid pretension, verboseness, and phraseology not characteristic of the common man"; are impatient with idealistic social reformers; "view government as a source of power to be used for individual, rather than social, ends"; are "charitably disposed toward most of the moral and situational shortcomings of others" except for "apostates, heretics, and marital infidelity"; believe that "justice must be tempered with a good deal of mercy, or charity for fallible man";* are tolerant of corruption, providing it doesn't get out of hand ("Making a buck is okay, but don't rob the poorhouse"); "place great emphasis on loyalty to the ethnic group, the party, and to each other . . . in highly personal terms . . . as related to people more than to something else . . . in individualistic and pragmatic terms"; are fascinated "with the intricacies and subtleties of power struggle

---

* An Irish politician, when asked if it was characteristic of Protestant Republicans to be charitable in politics, replies, "Oh, hell no! They want to take the guy out and slaughter him in the streets. The Irish want to give the guy a break every now and then. . . . Every guy is entitled to a fall, every dog to a bite."

from which they derived considerable satisfaction"; but are limited in their drive for power because, according to Daniel Patrick Moynihan, "The Irish did not know what to do with power once they got it. . . . They never thought of politics as an instrument of social change—their kind of politics involved the processes of a society that was not changing."

Professor Levine's description of the Irish political style reads like a catalogue of Richard J. Daley's political philosophy, political behavior, and career in politics. Daley has spent his entire life in politics. If, as Aristotle said, "Man is a political animal," Daley epitomizes Aristotle's political man. Politics has provided him, not only with a livelihood, but also with a life-style. It has been for him, not just a profession, but also a passion. As some men have been called to careers in the ministry, education, law, medicine, or business, Daley's mission on earth, in answer to the summons from his Lord, has been to do God's work on earth by manipulating the processes of politics and government to create the Good Society in the light of what he considers to be the Lord's will for him and for mankind.

Except for a brief period in his youth, when he worked in the stockyards on the South Side of Chicago, Daley has spent his whole life slowly climbing the rungs of the political ladder. Though he spent eleven long years studying law in night school while he worked full time during the day, he probably never seriously considered a career in law, except as an adjunct to his life-long ambitions in politics. Beginning as a precinct worker in his native 11th Ward, he slowly and steadily moved up through the ranks of public office and the local political organization with a single-mindedness of purpose until he achieved his goal of the mayoralty. In government he moved from the state house of representatives, to the state senate, to director of revenue for the state of Illinois, to county clerk of Cook County, and, finally, to the mayoralty in 1955, at age fifty-two. Simultaneously, within the political organization, he advanced from precinct worker to ward secretary, to ward committeeman, to county chairman, a position he achieved in 1953 as a necessary prerequisite to a bid for the mayoralty. Daley is a precinct captain who has learned the lessons of precinct work thoroughly and who has applied those experiences and maxims to his ward, his city, his county, his state, his nation, and, indeed, his world. He could well be described as "The Big Precinct Captain in the Sky."

While he has never been a student of philosophy, there are basic philosophic values and maxims that have guided Daley the politician throughout his political career. Those values and maxims are conservatism, parochialism, loyalty, tolerance, uncompromising morality (by his standards), acceptance of responsibility, attention to details, hard work, and a cautious skepticism about the trustworthiness of his fellowmen.

His conservatism is not a deep-rooted philosophy based on the teachings and traditions of the great political theorists but rather a kind of instinctive, innate cautious approach to his fellowmen and to his society and its problems. "He's like a fellow who peeks in the bag to make sure the lady gave him a dozen of buns," wrote old-time Chicago newspaperman, Ed Lahey, in an article he did on the mayor in the *Daily News* (July 11, 1966). Daley's conservatism is the old-line Irish Catholic acceptance of a world in which life is harsh, problems are normal, man is sinful, and struggle and hard work are necessary to obtain a foothold in this world and to improve one's status in society.

Daley's personal political philosophy is not the well-reasoned conceptual framework of Edmund Burke, the brilliant intellectualism of William Buckley, or the rugged individualism of Barry Goldwater. It is, rather, a kind of pragmatic approach to man and society which recognizes both the goodness and the evil of man, which is tolerant of the evil and cognizant of the good, and which accepts travail as a normal concomitant of man's existence on earth.

To survive in this world, men have an obligation to lift themselves up by their own bootstraps. But they also have a responsibility to help their fellow men who have not been successful in running the race through life but who have tried hard and done their best to make the most of themselves. Daley has little sympathy for those who do not try to raise themselves up, who are content to live off the sweat of the brows of their fellowmen, and who thus become an unwarranted burden on those who are carrying their fair share of the load. "Look, Sister," he told a Catholic nun who complained to him about the plight of blacks in the ghetto, "you and I come from the same background. We know how tough it was. But we picked ourselves up by our bootstraps." The Marxist concept of "From each according to his ability, to each according to his need" is totally alien to Daley's outlook toward society and its problems. Rather, Daley might say, "To each according to his ability, and to those in need who have striven to help themselves."

Although Daley has probably never read William Graham Sumner, he would agree with the Yale University philosopher who wrote in 1883, in *What Social Classes Owe to Each Other*: "Certain ills belong to the hardships of human life. They are natural. They are part of the struggle with Nature for existence. We cannot blame our fellow-men for our share of these. My neighbor and I are both struggling to free ourselves from these ills. The fact that my neighbor has succeeded in this struggle better than I constitutes no grievance for me. Certain other ills are due to the malice of men, and to the imperfections or errors of civil institutions. These ills are an object of agitation, and a subject of discussion. The former class of ills is to be met only by manly effort and energy; the latter may be corrected by associated effort."

Daley's political style is also affected by his parochialism. He has never left Bridgeport. He conceives his city and world as a series of Bridgeports—communities in which God-fearing, decent, hard-working people strive to keep the community stable, hold onto the values of their fathers, and fulfill their obligations as citizens to the neighborhood, the *polis*, and the nation. Thus, men in politics should be active in the neighborhood, should concern themselves with those in need in the community, and should stay out of other neighborhoods, where the people of those neighborhoods should deal with their own problems in their own way. The world is a Great Neighborhood made up of diverse peoples, each with their own cultures and customs to be respected, in which peace and prosperity can best be achieved by taking care of one's own problems at home, leaving others to do likewise in their respective neighborhoods. "We are a city of fine neighborhoods" he told a party rally in his first year in office in 1955. Eight years later, he still affirmed his belief in the character of his city. "I have lived in Chicago all my life," he told a press conference, "and I still say we have no ghettos in Chicago."

Daley's conservatism and parochialism are buttressed by a strong sense of loyalty to the people who are close to him by family ties or blood, to those who have worked for him, and to those who have supported him in times of stress. "What kind of world is this, if a man can't put his arm around his own son?" he asked in 1973, when he was criticized for ordering the city government to place an insurance contract through his son with an insurance firm where the son was employed. Sons of old acquaintances are rewarded with high political posts, widows of old political friends are cared for through appointment to decent-paying political positions, and old cronies are remembered when alive, eulogized after they have passed on, and sometimes sanctified by naming some civic public facility for them.*

Daley's political loyalty, however, transcends rewarding family, friends, and associates. He refuses to criticize or castigate associates and supporters who have become embroiled in legal or political difficulties. He will always find another spot in government or politics for a loyal supporter who has encountered severe criticism or difficulty in the position he holds. He has an elephant's memory for those who stood up for him or supported him in time of need or stress. But he also has a long memory for those who broke ranks, offered unwarranted criticism, or put their own private interests before the interest of the party or the organization.

Daley's political morality epitomizes the Irish Catholic sense of morality described by Professor Levine. He is "charitably disposed toward most of the moral and situational shortcomings of others except for apostates, heretics, and marital infidelity." He believes that "justice must be tempered with a good deal of mercy, or charity for fallible man." He recognizes that, inevitably, a certain degree of corruption exists in politics, as it does in all areas of human endeavor. But it should be kept within reasonable bounds.

While Daley may be a puritan in his social behavior, there is little sympathy for or understanding of the Protestant religious mentality which attempts to apply absolute moral standards to political behavior. Daley's political morality is, rather, rooted in the Irish Catholic attitude toward politics which reflects the Gelasian

---

* Of Chicago's five major expressways, one is named for the late President John Fitzgerald Kennedy; one is named for the late President Dwight David Eisenhower; one is named for the late governor of Illinois, Adlai E. Stevenson; one is named for a civic minded figure who envisaged the building of the expressway, Edens Expressway; and one is named for Dan Ryan, an old South Side Irish politician, who was a friend of Daley and who had served as president of the Cook County Board of Commissioners.

doctrine of rendering unto Caesar what is Caesar's and unto God what is God's. In other words, while man, the fallen creation, is commanded to be moral by his religious precepts, being sinful, he cannot follow his religious precepts in his daily life. In dealing with other men in a political milieu, it is necessary to follow the precepts of Caesar rather than God. It is not that God has no place at all in politics but that God's primary concerns are with the soul and salvation rather than with the mundane, everyday dealings of human beings with each other. Daley would agree with the German nineteenth-century theologian who wrote, "We do not consult Jesus when we are concerned with things which belong to the domain of the construction of the state and political economy."

This is not to say that men should not try to be as moral as they can in politics and follow God's law as much as they can, but that they often cannot because they are sinful creatures in an imperfect world. The purpose of politics, then, is to try to make men behave as morally as possible but also to recognize that they probably will not and cannot. "Look at our Lord's Disciples," Daley said, in answer to a charge that there had been corruption in city government, during his campaign for his fourth mayoral term in 1967. "One denied Him, one doubted Him, one betrayed Him. If our Lord couldn't have perfection, how are you going to have it in city government?"

Central to Daley's political style is his acceptance of responsibility for all matters which fall under his own purview. And he applies the same standards to all those who work for him or with him. If Daley assigns a job to a politician or city employee, he will not tell the person how to do the job. He will spell out the obligations of the position being offered, define the parameters of accountability, make it clear that with the title and the authority goes the responsibility, and define his own role in no uncertain terms. He normally will not give orders to an appointed or elected party or governmental official, give advice to those who come seeking it, or involve himself in a situation which has been brought about by the action of others. Woe to the party or public official who comes to him to ask what should be done about a particular situation. If you are working for the mayor, and you have a problem, and you come to him to ask him what you should do about your problem, chances are excellent that you will have a permanent problem with the mayor. If you have a problem, and you ask to see him to tell him about your problem, and then tell him what you think you should do about your problem, you are likely to get a monosyllabic grunt or nod, and leave the office, still not having received a yes or no as to what to do about your problem but recognizing that if you have a problem, it is still your problem. And you will know, too, that if you do not resolve that problem satisfactorily, you may be looking for another job in the very near future.

There is a great deal of research and analysis being done today in contemporary political science, psychology, and sociology on how decision makers in positions of responsibility and authority go about making decisions. Most of this research and analysis is irrelevant to professional politicians like Richard J. Daley. What the students of decision making have overlooked is that most successful politicians who have remained in office for any length of time are not decision makers. They are, rather, skilled practitioners in the art of not making decisions.

There is a simple explanation for the behavior of the nondecision makers who have managed to remain in public office for any period of time. They are generally professional politicians who, early in their political careers, learned the relationship between decision making and their chances for staying in office for any length of time. They know that every time a public official makes a political decision, somebody wins, somebody loses. They know, too, that those for whom they made the decision are ungrateful and will soon forget what was done for them. They know, further, that those against whom the decision was made will never forget the decision maker and will do their utmost to remove him from public office at the very first opportunity. They know, finally, that while an office holder must be held accountable and responsible for whatever happens in his office, there is no need for him to seek accountability or responsibility in somebody else's sphere of authority. Consequently, most successful politicians avoid making decisions whenever they can and make decisions only if they are forced to do so by a developing crisis or an aroused public opinion. And, even when they are forced to make a decision, they will do it at the lowest level of accountability in order to alienate and offend as few people as possible.

Richard J. Daley is a master of this political technique. While he accepts his responsibilities as mayor of Chicago and chairman of the Democratic party of Cook County, he will not accept the responsibility for the operation of any ward or political subdivision of the city, nor will he make decisions for those in the city bureaucracy who have been given responsibility or authority over a particular area of public policy. If backed against the wall, he will appoint a committee to study the problem or announce that it should be decided in accordance with the principles of Christian justice. In the meantime, he will be looking around for a successor to the unfortunate bureaucrat or politician who failed in his responsibilities at his level in the political or governmental systems that Daley controls. For example, when Superintendent of Schools James Redmond announced the Redmond Plan for busing black children in the city of Chicago into white schools, Daley was asked at his press conference what he thought of the Redmond Plan. Daley responded, "I'm not familiar with the specifics and details. I am not an educator. This is up to the educators of our country, the educators of our community, the board of education and their staffs to work it out." The reporter then asked if Daley was going to use his power as mayor to implement the Redmond Plan. Daley's response was, "Do you want the schools brought back into politics?" It was clear what the mayor was doing. He was going to run Superintendent Redmond up the flag pole and let him wave up there before he involved himself in such a controversial issue.

It is a fact of human behavior and human psychology that the talents of a successful politician are different from those of a successful administrator, and that men who are capable administrators usually have little feel for the realities of political life. Successful politicians are usually gregarious, hail-fellow-well-met types who enjoy shaking hands with the multitude, who revel in publicity, who are inveterate joiners, and who have legions of acquaintances and friends. Capable administrators, in contrast, are usually private men who shun the limelight, who gain satisfaction in working out problems, who are masters at shuffling papers and delegating responsibility, and whose thought processes are normally orderly, circumspect, and undeviating.

Daley is an exception to the rule. A rarity in American politics, he is a first-rate administrator who is also a master politician. He combines an unusual grasp of the administrative process with an uncanny sense of what is politically feasible and workable. His success is attributable primarily to the fact that he is essentially an administrator who applies his administrative know-how and techniques to the political organization he governs. His greatest strengths as a politician are his mastery of detail and his ability to work hard and inspire or convince others to do the same. While he is not really a gregarious man, he has great charm in personal relationships, a kind of innate decency and honesty that comes through, and sufficient poise on a platform to establish a rapport with audiences. But behind the facade of the politician lurks an iron will and an uncompromising administrative mind which demands rigid attention to details and specifications, and insists on neatness and order.*

Daley is still a precinct captain who applies the maxim of good precinct work to the political organization of which he has become chairman. He never forgets who holds the ultimate power in politics—the voters. He believes that they can be influenced most by ministering carefully to their daily and personal needs. He believes in dealing with people on an individual, personal basis, and he knows that great social issues are secondary at best and irrelevant at worst, in comparison to the day-to-day problems of the individual voter. He leaves great social causes and philosophic theorems to liberals and intellectuals, whom he does not understand, and for whom he has little sympathy. And he demands that every ward committeeman and every precinct captain in the organization be held accountable for his ward or precinct. He is an administrator loose in politics, who applies the principles of sound administration, responsibility, and accountability to his political organization.

Daley's own campaigns for the mayoralty are a reflection of his

* In 1972, I was retained as a consultant by the Chicago Home Rule Commission to study Chicago's government and make recommendations to the commission for necessary changes in the city's governmental structure. I secured an appointment with Mayor Daley in order to elicit the mayor's ideas on what changes he thought might improve the quality of government in Chicago. Daley's initial comment, when asked about the city's governmental problems, was, "I don't mean to tell you what to do, Milton. I have too much respect for you. But the steam boiler inspectors ought to be put under the Environmental Control Department." Not knowing what a steam boiler was, or what a steam boiler inspector did, I was flabbergasted at the mayor's depth of knowledge of and interest in the lower levels of the city's bureaucracy.

philosophy of politics. He spends almost no time cultivating the voters through the use of the media or the press. He does not raise emotional issues or cavort about the city trying to reach the masses of voters. His campaigns consist mainly of attending ward organization meetings, making contact with as many of the precinct workers in the 3148 precincts of Chicago as possible, and exhorting them to "work, work, work!" While he pays lip service to what he considers the issues of the campaign and will often recite the accomplishments of his administration, citing programs and statistics, those things are really secondary to his basic belief that good precinct work is the key to a successful election.*

He has few illusions about what wins or loses elections. When asked, after a campaign in which a Democratic candidate lost, the reasons why the candidate was unsuccessful, Daley invariably responds, "He didn't get enough votes!" As for postelection discussions of great social issues which may have influenced the election, Daley leaves those for intellectuals, liberals, and do-gooders in general, whom he generally regards as impractical amateurs, who can, at best, be tolerated and, at worst, ignored.

If Daley does have a basic political philosophy which governs his attitude and behavior, that philosophy is rooted in, and tied to, his membership in the Democratic party. It is the Democratic party, which has given him the opportunity to achieve the goals he set for himself in life, and which he believes is the party best suited for servicing the needs of the commonality of people he has associated with all of his life. Daley is not a reformer. His affiliation with the party began long before it became the party of the New Deal and the welfare state, and his continuing association with the party has had little to do with the national party's espousal of the welfare

* In 1970, when I appeared before the Cook County Democratic organization's slate-making committee, and presented my qualifications for office, I mentioned that I had been a precinct captain for several years and had carried the precinct in the 1968 presidential election but had lost the precinct in the 1969 election for delegates to the Illinois Constitutional Convention. After my presentation, Chairman Daley remained silent while the other committeemen asked questions about campaign finances, qualifications, and potential appeal to the voters. When I finished answering questions and prepared to leave the room, Daley spoke up and said, "Wait, I want to ask the professor a question." I wondered what the county chairman would question me about—background, abilities, fund-raising capability, or other matters relevant to my potential candidacy on the Democratic ticket? I was astounded when he asked, "Professor, why do you think you lost that precinct?" I thought, "There he is! The Big Precinct Captain in the Sky! He never takes his eye off the ball!"

state, civil rights, and an internationalist foreign policy. Daley's concept of the Democratic party is that of an instrument for ministering to people's wants and needs on an individual basis and as a vehicle for achieving the personal goals he has set for himself in life.

That rationale also governs Daley's relationship to the Democratic party at both the national and state levels. Daley applies the Gelasian doctrine of rendering unto Caesar what is Caesar's and unto God what is God's in a pragmatic way to his own relationship to his political party at the various levels at which the party operates. For him, the business of national policy is the concern of the national leadership of the party; the business of state issues and state public policies is the concern of the state Democratic party; and the business of gaining, maintaining, and utilizing political power at the city and county levels is the business of the local Democratic party. Just as he conceives of his city as a series of neighborhoods in which the people in each neighborhood should concern themselves with the problems and well-being of that neighborhood, so is his political world made up of concentric rings of political authority and responsibility which should be vested in those charged with ministering to the needs of society within their respective rings of the circle.

Thus, the president of the United States and the Congress are charged with looking after the interests of the people of the United States in the areas of foreign policy and national domestic policies. The governor of the state of Illinois and the state legislature are charged with looking after the interests of the people of the state of Illinois with regard to matters of statewide concern. County officials are responsible for public policies at the county level. And city officials should be concerned only with the well-being and governance of their city.

It follows that national leaders should not attempt to control state and local matters, except to offer assistance when called upon. Conversely, state and local officials should remain in their own bailiwicks and refrain from interfering with the prerogatives or criticizing the conduct of national leaders in their areas of responsibility.

Daley applies that conceptual framework to his own relationship to the people he encounters or deals with at all levels in his political world. Precinct captains are responsible for their precincts, ward and township committeemen are responsible for their wards and townships, the Democratic county central committee is responsible for party policy at that level, and he, as chairman of the county central committee, is responsible for providing leadership and supervision of the organization he was elected to direct. Consequently, Daley's interest in state and national party matters, policies, and candidates is subordinate to his interest in and responsibility for party matters, policies, and candidates at the city and county levels in Chicago and Cook County. This is not to say that Daley has no interest in state or national party policies, programs, and candidates. As a loyal Democrat, he considers it a part of his responsibility to interest himself in and involve himself in those matters. But, within the conceptual framework of his political world, those are secondary or tertiary areas of responsibilities for him in comparison to his responsibility as chairman of the Cook County Democratic organization.

This spatial conceptual framework, which governs Daley's relationship with his party at the state and national levels, has been modified to establish a special relationship with the national party insofar as procedures for choosing presidential candidates are concerned. Since 1960, when Chairman Daley played a major role in selecting and electing John Fitzgerald Kennedy as the Democratic presidential candidate and president of the United States, Daley has manifested an ever-increasing interest in presidential politics. When President Kennedy acknowledged his debt to Chairman Daley and his Cook County Democratic organization's role in electing Kennedy to the presidency in 1960 by publicly praising the mayor of Chicago and inviting him and his family to the White House on Kennedy's first day in office, Daley established a new role for himself in his party, that of kingmaker in selecting and electing Democratic presidential candidates.

Daley's interest in presidential politics, however, is not due to any overriding concern for national public policy or the national Democratic party. It is, rather, more closely tied to the sheer mechanics of politics and elections, and to a recognition of benefits to be derived for the local Democratic organization from a relationship with a Democratic president who would owe a debt of gratitude to that organization for its help in electing him to office.

That relationship can be parlayed into federal largesse for the city of Chicago and into power and prestige for Daley in the national councils of the party, which can affect his personal power and that of his local organization. And there is always the inner satisfaction that a professional politician derives from having played a major role in electing, not only his local ticket, but also the national leader of the party.

His concentration on the interests of the local party organization and on the subordination of national political objectives to local political interests, and the parochialism it engenders, were primarily responsible for Daley's miscalculations at both the 1968 and 1972 Democratic national conventions, and the buffeting he suffered from the national Democratic party in those years. In 1968, he overestimated the strength of the hippie-youth movement in the country, and of the anti-Vietnam War element in the Democratic party. He took at face value the inane mouthings of the hippie-youth movement and prepared to deal with them as if they were a major threat both to the national convention and the peace and order of his city. Instead of welcoming them to the city, allowing them to sleep in the park, and providing free hot dogs, drinks, and toilet facilities, he treated them as though they were a revolutionary force, capable of exerting a major influence on the convention and the party and of disrupting the life of his city. The resulting shambles of the 1968 Democratic National Convention in Chicago was a major contributing factor to the national defeat of the party and to the erosion of Daley's role as a national leader in the party.

In 1972, he did not take the McGovern Commission guidelines for the selection of Democratic delegates seriously. Instead of following those guidelines and electing his own slate of delegates (which he could easily have done), he ignored the guidelines on the assumption that he would not be called to account, and was unprepared to deal with the assault from the anti-Daley forces within the national Democratic party. He could not believe that he and his delegation of local stalwarts would be barred from taking their seats in the convention. When it occurred, he suffered what was probably the worst blow dealt to his prestige and pride in his entire political career.

However, it was a mark of Daley's professionalism that, both in 1968 and in 1972, he still supported the national ticket. In 1968, he carried the city of Chicago for Vice-President Hubert Humphrey by over 400,000 votes over Richard Nixon, despite allegations from uninformed pundits and observers that Daley had not delivered for the national ticket. In 1972, he emerged from a period of self-imposed isolation after the convention, made a tentative and uneasy peace with the party's candidate, Senator George McGovern, refused to bolt the party, and supported the national ticket, despite some defections from within the local organization by aggrieved committeemen such as Vito Marzullo and Tom Keane. Not that Daley threw all his power and prestige behind McGovern's candidacy. He did not. But he went along, maintained his party loyalty, made the best of a defeat for both himself and his party, and set about preparing to play a major role at the next Democratic national convention in 1976.

Daley's professionalism and party loyalty paid off when he was welcomed back into the party's national councils and treated with respect and warmth by the delegates assembled at the party's mini-convention in Kansas City in December 1974. After Daley's smashing victory in the mayoral primary in February 1975, Democratic National Chairman Robert Strauss said, "This means that the hero of the 1974 convention in Kansas City may also be the hero of the 1976 convention. It reestablishes that the mayor is still looked upon as one of the great leaders of this party." And presidential candidate Representative Morris K. Udall of Arizona told the press that "I wouldn't say Daley's the whole ball game any more, but he's still a good piece of it."

The 1968 and 1972 Democratic national conventions, however, pointed up Daley's major weakness as a national politician, the fact that he is somewhat out of touch with national trends in both his party and country. Daley does not understand several kinds of people. He does not understand young liberals, intellectuals, and the leaders of militant black and other minority groups. He is, in the twilight of his years as a politician, a prisoner of his Irish-Catholic-Bridgeport view of the world. The evolving behavior patterns and attitudes of the contemporary youth of America with regard to sex, drugs, religion, work, filial respect, and social goals are completely outside his conceptual framework, although he has tried to bridge the generation gap. It is too much to expect that at his age, with his background and deep religious feelings, that he could understand the youth of today, or that they could understand him. Similarly, with regard to liberals and intellectuals, Daley's innate conservatism, his Catholic-ethnic value system, and his professionalism as a politician make it difficult, if not impossible, for him to communicate with, empathize with, or understand what makes them tick. While he might understand the aspirations of the black and the Spanish-speaking minorities of his city and country, he cannot come to terms with their tactics, behavior, and intolerance for his world and his values. In his world, the blacks and the Spanish speaking are but the latest wave of ethnic immigrants to the New World and should emulate and benefit from the experiences of the ethnics who came before them. In that pre-New Deal, pre-welfare state, pre-War on Poverty society, individual effort and hard work were the keys to advancement and success. He cannot come to terms with an attitude and a philosophy that holds that welfare is a right, not a gift; that black and brown people are exploited because of their race; and that society is unjust rather than inefficient.

Despite some weaknesses such as those, Daley is unquestionably one of the master politicians of American urban political history. In a world in which political analysts and pundits propound the concept of a "new politics" which will replace something they call "old politics," Daley represents a school of thought which is as old as political society itself. That school of thought holds that there is no such thing as new politics or old politics but rather an area of human activity called "politics," which will never change. In that milieu there are no "new politicians" or "old politicians" but rather "politicians," professionals who play the game as it has been played since time immemorial. For them, politics is a process through which societies are best governed and conflicts and tensions are kept within bounds. But problems are hardly ever solved and great social movements always fall short of achieving their objectives. In their world, pragmatism, tolerance, and humility are the marks of the successful practitioners of the craft.

Although Daley has probably never read Thomas Hobbes, Niccolo Machiavelli, or Edmund Burke, his political outlook would probably reflect significant elements of the teachings of these three men. Daley would surely agree with the British writer T. E. Utley, who in January 1957 described the process of politics and the role of politicians in society in the *Twentieth Century*. "Politics," wrote

Utley, "does not consist in deciding in the void what is good for man and proceeding to do it." Further,

It has its own methods and conventions which are directed to maintaining divided societies in existence by reconciling conflicts within them or by keeping those conflicts within bounds. This is not to say that a politician may not legitimately influence the development of society according to his own moral prepossessions. But if he is to be a politician at all, he must start with the belief that he is managing a society which he did not make and that he is choosing between tendencies he did not initiate. If he cannot do this, he had better be a political moralist or a political columnist or a monk. It follows from this that the first duty of a politician is to submerge himself in the actual life of the community he is trying to manage. He must start his thinking by knowing that community thoroughly and must ask himself what can be made of it. He must not start by knowing what the good society is and then trying to make society into *that*. If he does, he will find that the people he is trying to manage want incompatible things and are perpetually disposed to quarrel. In trying to manage public opinion, he will discover that its bitterest disputes are not about morals but about circumstances; and that the study of circumstances (which includes an understanding and partial acceptance of prevailing errors about them) is the most important part of his discipline. Finally, he will learn that every society is potentially in dissolution: that the greatest force which makes for survival is affection for what is familiar and fear of what is not; and that although a society may sometimes perish through not adapting itself to change, it can never perish simply from not wanting change, and it can very easily perish from wanting change more than it wants survival. . . .

The first mark of a politician and the indispensable prerequisite of his trade is that he wants things which are politically practicable, and that he is fundamentally in sympathy with the fallen creation, and that there is a category of objects which are instinctively excluded from his ambitions and denounced by his affections because they are beyond the range of political possibility.

Utley's analysis could be a catechism of Richard J. Daley's political philosophy, behavior, and career. Daley is the practitioner *par excellence* of that kind of politics. As such, he epitomizes the outlook, aspirations, dynamics, successes, and failures of the Democratic machine in Chicago.

Daley the Mayor

When Richard J. Daley was sworn into office as mayor of
Chicago in 1955, at the age of 52, he had fulfilled a lifetime
ambition and achieved the ultimate career goal he had set for
himself. Daley, a life-long Chicagoan, has never had any ambitions
for himself in a public career that transcended the office of mayor of
Chicago. Daley's political ambitions have been inextricably bound
up in a personal relationship with the city he has always considered
to be the greatest city in the world. "Daley loves this city like you
love your wife and kids," a Republican politician told *Saturday
Evening Post* writer Milton Viorst in 1968. "He considers Chicago
his city. The sidewalks are *his* living room. The parks are *his*
backyard. He just doesn't want anyone to screw it up."

Daley has never suffered from the "second city" syndrome
which has traditionally plagued most Chicagoans when they are
comparing their city to New York. At various times he has
acclaimed Chicago "the melting pot of the nation," "the super-
market of the world," "the grassroots capital of America," "the
aviation crossroads of the world," "the greatest convention city of
the world," "the only city in the history of the civilization of the
world that is well on its way to solving its urban problems," "the
nation's most exciting city," "a place where our kids get involved
and go to the aid of a girl that is attacked or something else," "the
best-lighted city in the United States," "a cosmopolitan city which
is the largest and most highly diversified area on the face of the
earth," "the railroad center, the air crossroads, the trucking
terminal, the highway hub of the nation," and "a city that achieved
magnificence in a little more than a century, whereas other great
world metropolises took centuries." *

Daley's love for his city manifests itself most strikingly in his
determination to remake the face of the city, particularly those
areas which can be pointed out as showcases and which are most

* When President Richard Nixon arrived in Chicago to make a speech in 1972, and
alighted from his helicopter at Meigs Field, he was greeted by Mayor Daley and a Chicago
Fire Department band, which struck up a lively rendition of, "Chicago, Chicago, That
Wonderful Town," instead of the customary "Hail to the Chief," which traditionally precedes
a presidential appearance.

likely to be seen by visiting dignitaries and tourists—the Loop, North Michigan Avenue's Magnificent Mile, and the lakefront.

Daley is a builder, the greatest builder in Chicago's history, outstripping even former Mayor ("Big Bill the Builder") Thompson, who also left his mark on Chicago's physical appearance. "Daley likes to build big things," according to *Chicago Daily News* columnist Mike Royko. "He likes highrises, expressways, parking garages, municipal buildings, and anything else that requires a ribbon-cutting ceremony and can be financed through federal funds."

Chicago's fame as an architectural center, created by Louis Sullivan, Mies van der Rohe, Frank Lloyd Wright, Daniel Burnham, and numerous other architects, preceded Daley's election to the mayoralty. And Chicago's magnificent boulevard and park systems were laid out and developed before Daley even began his political career. But it can truly be said that the hub of the city, the Loop, has been revitalized and rebuilt under Daley; that a massive network of expressways geared to the needs of the age of the automobile and the rise of the suburbs has been constructed; that significant improvements in the public transportation system of the city have been made; that the lakefront has been continuously developed; and that the quality of city services such as street lighting, street cleaning, curb repair, rodent control, and garbage collection have been maintained at a high standard for a city of Chicago's size and character.

Daley is proud of his building accomplishments as mayor and is not modest in letting Chicago's citizens and visitors know who is responsible for the city's progress. He dedicates everything in sight when it is completed and has signs with his name emblazoned on them informing the citizenry of his responsibility for all public improvements and welcoming visitors to his city.

Although Daley is not an opera buff, patron of the symphony, or connoisseur of the arts, he has done everything in his power as mayor to improve the quality of cultural life in Chicago. His support for the arts has ranged from securing a Picasso statue for the plaza of the Civic Center, to promoting the Chicago Symphony Orchestra, one of the world's finest symphony orchestras; to helping publicize the Lyric Opera Company's efforts; to helping the Art Institute bring collections of world famous paintings for showings to

the citizens of Chicago. While the mayor may not appreciate the
opera, symphony concerts, or great paintings, he does have an
instinctive appreciation for the benefits that cultural institutions can
bestow on his city and its reputation in the nation and the world.

Daley has also undertaken and supported efforts on the part of
city authorities to provide a broad spectrum of cultural programs
for the citizenry. Those efforts range from symphony concerts in
Grant Park during the summer, to a Venetian Night boat show on
the lakefront, to promising to clean up the Chicago River so that
citizens who work in the Loop could catch their lunch in the river
during their noon-time break on the river bank, to providing
opportunities for all ethnic and racial groups to have a major parade
on one day of the year, to sponsoring a Catholic high school-public
high school championship football game in Soldier Field.° The
mayor is also a staunch supporter of the city's professional football,
baseball, basketball, and hockey teams, whose activities he considers essential to the city's reputation. Daley uses his power as mayor
to support all cultural activities from opera to football because he
believes they contribute to his city's reputation as a great world
capital, and provide worthwhile and healthy activity for the city's
citizenry.

Daley's critics, who are heavily made up of liberal, reform-
minded Democrats and Independents, rather than opposition
Republicans, recognize his achievements but fault him on other
grounds. Mike Royko says that Daley "isn't that enthusiastic about
small things, such as people. Daley does not like civil rights
demonstrators, rebellious community organizations, critics of the
mediocre school system, critics of any kind or people who argue
with him." According to Independent Alderman Leon Despres, a
long-time opponent of the mayor, "the immediate profit to the
central business area and the promoters outweighs the interest of
the majority of Chicago's citizens. The refusal to plan in the general
interest has done great harm to Chicago. . . . Get off the subway
anywhere in the central business area and you won't find a broken
city sidewalk. Get off the subway almost anywhere else, and you

---

° Daley told a Senate committee holding hearings in Washington on local programs for
cleaning up the nation's waterways that there would even be fish in the river for
Spanish-speaking citizens of Chicago living deep in the interior of the city close to the north
and south forks of the Chicago river.

will. Between the central business area and the outskirts lie large, almost uninterrupted grey areas of urban dry rot. This is where most Chicagoans live." In Chicago ghettos, according to Despres, "the segregation and oppression of Chicago's blacks in housing, jobs, schooling, and the quality of community life are crucial deterrents to general community improvement of any kind in Chicago. Self-organization of the ghetto; self-determination, and self-expression would soon end ghetto support of any political machine which tolerates such conditions. Under the Daley system of tight control, therefore, the party has to try to overrun, dominate, or starve every significant citizens' committee and community organization, especially in the ghetto. . . . The effect of the machine's systematic repression is the muting of protest, incalculable stagnation of the general citizenry, and loss of progress to Chicago." According to another liberal critic, Sidney Lens, "What Daley did was to change the tone of government—without changing its purpose. . . . Chicago government is of, by, and for the few thousand members of interlocking power elites. It is a government by manipulation, rather than participation, and its purpose—subtly hidden from public purview—is to preserve the social status quo. Mayor Daley builds great concrete ribbons—freeways—from one end of the city to the other; he stimulates business, particularly in the central district, and building, especially of upper-class and middle-class housing. But he predicates all this on sublimating the burning social problems of the day, principally the race issue. The common man benefits only minimally; his greatest needs are unmet. . . . The changes in Chicago, glossy as they seem to the uninitiated, are shallow, and they favor a small power elite. . . . The 'Daley' style of city politics may be a portent of the future and will bear watching; thus far the style presents a handsome visible front but glosses over or ignores the truly desperate social and economic problems of the people."

Daley's critics are probably, to a considerable extent, accurate in describing the Daley system of governing Chicago. However, the differences between Daley and his critics over the proper functions and purposes of the city's government are not much different than those which have traditionally divided liberals and conservatives, progressives and moderates, and, indeed, most of those who concerned themselves with the role and responsibility of government in human society throughout history. Those differences were incisively pointed out nearly a century and a half ago by Alexis de Tocqueville, the great French analyst of the American political system, in his classic study, *Democracy in America*:

We must first understand what is wanted of society and its government. Do you wish to give a certain elevation to the human mind and teach it to regard the things of this world with generous feelings, to inspire men with a scorn of mere temporal advantages, to form and nourish strong convictions and keep alive the spirit of honorable devotedness? Is it your object to refine the habits, embellish the manners, and cultivate the arts, to promote the love of poetry, beauty, and glory?

Would you constitute a people fitted to act powerfully upon all other nations, and prepared for those high enterprises which, whatever be their results, will leave a name forever famous in history? If you believe such to be the principal object of society, avoid the government of the democracy, for it would not lead you with certainty to the goal.

But if you hold it expedient to divert the moral and intellectual activity of man to the production of comfort and the promotion of general well-being; if a clear understanding be more profitable to man than genius; if your object is not to stimulate the virtues of heroism, but the habits of peace; if you had rather witness vices than crimes; and are content to meet with fewer noble deeds, provided offenses be diminished in the same proportion; if, instead of living in the midst of a brilliant society, you are content to have prosperity around you; if, in short, you are of the opinion that the principal object of a government is not to confer the greatest possible power and glory on the body of a nation, but to insure the greatest enjoyment and to avoid the most misery of the individuals who compose it—if such be your desire, then equalize the condition of men and establish democratic institutions.

De Tocqueville, in this selection, is pointing out the differences between democracy and aristocracy, and the advantages and disadvantages to be derived from each system for the state itself, and for the people. Daley's critics would opt for the advantages of democracy and forego the power and glory. "Instead of living in the midst of a brilliant society," they would rather "ensure the greatest enjoyment and . . . avoid the most misery to each of the individuals who compose it. . . ." At least, that is what they profess to believe the objectives of government should be.

But Daley is cut from another cloth. Although he is a man of the people who came from humble origins and really believes that he is a democrat as well as a Democrat, Daley's philosophy of government is, in many ways, closer to the tenets of aristocratic government than to those of democracy. While he pays lip service to the theory of democracy, many of its basic assumptions are at variance with his personal political philosophy. He cannot abide the diffusion of responsibility and authority. He does not believe that every man is as good as every other man. He cannot condone the excesses of behavior and irresponsibility which, as Plato pointed out in *The Republic*, are the inevitable by-products of granting freedom in a democratic political system. He recognizes the concept of majority rule, qualified by minority rights, but he has deep reservations about the quantification of power and the demands of minorities. He accepts the democratic belief in the dignity and worth of the individual, but, after a lifetime in government and politics, he has strong feelings about the need to subordinate individual need and greed to the welfare of society and the obligations of the state.

Daley would "give a certain elevation to the human mind . . . teach it to regard the things of this world with generous feelings," and "form and nourish strong convictions and keep alive the spirit of honorable devotedness." He would "constitute a people fitted to act powerfully upon all other nations, and prepared for those high enterprises which, whatever be their results, will leave a name forever famous in history." He would not "hold it expedient to divert the moral and intellectual activity of man to the production of comfort and the promotion of general well-being." He would "stimulate the virtues of heroism" over "the habits of peace." He would not "rather witness vices than crimes," or be "content to meet with fewer nobler deeds, provided offenses be diminished in proportion." He believes, in contrast to his critics, "that the principal object of government is . . . to confer the greatest possible power and glory upon the body of the nation," not "to insure the greatest enjoyment and to avoid the most misery to each of the individuals who compose it."

This is not to say that Daley is not a democrat with a small *d*. He is, and he has a deep-rooted respect for the efficacy and value of a democratic political system. But his democratic faith is strongly tempered by his conservative skepticism about the human species. A devout Catholic, he cannot accept a political system which glorifies material comfort, as well as human freedom, without instinctively juxtaposing that system against his Catholic belief in the virtues and responsibilities of authority and of the transient nature of man's short stay on earth. If the ultimate purpose of life on earth is to prepare for a hereafter in which men are ultimately rewarded or punished on the basis of fulfilling their obligations to God on Earth in order to reap their rewards in Heaven, then the definitive purpose of a political society cannot be the promotion of material well-being and the glorification of rights and privileges over duties and responsibilities. And, as a man of humble origin who has a healthy respect for those who succeeded in gaining power and authority through their own efforts, he is suspicious of reformers who believe that governmental authority and decision-making powers should be turned over without restriction to the masses in what has come to be called participatory democracy. Like the ancient Pharaohs in Egypt he believes that monuments and structures will endure long after the people who built them have passed on. Like the ancient Caesars in Rome he believes that circuses are as necessary as bread. And like the leaders of ancient Greece, he believes that the inculcation of patriotism and love for your *polis* are the solid foundations on which political societies survive and prosper.

In other words, Daley's philosophy of the role of government, which dominates his behavior as mayor of Chicago, is a complex potpourri of his Catholicism, his pragmatism, his conservatism, his liberalism, his working-class origins, his pull-yourself-up-by-your-bootstraps outlook, his fealty to democracy, his respect for ability and authority, his admiration of the symbols of power and glory, his acceptance of the values of the status quo, and an Edmund Burkeian rejection of violent change.

Daley applies this philosophy to his role as mayor of Chicago. He does not consider it his function as mayor to bring about great social changes in the relationships of the diverse economic, racial, ethnic, and religious groups which make up the population of his city. He does not believe that it is his obligation as mayor to make significant changes in the status quo of his city. He relies heavily on the cooperation and assistance of the elites who make up the power structure of the city. He is a power broker, balancing the interests of the various entities which make up the body politic in Chicago. He grants perquisites and prerogatives to those who have gained power and influence in his city. He is always prepared to reshuffle the deck, reallocate the spoils, and make concessions to those who have fought their way into the upper levels of the political and economic hierarchy which governs the city. But he will not undertake to lead a revolt against those who hold power and authority, or accept any attempt to radically alter the status quo in his city. He will not force racial integration on those who are opposed to it, put public housing units in white neighborhoods, allow hippies and radicals to take over the streets of his city, support any program which has as its purpose the diminution of law and order, or compromise with those who operate outside his system of values.

He will, however, support government programs for those in need when that need is genuine, allow dissent and protest as long as it remains nonviolent and nonrevolutionary, and accept changes in the status quo when those changes have been agreed to by those elements in the body politic which are most deeply affected by those changes.

His normal method for dealing with a problem in his city is to get it on his desk, then move it out to those in the community whose interests are most deeply affected by the problem. If they cannot arrive at a solution, he will use all of his authority as mayor to induce them to move in that direction. But he will normally not use his power and authority as mayor of Chicago to force on any side in a dispute a solution which that side is not willing to agree to and abide by. However, if the parties to a dispute can agree on a solution, he will put the city's authority behind it, and do everything in his power to implement and expedite the matter. He conceives of the public interest in such matters as one of recognizing, pacifying, and supporting the private interests of the various entities in the city's body politic when those private interests can agree on the resolution of conflicts which may arise between those private interests. But it is not the role of government to step in, lead the way, or force a solution on those who are unwilling to abide by it.

In accordance with his concept of the proper functioning of government, Daley's strategy as mayor is to deal with the business leaders of the city on matters of interest to the business community;

with labor leaders on labor problems; with religious leaders of the various denominations in the city on matters which concern their flocks; with ethnic spokesmen on ethnic interests; with sympathetic black spokesmen on racial matters; and with representatives of all interest groups who can demonstrate power, responsibility, and support from their constituents.

Thus, if a Greek judge is to be slated for the circuit court bench, leaders of the Hellenic American community in Chicago and the Greek Orthodox primate would be consulted before slating such a candidate. The B'nai B'rith, the Rabbinical Association, and influential Jewish political and business leaders would be consulted on the proper drafting of a city council resolution endorsing the actions of Israel. Leading real estate developers would be consulted in formulating plans for redeveloping blighted areas of the city. Bankers are brought into the business of buying and selling the city's municipal bonds. Cardinal Cody would be consulted on matters affecting the Roman Catholic faithful. The president of the Polish National Alliance would be invited to a reception for a visiting Polish dignitary. But the B'nai B'rith would not be consulted on Catholic matters, Cardinal Cody would not be brought into a discussion on Israel, labor leaders would not be consulted on bond issues, and bankers would not be consulted on prevailing wage rates for city employees. In other words, there is an implicit recognition of the principle of democratic representation and participation in governmental decision making, not on the basis of numbers or necessarily of the public interest, but rather on the basis of the need to pacify and deal with the private interests of the various entities that make up the body politic in the city. Inherent in this approach is an implicit recognition of Adam Smith's concept of an economic system which functions best in an environment in which private groups pursue their own interests and in which the pursuit of those private interests culminates in the overall good of the community. Daley applies Adam Smith's economic doctrines to the political and governmental systems he rules in his city.

Of course, some matters concern the general public or the city as a whole. On those matters, Daley's style is to select a broad-based, all-encompassing group of representatives of the various interest groups in the community who can bring some expertise to bear on the problem and who are safe politically from his own point of view. Known critics and opponents of his public policies or of a pending public issue have little chance of being consulted on any problem. And, once a group has been assembled, Daley will not move on the matter until a consensus has been built up and public support has been guaranteed.

Appointment of commissions and committees is also an effective way of dealing with controversial public issues which have not yet garnered sufficient support in the community or which threaten the status quo Daley has established in the city. On such issues Daley's style is to throw the ball to a commission or a committee appointed for the purpose of making recommendations to the mayor. Daley knows that on controversial issues it is difficult or impossible to build up a consensus in the commission or committee, and unlikely that a recommendation for action in the near future would be forthcoming. In the meantime, while the commission is debating the issue, newspapers and civic groups will probably turn their attention to other pressing issues which develop in the community.

While Daley recognizes the ability of elements of the body politic such as newspapers and civic organizations, who profess to represent the public interest, to stir up the community, he is also aware that they have special interests of their own, that their professions of concern for the public interest are often a facade for their own interests, and that they can usually be dealt with by pacifying their private interests or by muting or ignoring their attacks until such time as other matters of public interest come to the attention of the citizenry at large.

Daley also applies the Gelasian doctrine of rendering unto Caesar what is Caesar's and unto God what is God's to his dual role as mayor of Chicago and chairman of the Cook County Democratic Central Committee. To a considerable extent, he separates the business of the city from the operations of his political organization. He does not consult with ward committeemen on matters of public policy which are technical or governmental in nature. Nor does he involve department heads, bureaucrats, or his top governmental advisors in the planning and decision-making process of the political organization he heads. Ward committeemen and government officials are expected to concern themselves with their respective bailiwicks and responsibilities, and to stay out of matters which are not related to those responsibilities.

Daley is the key link in the chain of communication between the political organization and the city and county governments. He has centralized political and governmental power in his own hands to a degree that no mayor in Chicago's history has ever done before. All lines of authority and responsibility from the various agencies of the government lead into the office of the mayor. And, simultaneously, the avenues of communication from the various levels of the party organization also feed into Daley's office as chairman of the county central committee. The agility with which he has juxtaposed his role as mayor and party chairman is a testament to his abilities as both an administrator and politician. It has also made him the indispensable man in the city's political and governmental system. Politicians who need governmental assistance must come to him as mayor. City officials who need political support must come to him as party chairman. And business, labor, racial, ethnic, and religious leaders in the community who need either political or governmental aid must call on him for help.

Daley's ability to handle both his roles has freed him from many of the restrictions under which his predecessors as mayor had to operate. Former mayors of Chicago who did not control the party organization and who were beholden to the party leadership were inhibited in carrying out their tasks as mayors by the need to pacify politicians who had little or no interest in or concern with city wide problems. Conversely, party chairmen who did not hold public office had little understanding of and sympathy for the public problems which concerned the bureaucracy of the city government. But Daley, as mayor, is sensitive to the dynamics and problems of the bureaucracy and of the administrative process, and to issues of public policy which are of citywide concern. And, as party chairman, he is also cognizant of the realities and requirements of the city's political system. By centralizing the political and governmental power in the city in his hands, he has been able to use his political power to strengthen his office as mayor of Chicago and his governmental power both to strengthen his political organization and to limit the ambitions and powers of other politicians. In other words, Daley has been able to govern the city more effectively than any other mayor in Chicago's history.

There is, of course, another side to this picture. The concentration of political and administrative power in one man has served to put Daley, to a considerable extent, beyond the controls which normally inhibit the freedom of action of politicians and public officials. If the essence of a democratic system, as practiced in the United States, is a check-and-balance relationship between political and governmental entities, Chicago's political and governmental systems have operated for many years without the checks and balances which the founding fathers believed necessary for the protection of the general welfare and individual rights. As James Madison put it in *The Federalist Papers*, "If men were angels, no government would be necessary. If angels were to govern men, neither external nor internal controls on government would be necessary. In framing a government which is to be administered by men over men, the great difficulty lies in this: You must first enable the government to control the governed; and in the next place oblige it to control itself." How can this best be done? According to Madison, "Ambition must be made to counteract ambition. The interests of the man must be connected with the constitutional rights of the place."

In Chicago, under Daley's rule, few ambitions have been able to counteract Daley's ambitions, and the constitutional rights of the place have been subordinated to the interests of the man. In other words, Chicago's political, economic, and governmental systems under Daley have become appendages to one powerful man's ambitions and concepts of what is right and good for the city. This is not to say that Daley has not tried to do what he has considered to be best for his city and his people. He has. But, because he has come to dominate the city, the normal checks and balances which are the built-in protections of a democratic political system have, to some extent, been compromised in Chicago.

Since Daley dominates the legislative, judicial, and administrative branches of the city government, as well as the political system, the Madisonian concept of safeguarding individual rights and general welfare through checking power internally within a governmental system has not operated very well in Chicago, either. Again, according to Madison, "In order to lay a due foundation for that separate and distinct exercise of the different powers of government, which to a certain extent is admitted on all hands to be essential to the preservation of liberty, it is evident that each department have a will of its own; and consequently should be so constituted that members of each should have as little agency as possible in the appointment of members of the others." Daley has made it virtually impossible for potential opponents, critics, and opposing forces to check his ambitions for Chicago. Again, this is not to say that his ambitions for Chicago have necessarily been good or bad. But those ambitions and Daley's concept of what was good for his city have been, to a considerable extent, unchecked by the normal safeguards of a democratic society.

It is this fact which must be taken into account in evaluating Daley's record as mayor of Chicago. It is true that the city has made tremendous physical progress under his leadership, that the quality of public services has been considerably improved, that the city's financial status has been excellent, that racial tensions and conflicts have been kept under control so that the apocalypse which has so often been predicted for the city has not occurred, that the city's government has been made in many ways more responsive to the needs of the citizenry, that the city has made significant progress in dealing with its problems, and that Daley has unquestionably been the most effective and efficient mayor in Chicago's history. But it is also true that problems which Daley did not understand or consider important have often been sidestepped or ignored, that the processes of democracy in the city council have been somewhat subverted, that the judiciary has not always administered justice fairly, that the interests of the political organization have sometimes been placed before the interests of the general citizenry, and that the political and governmental systems in Chicago have often been utilized in the interest of powerful elites in the city's body politic rather than in the interest of those most in need.

What is probably true of Daley's five terms as mayor is that Chicago has lived for two decades under a constitutional monarchy, governed by a ruler who came to power, not through primogeniture or heritage, but rather through a combination of hard work, ambition, tenacity, ability, and civic pride. Despite the indisputable fact that he was a most unlikely candidate for the monarchy, Daley, like all such politicians, could not govern in any other way. Like Charles de Gaulle, Julius Caesar, Franklin Roosevelt, Lyndon Johnson, and other similar types, Daley could not have achieved what he has achieved as a politician and public official had he done it any other way. Like those men, Daley combines certitude of purpose, driving ambition, instinctive political sagacity, love of power and a willingness to use it, and a deep-seated Periclean civic patriotism. Such men fuse these qualities in an amalgam which makes common men into uncommon men.

Daley is one such common man who became an uncommon man. When urban historians chronicle the records of twentieth-century American cities and their political leaders, Daley will rank high with those who had a significant impact on their cities and their times. Whether he has been loved or hated, he will always be known and respected as a man who came very far from his humble origins, who had a significant impact on his environment, and who was worthy of study and analysis by those who are interested in the motivations, techniques, and ambitions of a breed of men called politicians.

✤ 3 ✤

Daley's Politburo

In room 208 of the LaSalle hotel, on LaSalle Street in Chicago's Loop, down the street from City Hall, is the nerve center of the Democratic party of Cook County. This is the headquarters of Daley's politburo, the Cook County Democratic Central Committee. In this suite of rooms decisions governing the party's policies are made, and from this office the perquisites of party control and influence are distributed to the faithful.

An out-of-town conventioneer, wandering down the hall of the hotel's second floor, and happening across Chicago's local equivalent of Soviet Russia's Kremlin, Hitler's Brown House, or Mussolini's Palazzo Venezia, would think that he had stumbled into the local sales office of a business firm that distributed literature and brochures advertising the company's product. There are no smoke-filled rooms reeking of cigars (Chairman Daley does not smoke), no jangling batteries of telephones, no authentic characters out of the *Last Hurrah* lounging around, no fresh-faced college students eagerly stuffing envelopes, and no well-dressed matrons fleeing the boredom of *Kinder*, *Küche*, and *Kirche* for the excitement of a campaign office. Except for a large Buddha-like photograph of Chairman Daley, smiling enigmatically down on all who enter, and pictures of the local candidates at election time on the walls, the decor is typical of any business office in the Loop.

Two offices to the left of the polite woman manning the reception desk is the inner sanctum, Chairman Richard J. Daley's private office, quietly furnished and dominated by pictures of his family. To the left of Chairman Daley's office is a large conference room, distinguished by montages of one of Daley's most respected American political figures, the late President John Fitzgerald Kennedy. Between the reception hall and Chairman Daley's office, guarding the door to the inner sanctum, is the office of the Madame de Farge of the local Democratic party, Mary Mullen. Miss Mullen (who is Mrs. Al Junquera but is almost always referred to by her maiden name) stands astride her domain, the county central committee's office, in the same way that her boss, Chairman Daley, stands astride his city. She is the person to see if you want an appointment with the chairman; if you want to be interviewed by the county central committee for slating for public office; or if you are running for public office and need advice, assistance, or contact with any of the organization's far-flung network of committeemen, office holders, or candidates.

Those who have come in contact with Miss Mullen have discovered that she is pleasant and gregarious but also discreet and tough. Powerful committeemen and major office holders treat her with deference and respect, and with good reason. A word from her can unlock or shut the door to anyone seeking entrance to the local Democratic party's inner sanctum. Daley has chosen well in his selection of his office manager at the county central committee. Miss Mullen has a sound grasp of administration, excellent political instincts, and keen insights into developing situations.

Only on election night, at the end of a political campaign, does the office present a picture of activity and power. By ten o'clock at night the outer office is crowded with newspapermen, powerful political figures, friends of the Democratic organization, and well-wishers who want either to be seen or to ingratiate themselves with the powers that be. Even when the results indicate a smashing victory for the local Democratic machine, there is no sign of jubilation, no celebration, and no partying. Everything is business. Those who have enough clout to get past the outer receptionist are admitted to the inner sanctum for a few minutes to congratulate the chairman and to offer well wishes and support for the future. Others stand around in the outer office, exchanging small talk with each other and observing the privileged few who go into the inner office. In some ways, the scene is reminiscent of a stockbroker's office with the ticker being watched, gains or losses recorded, and projections made. Those who wish to celebrate the party's victory with alcohol and food can go elsewhere, to the campaign headquarters of the various candidates or to the suites rented by the candidates for that purpose. By eleven o'clock at night, when the results are usually known, the chairman comes out and makes a short victory statement. Then everyone goes home. The business at hand has been completed, the results are in, and tomorrow is another work day.

Structure and Dynamics

To understand the nature of politics in Chicago and Cook County, one must understand the structure and dynamics of Daley's politburo, the Democratic Cook County Central Committee. There are 102 counties in Illinois, Cook and the other 101, with 5.5 million people in Cook County, and about 5 million people in the rest of the state. Cook County is made up of two parts—the city of Chicago, with approximately 3,300,000 people, and the suburban area of Cook County, containing over 2,200,000 people. The suburban area of Cook County is divided into 30 townships, and the city of Chicago is divided into 50 wards. The legal structure of the party in Cook County, like the party structure in the rest of the state, is regulated by the state legislature. Every four years, party members in each township in Cook County and each ward in Chicago elect a township or a ward committeeman in each party in the party primaries in alternate, even-numbered years. Thus, both the Democratic and Republican parties have a governing body of 80 committeemen—50 ward committeemen from the city and 30 township committeemen from the suburbs. Those 80 committeemen elect a county chairman, who in the Democratic party is the 11th Ward committeeman, Richard J. Daley, a position he has held since 1947. Daley was elected chairman of the Cook County Democratic Central Committee in 1953, and has been reelected regularly by his fellow committeemen ever since.

The county central committee selects candidates to run for office on the Democratic ticket in Cook County; acts as a coordinating body among all of the various elements of the party in Chicago, Cook County, and the state of Illinois; and is the agency for distributing patronage jobs, money, and party perquisites to the various elements of the party in the city, county, and state.

The power of a committeeman on the county central committee is directly related to his ability to deliver his ward or township for the party in an election. The number of votes he has on the county central committee and his influence in picking candidates and getting the best jobs handed out by the committee are governed primarily by the electoral results in his ward or township. Under Illinois law, a committeeman casts as many votes in the county central committee as he got for his party in his ward or township in the last election. For example, a committeeman who got 20,000 votes for the Democratic party in his ward or township in the last election casts 20,000 votes in the county central committee when a vote is taken, while a committeeman from a suburban township who got only 3,000 votes for his party in the last election casts only 3,000 votes.

In the Democratic party's county central committee, the real power is wielded by a bloc of committeemen from the inner-city wards in Chicago, the black and white working-class river wards on the north, south, and west sides of the city which carry heavily for the Democratic party in elections. The outlying middle-class wards on the far north, northwest, south, and southwest sides do not deliver the same blocs of votes for the party. The committeemen from these wards have much less power than the committeemen from the inner-city wards; and Democratic committeemen from the suburban townships, with a few exceptions, have practically no influence in the county central committee.

The converse is true in the Republican party county central committee, where the major influence is wielded by suburban township committeemen who deliver large blocs of votes for the Republican party in their townships, while Republican ward committeemen from the city have little influence in the party. In the past, this has led to a situation in some wards and townships in which Republican ward committeemen in the city and Democratic township committeemen in the suburbs have collaborated with the majority party committeemen in their wards and townships. It is a fact of life in many of the wards in Chicago that Republican ward committeemen do not exert much of an effort on behalf of their party, are controlled by the Democratic committeemen in those wards, accept some patronage from them, and possibly reap some other rewards as well. At one time, the same was true of a number of Democratic committeemen in some suburban townships. But with the great exodus of Democratic voters from the city to the suburbs, this practice of collaboration between Democratic suburban committeemen with the majority Republican committeemen in the suburbs has practically come to a halt.

The political dynamics of the Democratic county central committee do not always correspond to the requirements of the law. Decisions on party policy or on slating candidates are not made by counting thousands of votes as committeemen cast their ballots but rather on the basis of a consensus arrived at by an inner circle of powerful committeemen, most of them from the inner-city river wards. Within the group of eighty committeemen who constitute the county central committee, an inner group of about a dozen men dominate the party in Chicago and Cook County. In a sense, the situation in the county central committee is analogous to that in the Communist party of the Soviet Union, where, within the central committee of the Party, there is an inner group of powerful men known as the Politburo, the Political Bureau of the Central Committee of the Communist Party. While there is no formal politburo within the Democratic Cook County Central Committee, an informal politburo dominates the committee's proceedings, deliberations, and decisions.

The key figures in the inner group in the county central committee in 1975 are the Irish committeemen from the inner-city wards. Richard J. Daley of the 11th Ward, Tom Keane of the 31st Ward, Edmund Kelly of the 47th Ward, George Dunne of the 42nd Ward, and Neil Hartigan of the 49th Ward are the dominant Irish committeemen in the inner group. An Italian, Vito Marzullo of the 25th Ward; a Jew, Marshall Korshak of the University of Chicago's 5th Ward; two Poles, Congressman Dan Rostenkowski of the 32nd Ward and Matthew Bieszczat of the 26th Ward; a Croatian, Edward Vrdolyak of the 10th Ward; and two black committeemen, Cecil Partee of the 20th Ward and Wilson Frost of the 21st Ward, are the dominant figures of the other ethnic groups and blacks in the inner circle. Also carrying considerable weight are men like state central committee chairman John Touhy and Daley's alderman, Michael Bilandic, who, while not committeemen, are often consulted on important matters.

Old timers, who do not carry a great deal of weight but who are left alone in their domains and given sufficient perquisites, are D'Arco (1st Ward), Quigley (27th Ward), Girolami (28th Ward), Neistein (29th Ward), Brandt (33rd Ward), Marcin (35th Ward), Garippo (36th Ward), and Huppert (50th Ward). Middle-aged seniors, and juniors new to the committee, are men like Aducci (9th), Taylor (16th), Shannon (17th), Fitzpatrick (19th), Stewart (21st), Sims (28th), Lechowicz (30th), Laurino (39th), Congressman Pucinski (41st), Merlo (44th), and Tuchow (48th). Rising young men knocking on the door to the inner sanctum and competing with each other for notice downtown are the young Irish committeemen like Edward Burke (14th), Lyons (45th), Madigan (13th), and the chairman's cousin, John M. Daley (18th). A smattering of suburban township committeemen like Kirie of Leyden and Sutker of Niles are consulted as representatives of the "country towns" beyond the city's borders. Tolerated are most of the suburban township committeemen and a few relatively ineffectual and uninfluential ward committeemen. Ignored are suburban "reformers" like Williams of New Trier and Mugalian of Palatine.

Picking the Ticket

When candidates are to be slated for public office at the county level, an inner circle of thirty committeemen, predominantly from the city but with some representation from the suburbs, meet as a body to interview prospective candidates. A prospective candidate who is recommended by one of the Democratic committeemen is invited to appear along with all other would-be candidates for the office to make a presentation before the slatemaking committee. The presentation consists of appearing before the slatemaking group for anywhere from five to fifteen minutes to outline one's assets as a candidate and to answer any questions the committeemen may have relative to one's background and qualifications, and particularly to one's ability to raise campaign funds for the campaign.

An inner group of possibly eight to a dozen committeemen meet together to decide on who the party should back for the major offices. The slate that emerges from the deliberations of the inner circle is then presented to the slatemaking group of thirty committeemen for their approval, which is usually automatic. And, finally, the recommendations of the slatemaking group are then presented for approval to the full county central committee of eighty committeemen. Rarely is approval denied a candidate chosen by the inner group of slatemakers. Of course, another fact of life in the Democratic county central committee is that the chairman, Richard J. Daley, has the dominant voice in selecting candidates for any office of significance in the Democratic party in the city of Chicago, Cook County, or the state of Illinois. This is not to say that Daley picks the ticket alone or that the other committeemen have no influence on the final choice. But a suggestion from the county chairman will usually suffice to override the wishes or desires of any of the other committeemen, or any combination of committeemen, for any major office.

Two major considerations govern the committee's choice of candidates for public office. The primary consideration is, "Can the candidate win?" The secondary consideration is, "If he can win, can he do us any good?" If a candidate can't win, who needs him? If he can win and can't do the party any good, who needs him? If he can win and can do the party harm, who wants him? In other words, the interests of the party and the ability of a candidate for public office to serve the interest of the party come first in building the ticket.

Putting a ticket together requires taking into consideration the interests of the various groups which make up the local Democratic party. Every ethnic, racial, religious, and economic group is entitled to have some representation on the ticket. Thus, in Chicago, the mayor's job has been an Irish job since 1933. The city clerk's job belongs to the Poles. The city treasurer can be a Jew, a Bohemian, or a black. On the county ticket, the county assessor, the state's attorney, and the county clerk must usually be Irish, but the county treasurer, the county superintendent of public schools, or the sheriff can be a member of one of the other ethnic or racial groups. A judicial slate is made up of three or four Irishmen, two or three Jews, two or three Poles, several blacks, a Lithuanian, a German, a Scandinavian, several Bohemians, and several Italians. The basic assumption behind building a ticket is that, when the Poles see a Polish name on the ticket, they will vote for the Polish name plus all the other people on the ticket; when the Jews see a Jewish name on the ticket, they will vote for the Jew plus all the others on the ticket; when the blacks know that there is a black on the ticket, they will vote for the black and all others on the ticket, and so on. It would be inconceivable to the Democratic slatemakers in Cook County to construct such a ticket as was put together in 1970 in New York, where for statewide office three Jews and one black were slated. That would never happen in Cook County.

Constructing a ticket, then, is not a matter of chance or of personal preference on the part of the slatemakers. It is an exercise in science and art—in the science of constructing a well-balanced ticket and in the art of pacifying the various groups that make up the electorate in Chicago and Cook County.

This concern for the interests of the various ethnic, racial, and religious groups in the city and county goes deeper than just having the identification of the name on the ticket. A prospective candidate must be able to demonstrate to the slatemakers that he has some broad-based support within his community. A Pole who has been active in the Polish National Alliance, for example, would have much more attraction to the slatemakers than would a Polish lawyer who has had no interest in or concern with Polish affairs in the city or the county. A Jew who belongs to a half-dozen temples, who has excellent connections with the leading rabbis of the city, and who has contributed to the bond drives for Israel is much more useful than a Jew who belongs to the American Council for Judaism (an anti-Zionist organization) or who has not been active within the Jewish community.

A primary requisite for any candidate wanting to run for office in the Democratic party in Cook County is loyalty to the party. A candidate must be willing to subordinate his interests to the greater interests of the ticket and of the party as a whole.* The slatemakers

---

* When I appeared before the Cook County Democratic Slatemaking Committee in 1970, Congressman Dan Rostenkowski, chairman of the committee, asked me two questions after I made my presentation to the committee. The first question was, "Professor, if we slate you for office will you support the Democratic ticket?" The second question was, "Professor, you are being considered for county superintendent of public schools by this group. We may have to juggle this ticket. Would you be willing to run for some other office in the interest of the party?" Having been briefed in advance as to the proper answers, I responded to the first question, "Congressman, I'm a Democrat. I'll support every man on the ticket down the line." And, to the second question, "Congressman, I'm a Democrat. I'll run for any office where I can serve the party, provided I have the qualifications for the office." Evidently the answers to the two questions satisfied the slatemakers, since I was slated for the Cook County Board of Commissioners from the suburban area of Cook County, on what is euphemistically called "the suicide squad." The last time a Democrat was elected to the board from the suburbs was in 1930.

are also interested in candidates who, while they may not be able to win, may be able to help the rest of the ticket. Or a candidate can seriously be considered for public office if he has sufficient financial resources to make a major contribution, not only to his campaign, but also to the party. The party is always willing to listen to and possibly slate for an unimportant or difficult-to-win office a wealthy businessman or lawyer who has an interest in politics and who is willing to contribute to the party in the coming election.

Two factors that are not of primary concern to the slatemakers in putting a ticket together are the prospective candidate's qualifications for the office he seeks and his zeal for solving the problems of the city and county or for reforming government and public policy in the interest of all the electorate. This is not to say that the party is not interested in qualified people. But qualifications for public office and a concern for the public interest on the part of a candidate are secondary considerations to the slatemakers when it comes to making up a ticket. If one possesses the qualifications for a public office and if one has an interest in public service, so much the better, as long as one is prepared to subordinate those considerations to the primary interests of the party.

Once slated for office, the candidate is expected to carry his own load as a part of the ticket. The central committee does very little except to arrange appearances for him at the various ward and township organizations during the campaign. He is expected to raise his own campaign funds, establish his own campaign office, do his own advertising, and reach those segments of the electorate to whom he supposedly has the greatest appeal on behalf of the ticket. In fact, a candidate for a major office, rather than getting campaign funds from the county central committee, is expected to make a major contribution to the county central committee for the privilege of being slated for office by the party. He is also expected to buy tickets for every ward and township organization dinner dance, picnic, and golf day. And he is expected to contribute to the campaigns of other candidates for other offices as a part of his obligation to the party. A prospective candidate's financial situation and ability to raise campaign funds is an important criterion for being selected for office by the party. Many unwary, ambitious candidates have found themselves deeply in debt after a campaign. The party will come to the aid of candidates for public offices which are important to it. But it will not put any money into the campaign of a candidate for a public office which is not of any serious interest to the party.*

Getting on the ticket, however, even for relatively unimportant offices, carries with it certain prerogatives. There is a protocol similar to that established in diplomatic intercourse among nations and in court circles during the reign of Louis XIV in France. A candidate for county office is invited to sit at the speaker's table at the $100-per-plate dinner with President Johnson, to attend the private luncheon for the astronauts given by the mayor, to attend the VIP private receptions before the fundraising dinners for major candidates, and to sit in the front rows on the stage at the Auditorium Theater at the state convention. (Powerful committeemen and officeholders are relegated to the back rows or tables in the audience at such affairs). He is always introduced from the podium at all affairs he attends. To neglect or overlook the name of any candidate at any political function is considered an insult.†

A candidate who has done his bit for the party in a losing race and who has fought the good fight on behalf of the ticket may be rewarded by the party in a number of ways. He may be slated in the future for an office that he can win. He may be appointed to some significant post. Or he may be the beneficiary of the city or county government's largesse in securing contracts or contacts if he is a lawyer or a businessman. If one is asked to run for public office by the party and refuses, the chances of one's being slated for some other office in the future would be pretty slim. But if an aspiring candidate waits for his turn and runs for undesirable offices when the party needs him, the lightning may strike for a worthwhile office sometime in the future. James Reichley of *Fortune* magazine

---

* The party will, however, handle the mechanics of the electoral process for county candidates for all offices. When I was slated for the Cook County Board of Commissioners in 1970, and learned I needed several thousand signatures on petitions to legally qualify for the primary ballot, I had no idea how I could get the required signatures in time to file my petitions. Hastening down to the party headquarters I asked Mary Mullen how I could accomplish this task in time. She responded, pointing to a stack of petitions on a table, "See that pile over there on that table? Those are your signatures, 8,000 names. This is an organization we are running here."

† I once saw County Assessor P. J. Cullerton stalk off the speaker's platform and leave the room in a huff at a fundraising dinner for United States senatorial candidate William Clark in 1968. Although he had been introduced, his name had been inadvertently left off the printed program.

reported the story of a Chicago politician who, when he was well over seventy, was sent to the United States Congress by the Chicago machine. When asked by Speaker Sam Rayburn why in the world he had come to Congress at such an advanced age, and why in any case the machine had seen fit to endorse him, he is supposed to have replied feelingly, "Because it was my turn!"

Dealing with Dissidents and Troublemakers

Dissidents and troublemakers get short shrift from the party. The history of the Democratic party of Cook County is replete with incidents in which the party has punished dissidents or severed the ties to candidates or prospective candidates who either rejected the party's importunities or who went their own ways in their campaigns without regard to the interests of the party.

Two recent examples of candidates for major public office who alienated the party's leaders and went their own ways, either in office or in the campaign, and who were consequently cast out in the wilderness were Cook County board president Seymour Simon in 1966 and United States senatorial candidate William Clark in 1968. Simon had been elected president of the county board in 1962 and was considered one of the bright, coming young men in the Democratic party. An able but abrasive man, he pursued his own ambitions rather than the party's. Rumor had it, too, that he had crossed Tom Keane, a very powerful man in the machine, over a zoning matter and had also alienated Izzie Horwitz, the Democratic boss of the 24th Ward. A palace revolt within the Cook County central committee took place, and, when Simon presented himself for slating for a second term for the Cook County board presidency, the leaders of the opposition pulled the rug out from under him. Despite Daley's desire not to have an intraparty fight over such a critical office during an election, Daley finally had to give way to the wishes of the united committeemen, especially when he saw that not a single committeeman would speak in Simon's behalf.

Simon never got a seat at the speaker's table at political affairs, was never introduced, and was rarely invited to VIP receptions after his fall from grace. In 1971, when the city's wards were reapportioned by the city council, some of the best Democratic precincts in his ward were taken from him and reassigned to party regular committeeman Anthony Laurino of the 39th Ward, adjacent to Simon's 40th Ward. In exchange, Simon was given some Republican precincts on the east end of his ward. In 1974, Simon was slated for an appellate court judgeship in return for giving up the aldermanic seat he had won in the city council and his position as ward committeeman to a Greek, John Geocaris. (The party wanted a Greek committeeman in the ward, since the Greeks have moved into the ward in force.)

In 1968 Adlai Stevenson III alienated the slatemakers by declaring that he was the best candidate that the party had for governor of Illinois, and that he could not support President Lyndon Johnson's policy on Vietnam if he were slated for the United States Senate. There were rumors that the Democratic machine was not really interested in beating incumbent Republican Senator Everett McKinley Dirksen, who had a good working relationship with the machine, or Republican gubernatorial candidate Richard B. Ogilvie, who would have to vacate his office as president of the Cook County Board of Commissioners, thus enabling the Democratic majority on the board to elect a Democrat in his place. Stevenson was rejected as a candidate for either governor or senator. Incumbent Democratic Governor Sam Shapiro, a party workhorse who had succeeded to the office when Governor Otto Kerner was appointed to the United States Court of Appeals in 1967, was slated for governor, and William Clark, the popular Democratic attorney general, was slated as a sacrificial lamb in the race against Dirksen. Clark refused to conduct his campaign as a sacrificial lamb, conducted an independent campaign instead, crossed the party leaders publicly on a number of occasions, criticized Daley, and lost the race for the Senate. Since then, Clark has been in the wilderness, practicing law but nowhere to be seen at speakers' tables at major functions, and has not been considered for public office since 1968. Shapiro also lost to Ogilvie in an inept campaign, thus opening the door to the Democratic machine's recapture of the presidency of the Cook County Board of Commissioners.

A candidate can cross the party and be slated for office, however, provided the party needs him as much as or more than he needs them. That was the case with Senator Adlai Stevenson III, who alienated the party in 1968, and was denied slating for either governor or United States senator. But Stevenson was then slated for the Senate in 1970 when the party felt that he was needed at the top of the ticket to help carry the rest of the slate into office.

The Democratic slatemakers also consistently refused to consider Dan Walker, a politically ambitious civic leader and corporation attorney who had alienated the party leadership in 1968 with the Walker Report on the 1968 Democratic convention troubles in Chicago. Walker, who characterized the confrontation between the Chicago police and the demonstrators as a police riot, was anathema to the party leadership. In 1972 Walker defeated the organization candidate, Lieutenant-Governor Paul Simon, for the gubernatorial nomination in a bitter primary fight, and went on to defeat the incumbent Republican Governor Richard B. Ogilvie in the general election. Since Walker's election as governor, Daley and the machine have kept him at arm's length, and an uneasy truce has been established between Governor Walker and the Cook County organization. Since his election as an anti-machine crusader, Walker has muted his criticism of the machine at times and attacked its policies at other times, come to terms with Daley on some issues and opposed him on others, and has manifested considerably less zeal as an anti-machine reformer. The machine, for its part, has generally ignored Walker, blocked his policies, compromised with him when necessary, and has bided its time until the 1976 election, waiting to see how it can best deal with the Walker problem then.

Another bridesmaid who has never become a bride is R. Sargent Shriver, former director of the Peace Corps, director of the poverty program, and ambassador to France. Shriver, a Kennedy Democrat who lived in Chicago and served as president of the board of education, and who maintains a voting residence in the city, has had ambitions to run for governor or United States senator from Illinois for many years. But the party would not slate Shriver for any office despite his attractiveness as a candidate. In the eyes of the party leadership, Shriver has not served his apprenticeship in the ranks of the local party. His national experience in the Peace Corps, the poverty program, and the United States Department of State made no impression on the locally oriented leadership of the party. Shriver is the kind of personality about whom the party has second thoughts as a candidate. The party leaders are aware that Shriver would run a Kennedy-style campaign in the state, building his own organization independent of the party and pursuing interests which may not coincide with those of the party. Such a prospect has no appeal to the local Democratic leaders, who have no interest in a state Democratic machine in Springfield that would be a countervailing power center to the local Democratic machine in Cook County. They willingly supported Shriver, however, in 1972 for the unimportant office (in their eyes) of vice-president of the United States.

Again, all this is not to say that the party is not interested in attractive, dynamic, capable men who have excellent qualifications for public office and who are concerned with problem solving and the public interest. The party can and has slated and accepted such candidates in the past and certainly would again in the future. But the question would be, "Does this candidate serve or would he serve the interests of the Democratic party of Cook County if he were elected to public office?" If the answer is "No," then the prospects for such a candidate are fairly dim.

Another technique that the party has employed several times in the past has been to let an independent or party candidate for office lose rather than support or put into office a potential troublemaker or a man who would bring unfavorable publicity to the party. In 1967, for example, in two aldermanic races, the party either refused to help the Democratic candidate for alderman or helped the Republican or Independent against the Democratic party's candidates.* In Chicago's Near North Side 43rd Ward, after the Democratic organization's candidate for alderman had received unfavorable publicity in the newspapers and had been forced to retire from the race, two candidates were left in the aldermanic race, a reform Republican named Barr McCutcheon and a liberal reform Democrat named Jack Ringer, who was not a part of the local 43rd Ward organization. Under orders from the then Democratic 43rd Ward committeeman, Paddy Bauler, the Democratic organization supported McCutcheon for the aldermanic seat. McCutcheon won. That same year, in the black 2nd Ward on Chicago's South Side, Congressman William Dawson's ward secretary, L. C. Woods, became the candidate of the 2nd Ward organization for alderman. Woods also had received considerable

---

* Legally, aldermanic elections in Chicago are nonpartisan, but most voters in a ward know which candidates are Democratic, Republican, or Independent.

unfavorable publicity in the local press and had alienated many of
the precinct captains in the ward organization. The ward organization clandestinely supported the candidacy of an independent
reform black candidate, Fred Hubbard, against the local organization's own candidate, and Hubbard won the aldermanic seat.

The basic assumption behind these kinds of tactics on the part of
the organization is that it is better to lose an election temporarily
than to win with the wrong candidate from the standpoint of the
party's interests. The party could live with an independent reform
Republican alderman and an independent Democratic alderman in
the city council for four years fairly easily, especially in view of the
fact that the party has an overwhelming majority in the council.
Four years will give the party enough time to do one of two things,
either co-opt the opposition alderman and take him into the
organization or bide its time for four years and run a more effective
organization-oriented candidate against him in the next election.
The party is aware, too, that an alderman in the city council who
does not have cooperation from his Democratic ward committeemen has considerable difficulty in providing the kinds of services
that constituents in most wards in Chicago want from their
aldermen. Without patronage and precinct captains to support him,
it is hard for an alderman to maintain contact with the people in his
ward, to run for re-election, and to have any real influence in his
ward.

In both the aldermanic cases mentioned above, the party
strategy worked. Alderman Fred Hubbard, the independent black
alderman from the 2nd Ward, was co-opted by the Democratic
organization and appointed to a $25,000-a-year administrative
position, and he then cooperated with the organization in his
aborted term in the city council.° McCutcheon, the Republican
alderman from the 43rd Ward, was relatively ineffective in the city
council and decided not to run for office in 1971.

The organization can and has tolerated within its ranks, and also
somewhat on the periphery of the party, independent Democratic
candidates who do not always subordinate their interests to the
interests of the party. Such people as Alderman Leon Despres from

---

° In 1972, Hubbard was convicted of embezzling approximately $100,000 from the
funds of the Chicago Plan, the agency to which Daley had appointed him as director.

the 5th Ward, Congressman Abner Mikva, State representatives Anthony Scariano of Park Forest and Robert Mann of Chicago, and even Senators Paul Douglas and Adlai Stevenson III, fall into this category. The same holds true for Democrats in public offices about which the party is not particularly concerned such as county superintendent of public schools, or state superintendent of public instruction. Such office holders are generally allowed to go their own ways in their offices because the party does not make very serious demands on them. This was even true to a considerable extent when Democrats such as Otto Kerner and Sam Shapiro served as governor of Illinois. The party allowed them to conduct the state's business as they saw fit, as long as they collaborated with the Democratic organization in Cook County on state matters that affected the interests of the party in Cook County and the city of Chicago.

The major thrust of the party's effort in an election is directed toward the local offices. National and state offices are significantly less important to the party leaders than the county and city offices from which flow the perquisites and rewards of politics in which the local Democratic leaders are interested. Consequently, these offices are reserved for members of the party faithful of long standing who can be trusted and who can be relied upon to serve the party's interest as well as their own. But national and state offices, which have little appeal to the local party leadership, can be turned over to liberal, reform candidates who have an appeal to anti-organization Democratic voters who might thus be persuaded to vote for the local ticket, too.

4

The Ward Organizations

The most significant of all the party's relationships with any of the constituent parts of the organization are its dealings with the ward organizations in the city. Each of Chicago's fifty wards is an entity unto itself, a fiefdom ruled in the party's name by a committeeman who is a prince of the blood, a duke, a baron, an earl, or a mere knight. The ruling coterie in the party's hierarchy is analogous to the aristocracy of a sixteenth- or seventeenth-century medieval court.

The party is not a monolithic, totalitarian dictatorship but rather a feudal structure, dominated by Chairman Richard J. Daley. But Daley is neither an absolute monarch nor a totalitarian dictator. He is, rather, like Leonid Brezhnev, in the Soviet Politburo, a prominent figure who towers above all other members of the Politburo but does not stand alone. While Daley has gathered more power into his hands than has any other politician in Chicago's history, that power rests on a foundation of a shifting coalition of power groups and powerful figures, some within the political organization and some in the community at large. Daley governs in their names only so long as he keeps a stable balance of power among the groups which make up Chicago's body politic, maintains a decent level of order in the city, and provides sufficient perquisites to pacify the aspirations and demands of the city's political and economic aristocracy.

The Role of the Committeeman

The committeemen are the party's representatives in the wards, the link between the wards and the party headquarters, and the conduit through which party perquisites are distributed to the wards. Once a man is elected committeeman, it is almost impossible to dislodge him from his position unless the party leadership decrees that he step down from his post. Committeemen are elected in party primaries every four years by the registered voters of the party in what are known as precinct-captain elections, elections in which the machine vote is turned out by the precinct captains, and the unreliable voters are not disturbed.

An incumbent committeeman is protected against challengers by the law requiring a candidate for ward committeeman to get a petition signed by at least 10 percent of the party's vote in the last primary election. This is five times as much as the legal requirement for getting on the ballot to run for alderman (2 percent of the vote cast in the last aldermanic election) and twenty times as much as candidates for state representative or congressmen need. Candidates for those offices are required by state law to have petitions signed by only one-half of one percent of the registered voters in the party in those legislative districts. Securing that many signatures on a petition requires an organization, precinct captains familiar with the registered Democratic voters in the ward who are willing to distribute petitions on behalf of the candidate, and a substantial number of registered Democratic voters who are willing to alienate the ward committeeman by signing the petitions of a rival. While these conditions make it possible for an opposing candidate to challenge an incumbent ward committeeman, they make it exceedingly difficult for him to meet the legal requirements, not to mention the political hazards of challenging the incumbent. Few precinct captains will distribute petitions for a challenger to an incumbent ward committeeman, and not many registered Democratic voters will alienate an incumbent committeeman by signing his rival's petitions.

Once safely ensconced in his job, the committeeman is the absolute master of the ward organization. All party electoral funds are channeled directly through him, to be distributed by him at his pleasure. All patronage positions distributed by the county central committee to the ward organizations are funneled through him. All precinct captains are appointed by him and are subject to his summary dismissal without recourse to any other party authority. All favors dispensed by the party hierarchy and by city and county officials connected with the party require his approval before any party or governmental functionary will take action on such requests. No person from his ward can be hired in any patronage position at the city and county level without his sponsorship. And people who have been hired might be fired on his request from positions they hold with the city or county.* In other words, he holds in his hands the destinies and livelihoods of all members of his ward organization.

The position of ward committeeman carries with it not only perquisites but also responsibilities. In return for granting him absolute authority in his ward, the party expects him to support party decisions without question; to deliver for all party candidates, regardless of his personal feelings about those candidates; and to maintain an effective ward organization which serves the interests of the party as well as the needs of the committeeman's constituents. If one is given a leadership position by the party, one is expected to lead and produce or get out. There is little room in the relationship of the ward committeemen to the county central committee for sentiment, friendship, or failure. Powerful committeemen who have been high in the party hierarchy for many years have been cast aside when they lost control of their ward organizations or failed to deliver for the party in an election. For example, in 1970, County Clerk Edward J. Barrett, who was the long-time committeeman in the 44th Ward, was called down and raked over the coals by the party's hierarchy after he had lost the aldermanic election in his ward to a liberal reform Democrat. Barrett, who was seventy years old and who had been county clerk for sixteen years, was reslated for his office only on condition that he give up the committeemanship of his ward. There are numerous other examples of formerly powerful committeemen who held

---

* An order from a federal district judge in 1971 specified that city and county workers cannot be required to do political work to hold their positions. At this writing, it is difficult to evaluate the status of compliance with the edict.

elective or appointive offices under the party and who lost both their committeemanships and their offices when they failed to deliver in their wards.

Some of the most powerful and able committeemen such as Tom Keane of the 31st Ward and Vito Marzullo of the 25th Ward, as well as some lesser lights, also hold the aldermanic posts from their wards in the city council, but they are the exceptions rather than the rule. Most committeemen prefer to remain in the background, in control of the ward organization, its patronage, and its perquisites but out of the public eye. There they are not subject to criticism by the mass media and reform groups whose normal targets are public officeholders. But most committeemen select and control the ward's alderman in the city council and have a determining voice in the selection of the district's candidates for the state legislature and the national House of Representatives.

Most committeemen, however, hold either an elective post in an office fairly safe from scrutiny by the voters and the media, or an appointive office at a decent salary. A few committeemen such as Dan Rostenkowski, George Collins, Ralph Metcalfe, and Roman Pucinski have served in Congress; some serve in the state legislature in safe seats; several others, such as George Dunne, Matthew Bieszczat, John Stroger, and Jerome Huppert, serve on the county board; and others, such as City Clerk John C. Marcin, former County Assessor P. J. Cullerton, and former County Clerk Edward J. Barrett have held important but safe city or county offices.* Most committeemen who do not hold elective posts, however, hold major appointive posts such as attorney to the Chicago Park District, the Sanitary District, or the Forest Preserve District; superintendent of Water Collections of the City of Chicago; deputy commissioner of the Bureau of Sewers; general superintendent of the Bureau of Forestry and Parkways; vice-president of the Chicago Park District; city revenue director; and chief deputy clerks of the probate division, divorce division, and criminal division of the circuit court.

Other compensations can accrue to a committeeman in the city

---

* Barrett was convicted of mail fraud in 1972 and replaced as county clerk by Stanley Kusper, an able young Polish politician from Marzullo's ward organization. In 1974, when the party slated Kusper for county clerk, traditionally an Irish job, an Irish banker named Edward Rosewell was slated for county treasurer, an office which had been allocated to the Poles, thus balancing the county offices properly between the Irish and the Poles.

of Chicago and even in the suburbs. If he is an attorney, he can set up a law firm and get business for that firm from city and county agencies and from commercial firms and individuals in his ward. He can open an insurance office and sell insurance to commercial firms and major property owners in his ward. Since insurance rates are set by the state, the costs to prospective customers are no higher than other insurance brokers charge, and buying insurance from the committeeman might help to discourage building inspectors, electrical inspectors, fire inspectors, and sundry other city and county officials from disturbing the property. A diligent and enterprising ward committeeman might be able to sell performance bond insurance to contractors who are doing work for the city or county. There is the possibility of becoming a member of the board of directors of a bank or two in the ward, of having an interest in a commercial firm which sells materials or does business with the city or county agencies, or of getting tips on stock deals or beneficial business transactions from bankers or businessmen in your ward or in the Loop. He may even, if he is lucky, and close enough to the inner circle, be able to buy land which the city or county may become interested in for public purposes, and sell that land back to the city or county for a fair return on his investment. Finally, if he is exceptionally hardworking and willing to put in long hours, he may be able to hold several jobs at the same time, serving in the state legislature and holding a major appointive position with the county or city.

A committeeman's status in the pecking order of the county central committee, his influence in the selection of county or state candidates, and the allocation of patronage jobs to his ward, in terms of both number and quality of jobs, are directly related to his ability to produce votes for the party. These rules, of course, must be qualified by the preeminence of the Irish Catholic princes-of-the-blood committeemen in the power structure of the county central committee, who dominate the party organization. Even though the black wards in the city have become the bedrock strength of the Democratic party in Chicago, delivering massive percentages of Democratic votes in elections, black committeemen, as a whole, do not enjoy the power and prestige of their Irish counterparts. Since the death of the late Congressman William Dawson, who was the committeeman of the 2nd Ward, no black committeeman has achieved Dawson's status in the inner circle of the party, although several old Dawson political lieutenants have achieved substantial court status as dukes or barons. There is some chance, however, that they will become authentic princes of the blood in the near future, since several of the non-Irish ethnic committeemen such as Daniel Rostenkowski and Vito Marzullo have reached the charmed circle.

A review of the performance of every committeeman in his ward is conducted by the party leadership after every primary and every election. Every committeeman is required to give the chairman an estimate of the votes he expects to get in his ward or township before the election date, and his performance is weighed against that estimate. If he cannot deliver for the party he is in trouble. If he brings in a significantly higher vote total than the estimate he gave the county central committee, he could be in trouble, since it is then clear to the party leadership that the committeeman does not know what is going on in his ward. Losing the ward, or delivering a lower percentage of the vote than was estimated, can have serious consequences for a committeeman. He could lose his job, be "viced" and replaced by an acting ward committeeman selected by the precinct captains of the organization at the instigation of the county chairman, or he could have his patronage cut and have important jobs that he needs to reward his precinct captains taken from him.

There have been several significant changes in the makeup of the county central committee in recent years at the instigation of Chairman Daley. Older committeemen who have failed to deliver their wards for the party, or who have lost control of their organizations, have been dumped and replaced by ambitious, rising young committeemen willing to work to advance themselves and the interests of the party. Outstanding committeemen are rewarded by a significant elected office, a well-paying patronage appointment, seats close to the chairman at the speaker's table at important political dinners, better and more jobs for their precinct captains, a position at the front of the procession for their ward organizations in the annual St. Patrick's Day Parade, a position alongside the mayor in the front or second row of the marchers in the parade, or possibly even a position on the podium near the chairman when he reviews the troops.

The Patronage System

"This is my judge, this is my county commissioner, and this is my state senator," Alderman and Committeeman Vito Marzullo of the West Side's 25th Ward told me at lunch one day at his table in the Bismarck hotel. "I got an assistant state's attorney, and I got an assistant attorney general," Marzullo said to a *Chicago Daily News* reporter in 1967. "I got an electrical inspector at $10,500 a year, and street inspectors and surveyors and a $7,900-a-year county highway inspector. I got an administrative assistant to the zoning board, and some bailiffs and some process servers and a county building inspector at $8,400 a year. . . . I got fifty-nine captains and they all have jobs. I've got ten or twelve good jobs at the state department of highways, and others with the secretary of state, county clerk and county assessor and the city department of streets." The alderman was spelling out for the *Daily News* reporter some of the perquisites that flow to his organization, one of the most effective and efficient ward organizations in the city.

Few of the committeemen are willing to publicly confront the press with the realities of ward politics in Chicago, but Alderman Marzullo was only spelling out what is a privately accepted fact of political life by Chicago Democratic politicians. It is impossible to make an accurate analysis of the number of patronage positions distributed by the Cook County Democratic Central Committee to loyal workers, precinct captains, and supporters, but a fairly educated guess would be that there may be approximately 30,000 patronage positions available to the county central committee. The jobs range from $295-a-month clerks to $25,000-a-year directors of city commissions. They are located in agencies ranging from approximately 70 jobs in the county coroner's office to approximately 6000 jobs under the control of the county board and approximately 8000 jobs in the city of Chicago's departments and commissions. There are also many thousands of jobs in private industry throughout the Chicago metropolitan area which require the sponsorship of Democratic ward committeemen.°

° In 1938, when I graduated from Crane Technical High School and applied for a job with Sears Roebuck and Company's mail order house, whose headquarters was located in the

Estimates of the number of jobs available to individual committeemen range from a maximum of approximately 2000 jobs in Chairman Daley's 11th Ward to a dozen jobs in a heavily Republican township. Since there are 5463 precincts in the county, of which 3148 are in the 50 wards in the city, the patronage pool could average from 500 to 600 jobs per ward. If each job is worth 10 votes in an election, the machine has a running start of approximately 300,000 votes derived directly from the patronage system.

No person can be appointed to a patronage position at any level without the prior sponsorship of his ward committeeman. This maxim applies to all appointments, not only to local patronage positions but also to high-level federal posts such as federal judges and important positions in the federal bureaucracy. The level of appointment to which the system applies was recounted to me by a friend of mine, a young attorney in Chicago, who was working as a precinct captain in one of the Democratic ward organizations. He was being considered for an appointment to one of the major federal regulatory commissions in Washington. He was told in Washington, however, that he could not be appointed without Daley's approval. He could not get Daley's approval without the sponsorship of his ward committeeman. On a night when his ward committeeman was holding office hours at the ward headquarters, the attorney presented himself to the ward committeeman, who was sitting behind his desk with a big cigar sticking out of one corner of his mouth, and two precinct captains sitting on either side of the desk. The young attorney told his ward committeeman that there was an opening on one of the federal commissions and that he was being considered for the opening but needed the sponsorship of the ward committeeman. The ward committeeman took the cigar out of his mouth, and said to the young attorney, "You want to be a United States commissioner?" "Yes," replied the young attorney. Turning to the precinct captain seated on his left, the committeeman said to the precinct captain, "Do you want to be a U.S. commissioner?" "No," replied the precinct captain. Turning to the precinct captain

---

24th Ward on Chicago's west side, the employment office refused to give me an application. My precinct captain then secured a letter from Alderman Jacob M. Arvey of the 24th Ward, in which I lived. Upon presentation of the alderman's letter, the Sears employment office promptly produced a job application for me. The same relationship between ward committeemen and business firms still exists in many wards in Chicago today.

seated on his right, the ward committeeman repeated, "Do you want to be a U.S. commissioner?" "No," replied the second precinct captain. He turned back to the young attorney standing before him, and said, "Okay, you've got it. But you have to be cleared by the mayor. Go home and wait until I call you. I'll set up an appointment with the mayor." Two nights later the attorney's telephone rang. It was the ward committeeman, telling him to meet at the mayor's office in City Hall the next day at 9 A.M. The next morning the committeeman ushered in the young attorney to see the mayor, who was seated behind his desk. The committeeman made the introductions. "I understand, young man, that you are an outstanding attorney," said the mayor. "Well, your honor," said the attorney, "I'm not an outstanding attorney, but I'm a good one." At that point all conversation ceased. The mayor sat enigmatically, looking like Buddha. The committeeman sat expectantly, waiting for some further words of wisdom to drop from the lips of the mayor. After two minutes the young attorney realized that the mayor was not about to speak. Sitting there, in an embarrassed silence, the attorney had an inspiration. Turning to the mayor, he said, "Mr. Mayor, I want you to know that if I get this appointment, I will administer my position with every due consideration for the interest of the Democratic organization of Cook County." Smiling broadly, the mayor turned to the door and beckoned to his secretary, saying, "Call in the photographers!"

Patronage jobs are usually parceled out to precinct captains in a ward organization on the basis of their efficiency in their precincts, and their qualifications. Young attorneys seeking to climb the political ladder by manning a precinct in a ward organization can be appointed as an assistant state's attorney, assistant corporation counsel, or work in the state attorney general's office, if the office is held by a Democrat. The college graduate with accounting skills can work in the county comptroller's office, or in a comparable position in the city bureaucracy. A high school graduate without any particular skills or training can work on a highway crew, can be a sidewalk inspector, a house-drain inspector, a forest ranger, a tree cutter, a sewer inspector, or a street sign wiper.

A classic example of how the system works was recounted to me by a Chicago alderman. According to the alderman, Committeeman Bernard Neistein of the 29th Ward sponsored a man who was a minister in a storefront church for a position with a city department. The irate department head called Neistein to complain that the prospective job candidate could neither read nor write adequately. "Put him to work. I need him," Neistein told the bureaucrat. Turning to the alderman, Neistein showed him a picture of the minister's podium, where, facing the audience, was a sign bearing the following information for the edification of the worshipers: "———— Baptist Church. ———— Minister. Bernard Neistein, Ward Committeeman." ("Bernie Neistein," one high-level local bureaucrat told me, "is reasonable. If he sends you five guys to put to work, only two are illiterate. But Matt Bieszczat sends you five illiterates and wants you to take them all!")

In most cases, a precinct captain holds his patronage position as long as he delivers his precinct or covers the precinct to the satisfaction of his ward committeeman. Like his committeeman, a precinct captain is expected to carry his share of the burden for the party in his ward, as his committeeman is expected to carry the ward's share in city or county elections. Thus, power is delegated from the county central committee to the ward committeemen, and from the ward committeemen to the precinct captains. The entire system operates on the principle of autonomy of authority at each level in the political pyramid. When a man is given a precinct, it is his to cover, and it is up to him to produce for the party. If he cannot produce for the party, he cannot expect to be rewarded by the party. "Let's put it this way," Alderman Marzullo told me. "If your boss has a salesman who can't deliver, who can't sell his product, wouldn't he put someone else in who can?"

Like the ward committeeman, a precinct captain is required to estimate the results of the coming election in his precinct. And, like the ward committeeman, he is expected to predict accurately. Whereas losing a precinct may result in losing a patronage job, a captain who overestimates or underestimates the vote totals in his precinct also could be in trouble with his committeeman. Being unable to predict vote totals indicates to the ward committeeman that the precinct captain either is not working his precinct well or does not know what the voters in his precinct are thinking. Either reason is sufficient cause for disciplinary action such as the following incident recounted to me by a friend who spent election night, 1964, in the ward headquarters of former Alderman and Committeeman Mathias ("Paddy") Bauler of the 43rd Ward as the precinct captains came in to report. On the wall of Bauler's office was a tally board indicating which precincts had been carried and which had been lost in that day's election. A captain, who had lost his precinct that day, appeared before Bauler. "What kind of a job are you going to look for now?" asked Bauler of the abject precinct captain standing before him. As the unfortunate miscreant went out the door of the office, the next precinct captain appeared before the committeeman. "Your brother didn't vote," said Bauler to the precinct captain. "My brother didn't vote!" exclaimed the captain. "I'll kill him!" "Okay," said Bauler to the captain, "bring in the evidence, and you'll keep your job."

The party policy by which each captain or committeeman is expected to carry his precinct or ward, or suffer the consequences of failure regardless of the overall result of the election, forces each individual in the party's organization to concern himself only with his part of the action, not with the total result. For, even if the party wins the election, and he does poorly in his ward or precinct, the electoral victory will have little significance for him personally. Conversely, if he does well in his ward or precinct, he will stand well with the party hierarchy, even if the party loses the election. This policy forces every individual in the organization to think locally, to concern himself almost exclusively with his bit of turf, and to leave broad policy matters and directions for the party leadership. As a consequence, the machine in Chicago is not really one citywide organization but, rather, a composite of approximately 3148 local precinct organizations, each under the control of an individual responsible for his organization. There is no room in such a system for ideology, philosophy, or broad social concern. There is, instead, a pragmatic recognition of the need to concern oneself with one's little corner of the world, not with the interest of society as a whole, or mankind in general.

I became aware of this psychology in the election of 1968, when I worked a precinct for the Democratic organization in one of the North Side wards in Chicago. On election night at ward headquarters, I stood with my precinct co-captain before the big tally board which indicated the results in each of the ward's ninety-five precincts. Over the radio came the news of the developing results of the national and statewide elections for the Democratic party. It was clear that Vice-President Hubert Humphrey was losing the presidency to Richard Nixon, that Democratic Governor Sam Shapiro was losing the gubernatorial election to Republican Richard B. Ogilvie, and that Democratic senatorial candidate William Clark was losing the United States Senate seat from Illinois to incumbent Republican Senator Everett McKinley Dirksen. That night, even though I did not hold, and had no interest in securing a patronage job, and had taught political science for sixteen years, I found myself in the ward headquarters, my eyes intently fixed on the board carrying the tallies of my precinct, uninterested in the results in any other precinct in the ward, and almost totally unconcerned with the results of the city, county, state, and national elections for the Democratic party.

Working the Precinct

How does a good precinct captain carry a precinct in cities like Chicago? Not by stressing ideology or party philosophy, not by stuffing mailboxes with party literature, not by debating issues with his constituents, but rather by ascertaining individual needs and by trying to serve those needs. Good precinct captains know that most elections are won or lost, not on great national, ideological issues, but rather on the basis of small, private, individual interests and concerns. If they don't know this or have forgotten it, their ward committeemen remind them in ward organization meetings. "Distinguished citizens," Alderman Marzullo addressed his precinct captains on the eve of the 1971 mayoralty election, "civic leaders, and religious leaders. This ward is not depending on the kind of publicity given to troublemakers and the nitwits and crackpots. This ward is depending on the record for sixteen years of our great mayor and the people who will put their shoulder to the wheel because they love Richard J. Daley and what he has done for the city of Chicago with the help of the Democratic party. Bring this message to your neighbors in your own language. You don't have to be an intellectual. I'm not an intellectual and I don't intend to be one."

Four months after the mayoralty election, in which Marzullo carried his ward for the mayor by a heavy majority, Marzullo leaned back in the high-back leather chair in his City Hall office and told

Sun-Times columnist Tom Fitzpatrick, "I ain't got no axes to grind. You can take all your news media and all the do-gooders in town and move them into my 25th Ward, and do you know what would happen? On election day we'd beat you fifteen to one. The mayor don't run the 25th Ward. Neither does the news media or the do-gooders. Me, Vito Marzullo. That's who runs the 25th Ward, and on election day everybody does what Vito Marzullo tells them."

⌐What kinds of goods and services do precinct captains in ward organizations provide? According to Marzullo, his captains work 365 days a year providing "service and communication" to his people. This includes free legal service for the destitute, repair of broken street lights, intensified police squad patrol, special anti-rodent clean-ups in the alleys, new garbage cans for tenants provided for them by their landlords, and talks with the probation officers of youngsters who are in trouble. "Anybody in the 25th needs something, needs help with his garbage, needs his street fixed, needs a lawyer for his kid who's in trouble, he goes first to the precinct captain," says Marzullo. "If the captain can't deliver, that man can come to me. My house is open every day to him." New residents moving into Marzullo's ward get a welcoming letter from the alderman on 25th Ward letterhead stationery:

February 11, 1971

Dear Friend:

As you know, the City Council of Chicago has redistricted the Wards, and you are now a resident of the 25th Ward. As the Ward Committeeman and Alderman of the 25th Ward, I take pride in welcoming you into the official family of our Ward.

The 25th Ward is fortunate in being represented at all levels of government by people of all ethnic backgrounds. We are truly a cosmopolitan organization. As members of our organization, we have the Honorable Frank Annunzio, who is Congressman for the Seventh Congressional District; Honorable Thaddeus V. Adesko, Judge of the Appellate Court; Honorable Charles S. Bonk, County Commissioner; Honorable Anthony Kogut, Judge of the Circuit Court of Cook County; Honorable Sam Romano, State Senator; Honorable Matt Ropa, State Representative; and Madison Brown, Con-Con Delegate.

I would like to point out to you that the next nonpartisan aldermanic election will be held on February 23, 1971. At that time I am sure you will be visited by your Democratic Precinct Captain who will be most anxious to discuss any problems of mutual interest.

Our organization has always endeavored to meet the needs and wants of our people. I personally await the opportunity on behalf of all of the officials of the 25th Ward and myself, to be of assistance. Do not hesitate to let us know what your problems are, and if we can help, we are more than willing to extend our services.

With every best wish, I am

> Sincerely,
> Alderman Vito Marzullo
> 25th Ward Committeeman

Marzullo is a five-feet-six-inches seventy-seven-year-old grandfather, an Italian immigrant who came to Chicago at age twelve, who has spent fifty-five years in politics on the city's west side, who went only as far as the fourth grade in school but who lectures on politics at the University of Illinois, and who is one of the last authentic old-line ward bosses in the Democratic machine which has governed Chicago for more than forty years. On a winter night, in November 1974, I spent an evening with Marzullo in his ward headquarters on Chicago's west side. Seated behind his desk, Marzullo looked and sounded like Marlon Brando as the Godfather. "I always say, 'Vito, put yourself on the other side of the table. How would you like to be treated?'" Marzullo told me. "I'm not an intellectual, but I love people. I'm not elected by the media, the intellectuals or do-gooders. I'm elected by my people. Service and communication. That's how my ward is run."

Marzullo has run for office 18 times. Only once has he had an opponent. "I beat him 15,000 to 1000," Vito said. "I carried his precinct 3 and a half to 1. In 1940, when I first ran for state representative, I carried my precinct 525 to 14. The Republican precinct captain's mother and father voted for me."

"We got the most cosmopolitan ward in Chicago," said Marzullo. "Thirty percent black, twenty percent Polish, twelve to fifteen percent Mexican, five percent Italian, Slovenians, Lithuanians, Bohemians. We got them all."

"But I take care of all my people. Many politicians are like groundhogs. They come out once a year. On November fifth [election day], I visited every precinct polling place. On November sixth, I was in my office at City Hall at nine A.M. I'm there five days a week. On November seventh, I was here in my ward office at six-thirty P.M., ready to serve my people. My home is open twenty-four hours a day. I want people to come in. As long as I have a breathing spell, I'll go to a wake, a wedding, whatever. I never ask for anything in return. On election day, I tell my people, 'Let your conscience be your guide.' "

Marzullo's precinct captains were assembled in the rear room. After State Senator Sam Romano called the roll of the forty-eight precincts in the 25th Ward, Marzullo took the podium to remind his captains to maintain their efforts. "No man walks alone. Mingle with the people. Learn their way of life. Work and give service to your people."

After the meeting with the captains, Marzullo moved to the front office to greet his constituents. A precinct captain ushered in a black husband and wife. "We got a letter here from the city," the man said. "They want to charge us twenty dollars for rodent control in our building." "Give me the letter. I'll look into it," Marzullo replied. The captain spoke up. "Your daughter didn't vote on November fifth. Look into it. The alderman is running again in February. Any help we can get, we can use." "I'm looking for a job," the woman said. "I don't have anything right now," said the alderman.

The telephone rang. Marzullo listened and said, "Come to my office tomorrow morning." He hung up. "She's a widow for thirteen years. She wants to put her property in joint tenancy with her daughter. The lawyer wants a hundred dollars. I'll have to find someone to do it for nothing."

"Some of those liberal independents in the city council, they can't get a dog out of a dog pound with a ten-dollar bill," Marzullo snorted. "Who's next?"

Another captain ushered in a constituent. "Frank has a problem. Ticket for a violation of street sweeping." "Tell John to make a notation," Marzullo said. "You'll have to go to court. We'll send Freddy with you." The constituent thanked Marzullo and left. The captain said, "Alderman, how about that job in the Forest Preserves?" "You'll have to wait until after the first of the year," Marzullo responded.

The captain from the 16th precinct brought in a young black man who had just graduated from college and was looking for a job. "I just lost fifteen jobs with the city," Marzullo said. "How about private industry?" said the captain. "His family has been with us a long time." "Bring him downtown tomorrow," Marzullo instructed the captain. "I'll give him a letter to the —— Electric Company. They may have something." The young man left. "What about a donation to the Illinois Right to Life Committee?" asked the captain. "Nothing doing," said Marzullo. "I don't want to get into any of those controversies. People for it and people against it."

"We give a donation to thirty-five churches in the ward every year," Marzullo said. "One election day, I saw the priest from St. Roman's serving coffee and cake in the polling place. 'What are you doing?' I asked him. 'What the hell do you think I'm doing?' the priest replied. 'I'm trying to get some Democratic votes.'"

"Last time I ran, the Polish priest from St. Anne's took my petitions and got all the nuns to sign them," Marzullo said. "He had a paralyzed woman in a wheelchair who couldn't go to Mass because she couldn't get her chair over the curb in front of the church. I had the city build a ramp over the curb for her."

Marzullo pulled the ward organization's checkbook out of the desk. "Look at some of these donations—$100 to the City of Hope, $20 to St. Stephen's Holy Name Society, $20 to the Bennett Playground, $200 to St. Michael's Church, $100 to the American Legion, $125 to the West Chicago Florists, $600 for tickets to the Miko Howlett dinner, $25 to the New Trier Baseball Club."

"On election day, every captain gets $50 to $200 for expenses in his precinct," Marzullo explained. "We buy eight tables for the $100-per-plate Cook County central committee dinner. That's $8,000. We make contributions to all of our candidates and pay assessments for people running from our ward. When the mayor runs we carry the ward for him by at least five to one. He's a great family man. A great religious person. We've been together all the way. I got six married children. He came to every one of their weddings. He invited me to the weddings of every one of his kids. You don't go back on people like that."

"The money comes from our annual ward dinner dance," Marzullo explained. "We don't charge our patronage workers any dues, or take kickbacks. We sell ads for our ad book for the dance and clear about $35,000 from the ad book." Marzullo's ad book looks like a fair-size telephone book.

A Polish truck driver came in. "I was laid off three weeks ago," he told Marzullo. "I've got six children." Marzullo countered, "I lost two truck drivers and three laborers this week. The city budget is being held down. We have to keep taxes down. But come down to my office in City Hall tomorrow morning. I'll see if there is an opening in street sweeping or snow plowing." "We got ten votes in my building," said the man. "If we get you a job, let your conscience be your guide," the alderman advised.

Two more captains came in. "Can you do anything about garbage cans?" said one. "I need two." "I don't have anything yet," said Marzullo. "But we'll get forty or fifty soon as a donation from Trilla Cooperage." The second captain spoke up. "I got two goddamn sewers caving in. That goddamn Quigley!" (referring to City Sewer Commissioner Edward Quigley). "What are you yelling about?" asked Marzullo. "Give them to Johnny Domagala" (his efficient ward secretary).

More people came in. A Mexican crane operator who was getting his hours cut back, a captain who wanted a transfer from the blacksmith shop to an easier job, a woman computer operator who was being mistreated by her supervisor. To each of them, Marzullo said, "I'll see what I can do."

The last captain came in with a sickly looking black woman. "Mamie," he said, "I want you to meet my great alderman and your great alderman. If he can help you, he'll do it."

"Alderman," Mamie said, "I need food stamps. I've been in the hospital three times this year. They're giving me pills, but I can't afford to eat."

"You have to get food stamps from your case worker," Marzullo explained. "I can't help on that." Turning to County Commissioner Charley Bonk, "Charley, give her a check for fifty dollars for food." And to Mamie, "If you need more come back again." "God bless you!" Mamie responded as she went out the door. "I guess that's it for tonight," sighed Bonk wearily. "If you meet them head-on every day, you wear them all out."

In middle-class wards on the northwest and southwest sides of the city, precinct captains can help get tax bills appealed, curbs and gutters repaired, scholarships for students to the University of Illinois, summer jobs for college students, and directions and assistance to those who need some help in finding their way through the maze of government bureaucracy with a grievance. "See the four men on this wall to the right?" Marzullo once asked Tom Fitzpatrick. "There's Mayor Daley, Congressman Frank Annunzio, County Commissioner Charles Bonk, and the other man is Vito Marzullo. We put a lot of other judges on the bench, too. And don't think that these people are ingrates. They always cooperate with the party that put them on the bench whenever they can. You see what I mean? The 25th Ward has a voice in every branch of government. That's a hobby we have in the 25th. It's our way of providing service to our people."

Most of the work of a good precinct captain in providing services to his constituents is not fixing tickets, bribing officials, or getting special favors for people, but rather ascertaining the individual needs of his people, communicating those needs through proper channels to the proper authorities, and providing help to those who are unable to find their way through the massive layers of bureaucracy in twentieth-century American government.

"The days when you went to the ward committeeman for a bucket of coal or a sweater for Johnny were on the way out when we went to the welfare programs of a more compassionate society under Roosevelt," according to the number-two man in the Cook County Democratic organization, Committeeman Tom Keane of the 31st Ward. "The political organization today [in the 1970s] is a service organization, an ombudsman and an inquiry department. I consider my ward has fifty-seven community organizations doing public service," says Keane, who calls his fifty-seven precinct captains "community representatives." Keane's analysis is echoed by county board president George Dunne, the Democratic committeeman in the 42nd Ward. "To a great extent the service we offer now is referral," says Dunne. "People ask, 'How do I get this? Where do I go to get that?' In some instances a letter from me helps and I never turn them down. Some people feel a letter always helps, but I think they would get what they need without it in most cases. . . . Even though over the years times have changed, the success of a political organization depends on giving service to the people." °

° In 1950, when I was a graduate student at the University of Chicago and a full-time clerk with civil service status at the United States Post Office in Chicago, working forty hours a week on the night shift, I requested a change in status at the post office to substitute clerk, so that I could work only four or five hours a night. After going through all the proper channels in the post office, I was told repeatedly by the authorities that such a request could

For a good precinct captain, a patronage position is only one of the reasons for staying on the job. Precinct work, especially before an election, is hard work and sometimes sheer drudgery. The annual or semi-annual all-important canvass and registration drive requires a check of every house and apartment in the precinct to find out who moved out and who moved in, getting recalcitrant and uninterested voters registered, an on-the-spot psychological evaluation of every new voter who has come into the precinct, and a quick decision as to whether the new voter is a potential Democrat or Republican. If he is probably a Democrat, or might be encouraged to become one, he has to be registered. If he sounds like a Republican, he had best be ignored (who wants to register Republican voters?). Precinct work requires calculation of the way in which every potential voter in the precinct is likely to vote in the coming election. Good precinct work requires climbing stairs at night and on weekends, timing the visit properly so as not to interfere with the popular television programs, and learning the names, relationships, and attitudes of the voters. "Cover every home! Don't take nothing for granted!" Marzullo exhorted his captains at a ward meeting I attended. Good precinct work requires also an ability to blunt ideological prejudices, establish personal relationships, and adapt to the voters' peripatetic political perambulations. It further requires an ability to measure the depth of the voter's feelings, to push for the whole ticket when you can, but to be able to retreat gracefully when necessary. If the voters are angry at Hubert Humphrey or Richard J. Daley, will they at least vote for Matt Danaher for clerk of the circuit court and Edward Hanrahan for state's attorney of Cook County? If they don't like gubernatorial candidate Sam Shapiro's religion or vice-presidential candidate Edmund Muskie's ethnicity, can their hostility be overcome by appealing to their loyalty to the Democratic party, castigating the iniquitous Republican opposition, or asking them to help save the

---

not be granted, that a regular clerk could not be reduced to a substitute mail handler, even at his request. A subsequent brief conversation with my Democratic precinct captain resulted in a note from the precinct captain to the ward committeeman, a letter from the ward committeeman to my congressman, who was on the House of Representatives Post Office Committee, a letter from the congressman to the Postmaster of the Chicago Post Office, and a letter from the postmaster to me, notifying me of my immediate reduction to substitute mail handler.

precinct captain's job by voting right this time? A good precinct captain, according to Alderman Marzullo, "is a salesman, selling the party every day of the year."

After the sovereign voters are canvassed and registered, and after an estimate is made of the vote tally, the precinct captain still has the formidable task of getting the forgetful, uninterested, and lazy voters to the polls. Elections are won or lost in the precincts on election day after the preparatory work has been done. A precinct captain had better be in good physical condition to undergo the rigors of delivering the vote. "I've been on the street since 4 A.M.," precinct captain Al Chesser of the 31st Precinct in the 24th Ward told *Sun Times* columnist Tom Fitzpatrick on election day, November 4, 1970, "You know how it is. Polls open at 6 A.M. I've got to get out and put reminders on car windows of my voters that I know go to work early." By 6:30 A.M., Chesser's fifteen precinct helpers are working the neighborhood, knocking on doors, bringing out the voters, and reporting to Chesser at his station near the polling place. "I stand at this spot every election," Chesser told Fitzpatrick. "Everyone knows where I am. They all come this way and stop by so that I can give them advice on how to fill out their ballots." In Marzullo's neighboring 25th Ward, "The sun will rise over the 25th on Tuesday at 5:26 A.M.," a *New York Times* reporter told his eastern constituency after an interview with Alderman Marzullo. "By that time Mr. Marzullo's precinct captains will already be at the polling places in their precincts, ready to check the voters as they begin arriving at 6 A.M. On every major street corner their assistants will be posted, voices at the ready, to remind each resident as he starts to work that it is his duty to vote and vote right that day." "Politics," explained Marzullo, "is a matter of communicating. The people got to get the word. The 25th is ready to get it to them."

Such devotion to duty still pays off in the 24th Ward, which was the banner Democratic ward in the United States 35 years ago. In 1936, the ward, which was then solidly Jewish, gave Franklin Delano Roosevelt a 26,112 to 974 margin over his opponent Alfred E. Landon. In 1968, the 24th Ward, which had changed to an almost solidly black ward, gave Hubert Humphrey 16,498 votes to 369 for Richard Nixon. In the 25th Ward, Committeeman Vito Marzullo delivered 16,547 votes for the Democratic ticket to 3448 for the Republican ticket. Both wards, however, were topped by Committeeman Bernard Neistein in the 24th Ward's neighboring 29th Ward to the north. Neistein delivered his ward for the Democratic ticket, 19,570 to 507 for the Republicans.°

A classic description of how an efficient precinct captain operates in Chicago was contained in the *Chicago Daily News* on April 22, 1964, in a column by Jay McMullen, the *Daily News* City Hall reporter:

How One Democrat Gets Out the Vote

More than 1,000,000 Illinois Democrats voted April 14 in a primary in which their party had no major contests for nominations. There were no issues that drew them to the voting booths. There wasn't even anybody they could vote against. It was what is known as "the machine vote."

But the so-called machine is people. Each is a cog in the mighty machine. Like the machine itself, they are always in action, day and night, aiming at the next election.

They are, for the most part, people like Arthur W. Varchmin, 54, of 3636 West Diversey, Democratic precinct captain in the 21st Precinct of the 35th Ward in a heavily Polish area on the Northwest Side. Varchmin brought out 258 Democratic votes in his precinct against only 59 for his Republican counterpart.

How he did it is the success story of the machine.

In a sense, Varchmin started working on his voters a year ago. He informed them all, verbally and by letter, that the city budget was being reduced by the mayor and that next year their property taxes would be lower.

Meantime, Varchmin went to the city map department, obtained the legal description of every parcel of property in his precinct, some 208 in all. Then he went to the county assessor's office and got the tax bill for each. Only four of the 208 were increased. He then reminded his voters that what he had told them a year ago about their taxes was true.

"Some tried to argue with me, but I produced the figures right on the spot.

"Voting begins in a man's home," he explained. "Ninety per cent of his troubles are in his home, with his tax bill, why the garbage guys did this or something, debris accumulating, a water leak, or a building deteriorating in the neighborhood.

° A *Chicago Sun-Times* poll, taken before the 1970 elections in Illinois, gave Democratic United States senatorial candidate Adlai Stevenson III 99.1% of the vote to Republican candidate Ralph Smith's less than 1% in Neistein's 29th Ward.

"People in my precinct don't have to worry about a thing. All they have to do is call me. That's how I do business. I get the streets patched, for example. This morning I turned in a bunch of curbs that need repairs.

"I was out Saturday morning after the election checking up to see if the complaints I reported were taken care of.

"I do maybe 150 favors a year. I have 15 notebooks at home with the list of favors I've done for my voters. Each time a voter calls me for a favor I get his phone number. I helped one woman get her citizenship after she had been trying for five years. I made seven trips downtown with her.

"Every night I look through the alleys on the way home. People call at midnight, 1 A.M., 3 A.M. Somebody might have gotten arrested and needs bond money. Sure, you go to the station. You got to go there. You stick by your word. You don't tell the people one thing and not do it."

Election day is the time for the voters to return Varchmin's favors and he does a neat job of collecting. Before the election he has visited every household, followed up with a letter. Then a second letter of reminder hits each home the day before the election.

This isn't enough. On election day, Varchmin has seven people working for him. Several are "runners" who go to remind people who have not voted to come to the polls. Names of these are compiled by Varchmin's checkers at the polling place.

"I sent a letter out the day after the election thanking them for coming out and assuring them I'll continue to serve them. This is what gets people to come and vote. They find out you're strictly business."

Varchmin's wife is a big asset. She addresses envelopes, stamps them, answers phones because "this is my living."

What does Varchmin get out of it? Not exactly a cushy patronage job, but a comfortable one as assistant clerk of the Chicago City Council, working in the "bullpen" outside the council chambers. Easy work, good hours, enough pay to live on.

He sweats harder out in the precinct than he does on the job. If he didn't, his committeeman, John C. Marcin, who is also city clerk, would fire him.

That's why Varchmin always makes sure his committeeman always gets the most votes—242 in the primary to 235 for his congressman and 235 for Gov. Kerner.

"I don't need a governor," explains Varchmin. "Governors are for big guys. I need a congressman for citizenship cases."

Varchmin has bounced around on city, county, state and federal jobs for two decades. While he's not a gambling man, he'll give you almost any odds that he'll carry his precinct for Gov. Kerner over Charles Percy by 400 to 185.°

The Rewards of Politics

Election day, however, is not the end of anything for a precinct captain. It is merely a temporary interruption in a continuing process. There are voters to be thanked, services to be performed, records to be kept, a new canvass to be made, literature to be distributed, dues to be paid, political rallies to be attended, tickets to be sold, and preparations to be made for the next election. But there are the other rewards—membership in a social organization (the ward organization and the Democratic party), the opportunity to be something of a big fish in a small pond, some chance to serve your fellow man, and, of course, the possibility of advancing oneself to a better patronage job. For precinct captains, like committeemen and, indeed, like all politicians, are in politics for one of two reasons, or for a combination of those two reasons—to make a buck, to get into the limelight, or both. And politics, even at the precinct level in cities like Chicago, provides an opportunity for thousands of people to earn a living, to do something meaningful while earning that living, and to gratify their egos and personal needs.

The best ward committeemen in the organization—the Vito Marzullos, the Tom Keanes, the Richard Daleys, the George Dunnes, and the late William Dawson; and the best precinct captains—the Arthur Varchmins, the Al Chessers, the Sidney Steinmans, the George Winklers, and the John Domagalas—all

° After this column appeared in the *Daily News*, I tried for several years, at regular intervals, to get Mr. Varchmin to discuss precinct work with my class in urban politics at the University of Illinois. Mr. Varchmin always responded, "Leave your name and telephone number, Professor, and I'll call you." He would not say "yes," and being a good politician, he would not say "no," although it was clear he would not come. In 1970, when I was a Democratic candidate for the Cook County Board of Commissioners, I found myself seated next to City Clerk John C. Marcin, Varchmin's committeeman in the 35th Ward, at Alderman Vito Marzullo's annual 25th Ward dinner dance, the best political affair of the year. I recounted the story of Varchmin's unwillingness to appear before my class. Marcin's response was "I'm his committeeman, and he won't do anything like that without my permission." My response to Marcin was, "All right, will you tell Varchmin that he can come to my class?" Marcin responded, "Leave me your name and telephone number, Professor, I'll call you." The incident was a classic demonstration of the innate conservatism and caution of Chicago's Democratic politicians with regard to any form of public exposure.

consider themselves godfathers to their constituents, ministers to the wayward, and shepherds to their flocks. It is true that they expect their pound of flesh on election day in return for their services, and rewards from the party for their efforts. But it is also true that their motives are mixed, that they must be concerned with their constituents' problems as well as their own interests, and that good political work pays off in human satisfactions as well as in personal compensations. "How often," writes Hans J. Morgenthau, "have statesmen been motivated by the desire to improve the world, and ended by making it worse? And how often have they sought one goal, and ended by achieving something they neither expected nor desired? . . . Good motives give assurance against deliberately bad policies; they do not guarantee the moral goodness and political success of the policies they inspire."

If it is true that the road to hell is sometimes paved with good intentions, the converse is also true—that some good as well as some evil results from primary pursuit of self-interest, tempered by the necessity of concerning oneself with the welfare of others in order to achieve one's own selfish goals. It may well be true, despite the hard realities of political life in cities like Chicago and the primary selfish motives of the minions who serve the political machine, that a fair evaluation of the efforts of the machine's ward committeemen and precinct captains would result in some pluses as well as minuses, and that precinct and ward politics, as practiced in Chicago, is a mixture of good and evil, of service and selfishness, and of civic-mindedness as well as self-serving ambition.

Perhaps the best expository statement of the role of the precinct captain in the Chicago Democratic machine—a loyal party cohort, serving his party's and his own interests but also serving his fellow man—was an extemporaneous salute to his army of foot soldiers that the field marshal of the machine, Mayor Richard J. Daley, gave shortly before the April 1, 1975 mayoral election at a Democratic rally for the captains. Daley's words were taken down verbatim by Neil Mehler, the political editor of the *Chicago Tribune*, and printed in that newspaper on March 29, 1975:

He [the precinct captain] never gets in the newspapers unless he is criticized. He's as honest as the rest of us and he's a better neighbor than most of us, for partisan reasons. He has solicitude for the welfare of the family in his block, especially if they are a large family with dependable political loyalties.

He gets your broken-down uncle into the county hospital, if he lives in the slums. He's always available when you're in trouble. He's the salt of this democratic—small "d"—earth; and I wish the commentators and the writers and promoters of these high-minded civic organizations would stop picking on the Democratic Party organization because the people who make up the Democratic Party of the city of Chicago are always and will always be a reflection of the people in their respective neighborhoods.

Until someone devises a better method of Democratic political organization that has no broad base of precinct captains who punch doorbells and recite the virtues of their party and candidates, we ought to be more careful in our moral judgment about a political party.

To all you fine men and women who have thruout the years carried aloft this banner of the Democratic Party and programs, we know what you have done and we're grateful and thankful and I'm personally grateful to you individually and collectively because you have provided the service that makes life worth living.

You have been available to the young and to the old; you've sponsored and I hope you will again sponsor softball and basketball teams and baseball teams for the young of your community. You've consoled and helped the widow when she was in trouble and she lost her husband.

You've taken into yourself guidance for the young that many times were fatherless. This is the real strength of our party and they'll never take it away from us. As long as we have the kind of an organization we have in the city of Chicago, we will time and time again be victorious.

One week after Daley's speech to the precinct captains, an item in the *Chicago Tribune* (May 4, 1975) recounted a graphic illustration of the lengths to which a good precinct captain would go in order to service his constituents:

The Democratic Party of Cook County, known fondly as The Machine, has always contended it stays in power because it provides services to residents, who also happen to be voters. An example from the 39th Ward: An elderly man stashed $100 in a roll of paper towels to hide it from some workmen. His daughter, Joan Smith, then accidentally threw the roll into the garbage. Off it went in a city truck. After several calls, she got the number of John D'Amico, the ward superintendent and son-in-law of Ald. Anthony Laurino (39th). D'Amico, in the best "I Will" tradition, picked up father and daughter and dashed to the dump. Unfortunately, the truck had been emptied, so D'Amico and four other men sifted thru the garbage until they found the money. "The look on dad's face, including tears, was worth a million," Joan said. "I wanted to tip the men, but they didn't want anything." D'Amico said: "We're here to help the people."

"I have office hours every Tuesday and Thursday night," Alderman Marzullo told reporter Fitzpatrick. "One night this group of guys come in and stand before me and tell me they got twelve demands to make. "You got demands to make? I ask them," said Marzullo. "Who's your precinct captain? They tell me they're acting for themselves and that they represent 2,000 people. You make no goddamn demands to this old man, I told them. Who died and elected you guys boss? I'm the elected boss. You get out, you sons of bitches, and don't come back."

"Sometimes I feel just like Abraham Lincoln," Marzullo told Fitzpatrick. "He's the one who said you can only fool some of the people some of the time. But my people got confidence in Vito Marzullo all of the time."

❧ 5 ❧

The Machine and the Democratic Party

To maintain its power in Chicago and Cook County, and to secure the prerogatives of politics—influence, money, and status—the Chicago machine must maintain good relations with the Democratic party at three levels outside its home turf: the suburban Democrats, the state party, and the national party. How does the machine deal with its fellow Democrats in the suburbs, state, and nation in order to insure its hegemony in Chicago and Cook County?

The Machine and the Suburban Democrats

Traditionally, politicians in the two parts of Cook County, Chicago and the suburbs, have dealt with each other in two ways. First, Democratic politicians in the city and Republican politicians in the suburbs treated the other part of the county as foreign territory to be ignored, tolerated, or negotiated with in the manner of dealing with a foreign state. Second, left to their own devices by their party colleagues across the border, city Republican and suburban Democratic politicians resorted to the practices of minority politics in majority-party territory. They recognized the status quo, did not disturb the equilibrium, did not seriously challenge the power structure, accepted the crumbs from the table, and practiced a degree of collusion, if not outright collaboration.

For suburbanites, Chicago was a place to work, to leave at five o'clock and return only occasionally for cultural stimulation. The city's problems were no concern of theirs. The major exceptions to this rule were the Protestant businessmen, who dominated the economic life of the city and concerned themselves with its problems for a combination of reasons—economic considerations involving their industries and a moral sense of *noblesse oblige.*

For most Chicagoans, the suburbs were foreign territory beyond their range of understanding or interest. For an ethnically oriented neighborhood dweller, to whom other parts of the city were strange, the suburban ring was completely beyond the pale.

The city organization Democrats, for their part, have had little or no understanding of or sympathy for the suburban Democrats. They regarded the suburbanites with suspicion or, at best, tolerance, consulted with them infrequently, ignored them often, and made practically no effort to bring them into a more important role in the party's inner councils. Very little has been done in the past few years to bridge the gap between the old-line city Democrats and the growing suburban Democratic party. Nor is there any indication that the Democratic politicians in Chicago are doing anything at present, or will be doing anything in the future, about the growing suburban population and the relationships of the city machine to the needs and interests of that population and of the Democratic party in the suburbs.

City-suburban relationships operate on three levels—community relationships between the populations of the two areas, political relationships between the political parties in the city and the suburbs, and governmental relationships between city and suburban governments. On none of these levels has there been much interest in or cooperation with suburban Cook County by city community leaders, politicians, and governmental officials.

The Chicago community leaders' lack of concern for suburban problems and interests is understandable. Plagued with numerous problems in the city, they can hardly be expected to manifest an interest in what they consider to be the less significant problems of the suburbs. And, of course, that lack of interest has been a two-way street. Few suburbanites have manifested anything more than a passing interest in the community problems of the city, since they fled the city to escape from its problems and are more concerned with the new communities into which they have moved.

The same lack of concern has manifested itself at the governmental level between city and suburban elected public officials. They would be foolish to spend much time and effort concerning themselves with the needs and interests of people who are not their constituents and who have nothing to say about whether they are returned to office.

Since meaningful relationships between groups at any level in the body politic must be based on mutual interests, the lack of collaboration between suburban and city community leaders and governmental officials is a tacit recognition of the divergent interests of the two parts of Cook County. Despite a great deal of well-meaning cant about the need for cooperation, there is little of common interest between the populations and governments of Chicago and the suburbs. Chicago's community problems manifest themselves most critically within the context of the relationships between rapidly growing black and Latin minorities in the city and a steadily dwindling white population. The question of race dominates the life of the city today in the same way that ethnicity once did in the past. At a second level, the interests of the segment of the population which is poor and in desperate need of expanded city services conflict with the resistance of the lower-middle- and middle-class taxpayers in the city to the use of their tax monies for the support of the poor. In other words, Chicago is divided between blacks, browns, and whites, and the poor and the lower-middle class.

Neither of these two conflicts exists in quite the same way in suburban Cook County. Rather, because of the economic, racial, and class homogeneity of the population of most suburban municipalities, racial conflict and competition for the use of tax money between a welfare-demanding poor and a taxpaying middle class does not exist. Most suburbanites are taxpaying lower-middle- or middle-class homeowners who share basically the same interests in the use of their tax dollars by governmental bodies. This is not to say that suburban municipalities do not have tensions, conflicts, and major differences within their communities. But the tensions and conflicts are different from those of the city. Since there are few blacks, not too many poor, and a common interest among home-owning taxpayers, suburban public officials are not subjected to the same kinds of pressure as city public officials are, and are much more concerned with and oriented to administrative problems rather than political conflict. Consequently, since there is little to collaborate about between the public officials in the suburbs and Chicago, the two groups of officials live on different sides of a Chinese wall which divides the city from the suburbs.

At the political level, however, one would assume a commonality of interests between city and suburban Democrats and Republicans within the confines of their respective parties. Since the politicians in both parties ostensibly have the same interests—capturing and retaining public office—one would assume a degree of cooperation between city and suburban politicians. This assumption, however, does not fit the realities of politics in Cook County. If one goes back over the history of city-suburban Democratic and Republican relationships over the past few decades, it is clear that politicians in both parties in the city and the suburbs have no more interest in collaborating with and contributing to their counterparts on the other side of the fence than do community leaders and government administrators, and may have even less interest in improving the lot of their cohorts in their parties on the other side of the city-suburban dividing line.

Why is this so? Primarily, because city Democratic politicians are not much interested in the resolution of county problems and are less interested in their party's winning elections than in winning an office for themselves, they are always willing to subordinate the party's interests at the county level to their own interests in their own bailiwicks. Consequently, Democratic city politicians have little interest in Democratic suburban politicians' winning office simply because they belong to the Democratic party. Democratic city politicians are willing to sacrifice the party's interests in the suburbs to further their own interests in the city. The same thing holds true for Republican politicians in the suburbs with regard to their Republican counterparts in the city.

Because of this attitude suburban Democrats are almost never slated for any major county office. Democratic candidates for major county offices such as president of the county board, state's attorney, county clerk, county treasurer, member of the board of appeals, county assessor, and clerk of the circuit court are always city Democrats. The only countywide offices for which suburban candidates are usually slated are for county superintendent of schools, an office in which the city Democrats have absolutely no interest, and six candidates for the Cook County Board of Commissioners from the suburban area, offices which no Democrat has any chance to win. One or two suburban committeemen may be put on the bench as judges of the circuit court, several of them may be sent to the state legislature to represent their districts, and a minor administrative post such as civil defense director of Cook County may be allocated to a suburban committeeman. But in the allocation of party funds, distributing patronage positions to the faithful, and electoral support, suburban committeemen are left to shift for themselves or given minimal assistance at best. So low do suburban committeemen stand in the party hierarchy that few demands are made on them in producing votes, or in selling tickets for the party's major dinners. The general attitude of the party leadership in the city toward the suburban committeeman is "Well, do the best you can and we won't expect too much of you anyway." *

The refusal of the Cook County Democratic organization to slate suburban Democrats for major county offices is buttressed by a refusal to alter the legal makeup of the county central committees to conform to the changing population and registration patterns in Cook County. When the population of the city was over 3,500,000 and the population of the suburbs was less than 1,000,000, the county central committees were made up of 50 ward committeemen from the city and 30 township committeemen from the suburbs. But with the decline in city population and the population explosion in the suburbs over the past thirty years, the makeup of the county central committees has remained exactly the same—50 ward committeemen from the city and 30 township committeemen from the suburbs. Nor was there any change in the makeup of the county board, which was created with 15 commissioners, 10 Democrats from the city, and 5 Republicans from the suburbs. With

---

* In 1969, when a Republican suburban county commissioner died, the county board had the legal authority to select a commissioner to replace him for the balance of his term. The ten-man Democratic majority on the board gave the remaining four Republican suburban county commissioners the power to choose a Republican to replace their late colleague. Had a suburban Democrat been selected by the Democratic majority for the vacancy, he would have had the opportunity to run for the county board from the suburbs as an incumbent commissioner, but the powers that be in the Democratic organization decreed otherwise.

the city's population declining from 3,600,000 in 1950 to 3,300,000 in 1970, and with the suburban population going up from 1,000,000 to 2,200,000 in 1970, neither political party moved to alter the system of political and legal representation to conform to the population statistics. The number of registered voters in the city, which was 1,688,835 in 1938, increased by 1966 to only 1,701,088, a total increase of less than 13,000. Suburban registration, however, which was 182,867 in 1938, rose to 935,550 in 1966, again without any increase in suburban representation on either the Cook County central committees of the two major parties or on the county board. In 1973, however, with countywide elections for the board scheduled the next year, the county board, under the threat of a court suit, allocated one more commissioner to the suburbs without reducing the city's representation, thus satisfying politicians in both parties in both areas.

The problems of the suburban Democratic committeemen vis-à-vis their city counterparts are further multiplied by the fact that the governmental structure does not coincide with the political structure in the suburbs. In the city, which is divided into fifty wards with fifty ward committeemen on the county central committee, the fifty wards also elect an alderman from each ward to the city council. So, in Chicago, there is a governmental body, the city council, which provides legal representation in government for the voters of the fifty districts in the city. There is no comparable governmental agency at the county level. Suburban township committeemen rule a domain which may have within it five or six separate municipalities, each with its own governmental system over which he has little influence or control. Their power is township-wide. Governmental power in the suburbs is municipality-wide. This makes for a situation in which suburban township committeemen have little opportunity to control government offices which might provide some power and patronage for them through which they can build a political organization. Except for a few townships, the boundaries of most townships in Cook County do not coincide with any municipality. Consequently, there is a fragmented, legal governmental structure in the townships alongside the political structure. In the city, political and governmental boundaries coincide, making it possible for a ward committeeman in the city to have significant influence and power in city government, since he usually chooses the alderman from his ward.

Suburban Democratic township committeemen are also confronted with a situation in which city Democratic candidates for county offices are generally considered to be machine hacks by their suburban constituents, and have little appeal to suburban Democratic voters. In county elections, it is difficult for a suburban Democratic committeeman to sell the party's candidates to his voters. A poor showing for the county ticket inevitably reduces his influence at the county central committee in the La Salle hotel. The fact that he can deliver a substantial Democratic vote for national Democratic candidates for president and United States senator has little influence with the ruling powers in the Democratic county central committee, since they are really not much interested in those offices. Thus, suburban Democratic committeemen are prisoners of a political situation in which they find it difficult to turn out a good party vote for the local ticket, which is all important to the county central committee, and can turn out a substantial Democratic vote for national or statewide candidates in which the party's governing body has little interest. This anomaly is further aggravated for suburban Democratic township committeemen by the fact that their better-educated, more economically secure constituents are less amenable to organization control, are much more likely to split tickets for attractive Republican candidates, and by the fact that without patronage it is difficult to man precincts in the townships, except with volunteer workers. And every politician knows that a volunteer worker cannot be dictated to or controlled as can a precinct captain who is on a patronage payroll.

An interesting phenomenon of the relationship of the county board to the suburbs is that, while many of the important functions of the county board are important to the people of suburban Cook County, the ten-man Democratic majority on the county board are all city Democrats, who have little knowledge of or interest in the suburbs. And Democratic presidents and finance committee chairmen of the county board are always ward committeemen from the city. While some of the board's functions are countywide, other major functions such as governing the unincorporated areas of Cook County, maintaining the road and highway system in the county, and controlling most of the recreational areas and facilities in the

suburbs are vested in a county board which is completely dominated by city Democrats.

A more significant feature of the relationship of suburban
committeemen to the county central committee and county government is that practically all the county patronage jobs are controlled
by city Democratic committeemen. The thousands of patronage
jobs vested in the office of the president of the county board, the
Forest Preserves District, the county clerk, the county assessor, the
county treasurer, the sheriff, the clerk of the circuit court, and
the state's attorney are all controlled by city Democrats. Through
their control of these offices, and of the presidency, the finance
committee, and the ten-man Democratic majority on the county
board, the city Democrats maintain absolute domination of a board
and offices which could help Democrat suburban committeemen
build up stronger organizations in their townships. But, since the
city Democrats have no interest in building up suburban Democratic power, they will not surrender any of these prerogatives to
suburban Democratic committeemen, except for minor offices and
patronage.

There is a deeper, more hidden power in the control of the
major county offices by city Democrats. The county treasurer
determines how and where the hundreds of millions of dollars in
county funds will be deposited. He can deposit those funds in city
banks rather than in suburban banks, and sweeten relationships
between the Democratic political organization in Chicago and the
major banking interests in the city. The county clerk controls the
election machinery in Cook County, and can use his power of
determining places on the ballot of the various candidates, selecting
polling places, hiring election-day personnel, and enforcing the
election laws to diminish the power of suburban committeemen and
politicians who oppose the city Democrats and to increase the
power of those suburban Democrats who work with the city
machine. The enforcement powers of the sheriff and the state's
attorney can also be used to protect the interests of city or suburban
Democrats in Cook County who cooperate with the city machine,
and to harass or punish suburban Democrats who are opposed to
the city machine.

The most significant powers, however, of all of the county
officeholders besides the county board president probably are in the

county assessor's office. That official, who is always a city Democrat, assesses all real estate property in Cook County. He can raise or lower assessments of commercial firms, industrial complexes, newspaper publishers, real estate developers, banks, and other property owners. The real power in the assessor's office, buttressed by the city Democrats' control of the board of tax appeals, is that the office can be used to encourage campaign contributions to the party from corporations, individuals, financial institutions, and other organizations and individuals. In fact, it can seriously be argued that the most important office in the state of Illinois is not the governorship of the state, the presidency of the Cook County board, or the mayoralty of Chicago but, rather, the office of county assessor of Cook County. For with control of that office comes the ability to raise massive campaign funds for the party for offices and campaigns in which the party has a major interest.

There is still another facet to the city Democrats' control of the county board and of the major county offices. The county board and the major county offices not only have regulatory powers over various aspects of life in Cook County but also provide goods and services to the people of the county. This requires letting contracts to build roads and construct institutions, leasing property, and purchasing significant quantities of materials needed by the county. Schools need supplies, the county jail needs food, highways must be constructed and maintained, and the forest preserves require development and maintenance of recreational facilities and areas. The allocation of contracts for all these goods and services to private firms is under the control of county officers. This is not to say that any of the county officers are corrupt or not corrupt. But contracts can be given to firms and individuals who have relationships to and influence on public officials in the county offices. The city Democrats' control of county offices which allocate contracts inevitably increases the power and influence of those city Democrats vis-à-vis the potential power and influence of suburban Democrats in the organization.

Thus, it is clear that the relationship of the city Democratic machine to the suburban area of Cook County, and to suburban Democrats, is based on a many-faceted, complex set of factors. Those factors are political, financial, governmental, and psychological. Two major motives govern city Democratic machine politicians' relationships to their suburban counterparts—making sure that no major suburban power base that would be a countervailing power center to the Democratic city machine within Cook County is built, and protecting the political, financial, and patronage powers of city Democratic machine politicians from significant inroads by their suburban counterparts.

The city Democratic machine's relationship to the suburbs of Chicago and Democrats in those suburban areas is analogous to the machine's relationship to the state of Illinois and downstate Democrats, and to the United States Government and the national Democratic party. The major objective is to insure continued control of the city of Chicago and of those offices in Cook County which have political, patronage, and financial significance to the city Democratic machine. In pursuit of that objective, the machine is willing to write off suburban Democrats, downstate Democrats, and national Democrats, or at least subordinate the interests of the Democratic party at those levels to the interests of the Democratic organization in the city of Chicago.

The longtime Democratic domination of the city of Chicago and of the major Cook County offices could not exist without a tacit acceptance of the situation by the Republican party in Chicago, Cook County, and the state of Illinois. In return for Democratic domination of the city and the major Cook County offices, the Republicans often control the state government and state patronage, almost always control municipal and township governments in Cook County and downstate, and get the political, financial, and patronage perquisites that go with control of those governments.

Given the massive population explosion in the suburbs and the defection of suburban Democrats from the city machine on the county ticket, the Republican party in Cook County could almost certainly capture major county offices regularly in elections if it made a serious effort to do so. But the Republican party traditionally runs for countywide offices unknown Republican politicians from the city who have no appeal to suburbanites, or runs little-known, suburban, amateur Republicans who have no organization support. On its part, the city Democratic machine insures Republican dominance of the suburban municipality and township governments by refusing to give Democratic suburban committeemen the kind of financial, political, and electoral support that they need to make serious efforts to capture municipal governments in suburban Cook County. While it is true that city Democratic machine support for suburban candidates in municipal elections in the suburbs could possibly damage the chances of such candidates, clandestine financial, patronage, and electoral support could be given to suburban Democrats without seriously damaging their influence in their communities. And without such support from the Democratic organization in the city, suburban committeemen have little chance of building the kind of effective organizations they need to capture municipal and township offices in suburban Cook County.

The great question for the future is "How long will the arrangement work, given the population growth of the suburbs, the erosion of the city's population, and the changes that will take place within the city machine as the aging Irish politicians leave and as black politicians who must represent the interests of the burgeoning black population of the city come to power in the machine?"

The Machine and the State Democratic Party

The history of the relationship of the Chicago Democratic machine to the Democratic party in the state of Illinois is a record of subordinating statewide Democratic interests to the interests of the Chicago machine. The major thrust of the Chicago machine's policies toward downstate Democrats has been to try to make sure that no powerful statewide organization is created as a countervailing power center to the Chicago organization. In pursuit of that primary goal, the Chicago organization has always been prepared to deal with downstate Democrats and Republicans on a *quid pro quo* basis of dividing up the political spoils so that politicians in both parts of the state can remain secure in their power bases and benefit from state policies which would protect those bases.

At the state level, the party is willing to slate candidates like Otto Kerner for governor, Adlai Stevenson or Joseph Lohman for state treasurer, Donald Prince or Michael Bakalis for state superintendent of public instruction and to give powerful patronage offices like the secretary of state to a downstater, since the downstate Democratic party is entitled to a fair share of the state patronage jobs and since the state ticket must be balanced with some downstaters.*

However, no independent, powerful political figure can be slated for the governorship. Since the governor controls thousands of patronage jobs, he has at his disposal the wherewithal to build a powerful Democratic machine, centered in Springfield, which could have interests inimical to those of the Cook County organization and which could replace the Cook County organization as the dominant Democratic organization in the state. Consequently, only candidates who do not possess the potential for building a statewide machine or who, if elected governor, would be willing to collaborate with the Democratic organization of Cook County can be slated for the governorship. In every instance, when independent, liberal, strong-minded Democrats have appeared before the slate-makers, seeking the endorsement for the governorship, they have been denied that endorsement. Men like Sargent Shriver, Joseph Lohman, Steven Mitchell, Adlai Stevenson III, and Dan Walker have never been able to secure the backing of the Democratic organization of Cook County for the governorship. However, capable, decent, hardworking men like Otto Kerner and Sam Shapiro have received the organization's endorsement. The organization can be quite sure that, if elected governor, men of this type will not attempt to build a countervailing political organization in Springfield.

There is considerable evidence, also, that the Democratic organization of Cook County has not always been seriously interested in winning the governorship. Since the Civil War, only six Democrats have been elected governor of Illinois, Peter Altgeld, Edward Dunne, Henry Horner, Adlai Stevenson, Otto Kerner, and Dan Walker. Two men completed unexpired terms of incumbent governors: Lieutenant-Governor Sam Shapiro, who succeeded to the governorship when Governor Kerner resigned one year before his term came to an end in 1968, and John Stelle, who completed Horner's second term when Horner died in 1940.

---

* Formally, the Democratic state central committee, made up of twenty-four elected committeemen, one from each congressional district in the state, chooses the party's candidates for statewide office. But since the great bulk of Democratic votes in a primary election comes from Chicago, the Cook County central committee has the dominant voice in selecting statewide candidates, too.

Some interesting gubernatorial races in the past several decades have indicated the possibility of collusion between the Democratic organization of Cook County and the Republican party in the state. In fact, there is evidence that an understanding has existed from time to time between the two parties, an understanding by which the Democratic organization keeps control of Cook County and the city of Chicago, and the Republican party is allowed to keep control of the state government. Since Cook County is half the state, with at least the equivalent number of patronage jobs and other perquisites that the state government in Springfield has to dispense to the party faithful, such an arrangement can be advantageous to the professionals in both parties.

The only Democratic governors elected in the past fifty years have been Horner (in 1932 and 1936), Stevenson (in 1948), Kerner (in 1960 and 1964), and Walker (in 1972). In those elections, except in 1972, it was practically impossible for a Democratic candidate to lose the governorship because of the political situation in the country or in the state. In 1932, with the country in the throes of the Great Depression and with Franklin Roosevelt and the New Deal coming into office nationally, the Democratic candidate was sure to be elected governor of Illinois. The party slated Henry Horner, a probate court judge, who was a hardworking, intelligent, decent, and capable man. Horner was not a politician in any real sense of the word, and the Democratic organization felt sure that he would not build a machine in Springfield. However, after Horner crossed the party leadership over several matters, the Democratic organization backed Herman Bundensen, the commissioner of health of the city of Chicago, against the incumbent governor. Horner fought back, and, with some support from dissident committeemen from the Cook County Democratic Central Committee and a good deal of support from downstate Democrats, Horner won the gubernatorial primary and went on to win his second term in office. The Democrats managed, however, to lose the governorship back to the Republicans in 1940 and 1944, to Dwight Green, a Republican politician who worked well with the Democratic organization in Cook County in dividing the state up fairly between the two parties.

In 1948, with President Harry Truman running as an underdog for his second term in office, the Democratic slatemaking committee decided that they could slate two top-grade, reform liberal candidates for the two major state offices on the ticket, governor and United States senator, in what was thought to be a losing election. In the original slating, Paul Douglas, a distinguished liberal economist from the University of Chicago, who had served in the Chicago City Council and who had established a war record as a Marine hero in the Second World War after having been a conscientious objector in the First World War, was slated for the governorship. Adlai Stevenson, a native son of Illinois who had served in several high federal posts and diplomatic missions for the United States, was recommended to the slatemaking committee by Colonel Jacob Arvey, the chairman of the Cook County Democratic Central Committee and was slated for the United States Senate, a post for which he was well qualified by background and experience. After thinking the matter over, the slatemakers reversed the ticket for the two top spots, slating Stevenson for the governorship, for which he had little background, and slating Paul Douglas for the United States Senate.

The switch was probably due to some second thoughts on the part of the slatemakers. Douglas was the kind of candidate who, if he won the governorship, would be very difficult to control. In the Senate he would be safe. He could go his own way, pursuing his liberal inclinations, without any serious effect on the local Democratic party. For, as one of the Democratic politicians high in the party at the time said, "How many jobs does a United States Senator have to hand out anyway?" And Douglas would give the party the kind of liberal, independent, reform image at the national level that the local party could both tolerate and utilize. Conversely, Stevenson was an unknown, both to the slatemakers and to the voters of Illinois. His chances of winning the governorship were considered slight, and, even if he won, given his lack of experience at the state level, the Cook County organization could feel quite safe with Stevenson in Springfield.

Both men won, Douglas by over 400,000 votes and Stevenson by almost 600,000 votes in the Democratic victory of 1948, in which Truman surprised the experts and defeated Thomas E. Dewey for the presidency. However, Truman carried Illinois by only 30,000 votes. One of the major factors contributing to Stevenson's electoral victory was the record of the incumbent Republican governor,

Dwight Green, who insisted on running for a third term with an eight-year record of alleged corruption in office and who was actually unelectable in the state. Stevenson turned out to be a capable, fairly effective reform governor, who worked with the Democratic organization of Cook County but who was not always subservient to its dictates or its demands.

What to do about such a reformer? Run him for the Presidency of the United States in 1952 against Dwight D. Eisenhower in an election which he could not possibly win. That, at least, got him out of Springfield. In Stevenson's place, the Democratic organization slated Stevenson's lieutenant-governor, Sherwood Dixon. Hardly a voter in the state of Illinois had heard of Dixon by 1952. He was a decent, honest man who had served in an undistinguished office for four years and who had no political power base of his own. The Republicans slated William G. Stratton, who rode into office on Eisenhower's coattails in the 1952 election.

After a four-year record of alleged corruption which matched Green's, Stratton ran for his second term in 1956. The Democratic organization slated as its candidate for the governorship, one Herbert Paschen, who was serving as the treasurer of Cook County. Paschen, like Dixon, was an undistinguished, unknown Cook County politician, who had no statewide recognition or appeal. In the middle of the campaign, about three months before the gubernatorial election was to take place, a scandal broke over the Stratton administration. Orville Hodge, the Republican state auditor in Stratton's administration, was indicted for defrauding the state of well over two million dollars during his term of office.

How could Governor Stratton survive a scandal of such magnitude three months before the election? A way was found. In September, six weeks before the election, a flower fund was discovered in Paschen's office as county treasurer. Employees had been forced to contribute a small percentage of their salary to a "flower fund," which was to be used to buy flowers and gifts for employees of the office who were in the hospital. A great outcry arose over the "corruption" in Paschen's office. Paschen resigned from the ticket. A new candidate had to be found. First-rate independent candidates like Joseph Lohman and Steven Mitchell presented themselves to the slatemaking committee for consideration, but the slatemaking committee would have none of them.

Instead, Richard Austin, a local judge of impeccable reputation but with absolutely no charisma and no statewide electoral recognition, was thrown into the arena. President Eisenhower carried the state by over 800,000 votes, while Governor Stratton squeaked by Austin by 36,000 votes and the governorship was saved for the Republicans for another four years. According to the political scuttlebutt, the Cook County Democratic machine had made a deal with Stratton and had sold Austin out in the election. Austin, who, for his unknowing willingness to run as a loser in the campaign, was rewarded by being appointed to the federal bench as a district court judge, has never forgiven the machine for what it did to him and has been a bitter critic and opponent of the machine for two decades.

In 1960, after another four-year record of corruption and neglect of the state's major problems, Governor Stratton, like Governor Green before him, was determined to run for a third term despite considerable opposition from within his own party. With Richard Nixon replacing Dwight Eisenhower as the Republican candidate for president, the Republican party in Illinois did not have a powerful vote getter at the top of the ticket, capable of pulling in the local ticket. The Democratic party in Illinois again had a golden opportunity to elect a governor to office in Springfield. Again, independent, liberal candidates like Shriver and Mitchell offered themselves to the Democratic slatemakers. But the slate-makers chose instead county judge Otto Kerner. Kerner, a handsome, personable, well-educated attorney, who was the son-in-law of former Mayor Anton J. Cermak of Chicago, had served as United States Attorney for Northern Illinois and had been twice elected as county judge of Cook County. In that office he had established a record of efficiency, integrity, and exemplary public service. But he was not a politician, had no political power base of his own, and consequently could be no threat to the Democratic organization in Cook County if he were elected governor of Illinois.

Kerner defeated Stratton in 1960 in a landslide, winning by over 500,000 votes, and was re-elected in 1964, defeating Republican candidate Charles Percy. Kerner served as governor for seven years, resigning one year before his term ended in 1968, to accept an appointment to the United States Circuit Court of Appeals in Illinois. As governor, Kerner was left relatively free to run the state according to his own philosophy, to devise his own programs, and to pursue whatever political ambitions he might have in his own way. But he made no attempt to build a political organization or to challenge Mayor Daley and the Democratic leaders in Cook County for control or leadership of the Democratic party in the state. He was content to govern the state well administratively, cooperate with Mayor Daley and other Democratic leaders politically, and concern himself with the interests of the people of the state in an almost nonpartisan way. When he resigned as governor in 1967 to accept the federal judicial appointment, his lieutenant-governor, Samuel Shapiro, an amiable downstate Democratic politician who had served many years in the state legislature, became governor. In 1973 Kerner was indicted and convicted of bribery, mail fraud, conspiracy, and income tax evasion in a federal court for buying and selling race track stock while he was governor of Illinois.

In 1968, proven vote getters like State Treasurer Adlai Stevenson III, and liberal, independent downstate State Senator Paul Simon sought the gubernatorial nomination from the slatemakers but were ignored. The party selected incumbent Governor Shapiro. In a campaign marked by a singular lack of interest in and concern for both Shapiro's campaign for the governorship and William Clark's campaign for the United States Senate seat, the local Democratic party concentrated its effort on two local offices, state's attorney of Cook County and clerk of the circuit court. The two candidates for these offices, Edward Hanrahan from the 36th Ward and Matt Danaher, the alderman from Daley's 11th Ward, were authentic members of the local Irish Mafia. Hanrahan and Danaher won easily in Cook County whereas Shapiro and Clark lost their statewide races for senator and governor.

According to the political scuttlebutt, the party was not seriously interested in either Clark's winning the senate seat or Shapiro's winning the governorship. Mayor Daley had had a fairly good working relationship with incumbent Senator Everett McKinley Dirksen for many years. In fact, according to some pundits, Daley did not need a Democratic senator in Washington as long as he had Everett Dirksen there. Nor was it too important to the organization to hold the governor's chair in Springfield, for, when Republican Richard B. Ogilvie was elected governor, he had to give up the presidency of the Cook County board. With a two-to-one majority of Democratic commissioners on the county board, the

Democratic members of the board then elected George Dunne, the Democratic committeeman of the 42nd Ward, who was chairman of the board's finance committee. So while the party lost the senate seat and the governorship, it regained the county board presidency and held the offices of state's attorney and clerk of the circuit court. The president of the Cook County board controls (according to some estimates) about six thousand patronage jobs in Cook County. The clerk of the circuit court controls approximately fifteen hundred patronage jobs in Cook County, and the state's attorney is in control of the machinery of prosecution in the county. An interesting sidelight of the 1968 election was the unprecedented victory of State Senator Paul Simon, who had been rejected for the gubernatorial nomination but had been slated for the lieutenant-governor's spot on the ticket. Simon demonstrated his vote-getting power by getting elected lieutenant governor while the Republican gubernatorial candidate won, the first time any candidate for that office in the history of Illinois' politics had accomplished such a feat. It was clear that had Simon been slated for governor he would have won the office. But who needed a governor like Simon in Springfield?

For their part, the Republicans in Illinois have never seriously attempted to challenge the Democratic organization in the city of Chicago since the Democratic party captured control of the city in 1931. Republican candidates for mayor since 1931 have generally been either political unknowns, sure losers, or liberal Democratic reformers who saw no future for themselves in the Democratic party and leaped across the fence to accept the Republican party's invitation to become a sacrificial lamb in running for mayor of Chicago.

If one goes back over the list of Republican candidates for the mayoralty in Chicago for the past forty years, one finds such names as Roger Faherty, Emil Wetten, Russell W. Root, George B. McKibbin, Timothy P. Sheehan, and John Waner. Whereas some of these were able men, all were traditional, old-type Republican politicians who were not attractive candidates and who had practically no chance to win an election in the city of Chicago. Three times over the past twenty years, the Republican party has nominated Democrats who left the party. Robert Merriam, a Democratic reform alderman from the 5th Ward in Chicago, left

the party to become a Republican candidate for mayor against
Daley in 1955; Benjamin Adamowski, a frustrated Polish Democrat,
left the party in 1956 to run as a Republican for State's Attorney of
Cook County and then ran against Mayor Daley in 1963; and
finally, in 1971, Richard Friedman, a liberal, young reform Democrat who had served in the Democratic attorney general's office in
Springfield for a number of years and had been executive director of
the Better Government Association in Chicago, undertook a suicidal
race against Daley. In 1975, after unsuccessfully importuning over
one hundred civic leaders, politicians, and media personalities to
run against Daley, the Republicans slated the lone Republican
alderman in the city council, John Hoellen. Hoellen agreed to run
on the condition that he could also run for his aldermanic seat at the
same time, and began his campaign with the announcement that "I
am sixty years of age. I have no hair on the top of my head. I am fat.
But there is no one who knows the workings of City Hall better
than I do. I pledge it will be a good fight."

The "good fight" began inauspiciously for Hoellen. On February
25, 1975, when the results of the mayoral primary and aldermanic
election were in, Hoellen had not only run an abysmally poor race
in his party's primary, getting 17,723 votes out of approximately
30,000 cast, including over 12,000 votes for his opponents (a Good
Humor ice cream salesman and a railroad engineer who promised to
run the city like a locomotive), but had also lost his aldermanic seat
in the city council, leaving the council with a solitary Republican
alderman. Daley, who faced a serious primary challenge from three
opponents for the first time since his first run for the mayoralty in
1955, received 463,623 votes, or 56.5 percent of the Democratic
primary vote, compared to a total vote of 337,819 for all three of his
opponents. The outcome of the 1975 mayoral election was foreor-
dained. When the results were in for the April 1, 1975 election,
Daley had won a smashing victory, with 536,413 votes to Hoellen's
136,874. Daley carried all 50 wards in Chicago, with 78 percent of
the vote, compared with Hoellen's 20 percent. The machine also
retained overwhelming control of the city council, winning 44 of the
50 aldermanic seats.

All these men ran against Daley without any significant support
from the Republican party organization in the city or the Republican party in the county and state. Since the Republican party in the

city cannot possibly mount an effective campaign without substantial support from the statewide and countywide Republican organizations, the denial of such support helped insure the defeat of the Republican candidate. Only two candidates have come close in the mayoral elections over the past forty years in Chicago—Robert Merriam, in 1955, running against Daley for Daley's first term, and Benjamin Adamowski, in 1963, running against Daley when the mayor ran for his third term. The relative closeness of both of these races can be attributed to special circumstances in the two elections. In Merriam's case, after Martin Kennelley's two terms in office, the major newspapers in the city and most of the reform elements in the city were suspicious of Richard J. Daley, whom many of them considered to be an organization hack. They feared a return to the good old days of the Thompson-Cermak-Kelly era. Consequently, Merriam had a lot of support that a Republican candidate in the city normally does not get. Once Daley had proved himself in office and dispelled the fear of a return to the good old days, much of that support has gone to the mayor in his campaigns for re-election, although the *Sun Times* and the *Daily News* endorsed Daley's opponent, Alderman William Singer, in the 1975 mayoral primary election on the grounds that Daley had been in office long enough, was too old, and had become unresponsive to Chicago's needs.

Adamowski came fairly close in 1963, only because he was Polish. In a city with a population of 600,000 Poles, a dynamic Polish candidate can pull a heavy ethnic vote. In that election, Daley won thirty-one wards and lost nineteen. The wards that Daley lost were heavily ethnic wards with a strong concentration of Polish voters. But if Adamowski had been Lithuanian, Croatian, or Jewish, his vote total would have been significantly lower.

This is not to say that the arrangement between the two parties is necessarily good or necessarily bad. It may well be a tacit recognition of the political facts of life in the city of Chicago and in the state of Illinois on the part of the leadership of both major political parties. Illinois, like many other American states, has traditionally been divided between a major industrial big city and a rural hinterland. Like most other such American states, the marriage has not been a union of compatible partners but rather a shotgun wedding of contending parties.

In contrast to Catholic, ethnic, black Chicago, downstate Illinois has traditionally been white, Protestant, small-town, Republican, and conservative. It is the land of the Lions, the home of the Kiwanis, and the territory of the Elks. The sanctity and validity of traditional rural American values guides the outlook and the aspirations of the majority of its population, except for a few industrialized small cities. The state government in Springfield has been the private province of this part of Illinois. Chicago, the colossus of the North, with its blacks, Catholics, Jews, crime, delinquency, and corruption, has always been regarded as the Babylon of Illinois, a place to visit but not to live in. Indeed, there has usually been as much crime, delinquency, and corruption, proportionately, in the towns of downstate Illinois as in Chicago, but this fact has been conveniently overlooked by the local citizenry.

Castigating the northern colossus has been a way of life for generations in rural Illinois. Protecting the state government from undue influence by the big-city slickers has been a self-appointed holy mission. Exploiting the urban masses financially and politically in the interests of the rural section of the state has been regarded as proper. If this violated the state constitution, if it deprived Chicago's citizens of a fair share of the state's revenue, if it discriminated against Chicago's children in providing equal educational opportunity, and if it denied equal representation or consideration for their interests to Chicago's population, it was all being done in the name of the sanctity of the real American values, which happened to coincide with the interests of the economic and political leadership of the downstate areas.

The major problem has been a steady growth of population and political and economic power in Cook County, in Chicago and its suburban ring. Cook County, with over five million people, has a population equal to all the other 101 counties, and a disproportionate share of the industry and wealth. Keeping some balance between downstate's politics and economics and the growing power of the giant northern county is, of necessity, a major political consideration. The success with which downstate Illinois has accomplished this task is a testament to the dedication of the downstate political leadership.

Downstate Illinois has many problems of its own, some similar to those in Cook County and many different. Saving the towns from deterioration, keeping industry from leaving, bringing in industry, offering the young people adequate opportunity at home, trying to compete culturally with the big urban area, and maintaining and protecting a way of life and traditional values are of major concern to the downstate residents. Like their northern counterparts in Chicago, downstate politicians not only represent but also reflect the aspirations, needs, and values of their constituents. Like their big-city brethren, their behavior and policies are based on a mixture of self-interest and honest belief in the value of what they defend. And who is to say that they are not partially correct in what they do, that what they strive to maintain is not in the best interests of their constituents and of the state?

Since the politics of downstate does not and cannot resemble the politics of Chicago and Cook County, and since the interests of the two areas are different, political arrangements must, of necessity, reflect those conflicting interests. Illinois' most populous city, Chicago, and county, Cook, constitute respectively one-third and one-half the population of the state. Chicago and Cook County are controlled by a disciplined Democratic organization interested primarily in its local needs and prerogatives and only secondarily in the problems of the state. The other half of the state is dominated by a Republican party which traditionally has no central direction or control and which is fragmented by periodic internecine bouts and lack of direction. The party attempts to maintain control of its half of the state by playing on downstaters' fear of Chicago, with its racial and religious minorities, and the bogeyman who will take away their liberties—Mayor Daley. In such a milieu the astounding thing is that anything at all is accomplished at the state level.

One reason why the system sometimes worked in the past was that the informal understanding between the two opposing forces kept the pot from boiling over. When a politically able and astute Republican governor sat in Springfield, it was possible to work out a *modus vivendi* in which the interests of both sides and, to some extent, the people of Chicago, Cook County, and downstate could be given consideration. But when there is no Republican governor or strong leader, the possibility of political collaboration in the interests of both the politicians and the people diminishes and sometimes breaks down, particularly since the office of governor of Illinois does not have the power to enable its occupant to coerce the

legislature when necessary. The governor is essentially an administrator, an executor of the will of the legislature. Any real power in
the governor's office stems from whatever political pressures he can
bring to bear.

A Democratic governor has the particular problem of dealing
with the powerful Democratic politicians in Chicago's City Hall,
who have their own interests to protect and axes to grind, but a
strong Republican governor, unencumbered by a similar relationship to City Hall in Chicago, can normally coerce the legislature
more effectively than can a Democratic governor, as even Governor
Stratton demonstrated in his eight years in office. A Republican
governor, of course, has his problems in coming to terms with the
Republican satraps in the state senate who are comparable to what
Murray Kempton calls "the great bulls" in Congress. But if he can
pacify them, and establish a working relationship with City Hall in
Chicago, he is relatively free to build his own organization and
pursue his own interests without much interference from the
legislature or from the "big boys" in Chicago.

Within the context of these realities the game of politics has
been played in the state of Illinois, the county of Cook, and the city
of Chicago. And within those realities the professional politicians in
both parties have functioned. Whether the dynamics of the game as
it has been played in Illinois has served the interests of the citizenry
of the state, county, and big city is a moot question, but those
dynamics have served the interests of the politicians better than has
any alternative arrangement.

The arrangement was seriously challenged for the first time in
recent history by the candidacy and election of Dan Walker as
governor of Illinois in 1972. Walker, who had been denied a place
on the ticket by the Democratic organization slatemakers a number
of times, refused to appear before them in 1972 and challenged the
organization gubernatorial candidate, Lieutenant-Governor Paul
Simon, in a bitter primary fight. Simon, who had been anathema to
the machine for years during his career as a state legislator, had
finally been accepted as a safe candidate for governor in 1972, after
a distinguished career as lieutenant-governor. But, despite the
machine's support, Simon lost the primary election to Walker, who
ran as an anti-machine reform candidate. Walker's victory was due
to three major factors—Walker's masterful public-relations efforts,

Simon's ineffectual campaign, and a massive crossover of anti-Daley Republican voters into the Democratic primary when the Illinois law prohibiting such a switch was voided by a federal court a few weeks before the primary election date. Walker then went on to defeat the incumbent Republican, Governor Richard B. Ogilvie, in a close election.

However, since Walker's ascension to the governor's chair, he seems to have worked out a *quid pro quo* relationship with Mayor Daley and the Chicago machine. While still occasionally expressing anti-machine sentiments and attempting to build a statewide personal organization, he seems to have accepted a relationship of giving Daley what he wants for Chicago and the Cook County Democratic organization in return for Daley's support for his efforts to establish a national reputation as an effective governor as a prelude to a try for the Democratic presidential nomination in 1976.

Under the peculiar rules of Illinois politics, Walker and Daley may have a great deal in common in their mutually tolerable ambitions. If Walker is willing to give Daley what he wants, Daley could well be persuaded to support Walker's presidential ambitions for 1976 as a means for accomplishing two of his own objectives simultaneously—getting what he wants for his city and local organization and getting Walker out of Springfield. That could open the door to electing a Daley stalwart as the next governor of Illinois. Only time will tell if the deal can be worked out to the mutual benefit of all of the major parties involved at the time of this writing.

The Machine and the National Democratic Party

In its relationships with the national Democratic party, the local party has also pursued a consistent policy of subordinating national Democratic politics to the interests of the local organization. Since 1932, the city of Chicago has voted consistently Democratic in national elections, with the exception of President Eisenhower's two campaigns in 1952 and 1956. The Great Depression of the 1930s and the coming of the New Deal insured the hegemony of the local Democratic party in a city which had gone Republican as often as it had gone Democratic in local as well as in national elections. Chicago, like most of the big northern cities, became an essential ingredient in the formula for Democratic victories in national elections. Holding the South and delivering thumping majorities in the big cities of the North insured national hegemony for the Democratic party. Chicago became a bulwark of the party of the Democracy in 1932, and has remained so ever since.

However, there has always been a built-in ideological conflict between the interests of the local Democratic organization and the interests of the national party. The theoretical, liberal foundations of Franklin Roosevelt's New Deal had no appeal to the conservatively oriented local ethnic politicians. They embraced the Democratic party and the New Deal because it offered them material rewards and opportunities which served to buttress their local influence and control. The welfare state was, and still is, for them not a condition of society or a direction in which society should move because of its emphasis on middle-class, liberal, Democratic ideas. They were, and on the whole still are, unfamiliar with and unsympathetic and unresponsive to eighteenth-century Benthamite and Millsian concepts of what the good society should be like.

In essence, the Democratic organization in Chicago is nonideological. It is dedicated primarily to gaining and retaining offices and reaping the rewards of office. Its movers and shapers are relatively unconcerned with philosophical terms like liberalism, conservatism, or any other "ism" except pragmatism and materialism. But the basically conservative orientation of the local leadership gives the Democratic party in Chicago a kind of schizophrenic character. The party has for forty years been riding the crest of a national Democratic liberal image but has remained essentially conservative locally. Federal welfare programs have been embraced and utilized, not out of any deep commitment to their intrinsically liberal character, but out of deference to their practical political results. Civil rights legislation has been supported, not primarily out of any inherent sympathy for the underprivileged blacks, but mainly because it was good politics. Liberal candidates for national office have been slated only when their candidacies serve the local needs and interests of the party.

The relationship of the essentially conservative local Democratic organization with the more liberal national leadership of the party has been a two-way street. Democratic presidents like Roosevelt, Truman, Kennedy, and Johnson have collaborated with the local organization, funneling federal funds through it and bailing it out of trouble when necessary. The organization, for its part, has consistently delivered large majorities in the city for Democratic presidential candidates, except Adlai Stevenson. Even Hubert Humphrey carried the city by over 400,000 votes in the 1968 presidential election.

The party is willing to support national liberal Democratic candidates for the presidency, and deliver thumping majorities in the city for them, as long as those candidates are willing to collaborate with the local organization, using federal power and money to support the interests of the organization in Chicago and Cook County. But the local organization will not support a national Democratic candidate for the presidency whose candidacy threatens the local organization's interests. The price tag for the heavy Democratic majorities delivered in the city for national candidates is a recognition on the part of those national candidates that the federal government will normally not intervene in matters of local concern which are of importance to the local party.

The local organization has consistently demanded and received its pound of flesh from Democratic presidents for the past forty years. When the city of Chicago built a skyway to Indiana which turned out to be a white elephant, the federal government, at the instigation of President Lyndon Johnson, offered to take the white elephant off the hands of the city. When federal officials from the Department of Health, Education and Welfare threatened to cut off educational funds to Chicago's school system because of allegations of segregation in the city in 1967, a telephone call from Mayor Daley to the White House sufficed to overrule HEW's recommendation. Traditionally, the last major public appearance of a Democratic presidential candidate on the Saturday night before the Tuesday election is in the city of Chicago. On that night, Mayor Daley mobilizes tens of thousands of his loyal workers and supporters to march through the city to the Chicago Stadium, and a million Chicagoans to stand in the streets and cheer the presidential candidate on his way to the rally. On January 20, 1961, one of the first things President John F. Kennedy did on entering his office at the White House was to place a telephone call to Mayor Daley's hotel suite to invite the mayor and his family to come over to the White House for a visit. And, of course, Daley has always had a "hot line" to the White House when a Democratic president sits there. When Daley needs a speaker for the annual $100-a-plate county central committee dinner, the president is normally happy to oblige the mayor. For his part, the mayor is normally happy to deliver seven Democratic votes from the city of Chicago in the House of Representatives and one Democratic senator from the state of Illinois on legislative matters in which the president is interested. The philosophical thrust of those matters is of little interest to the mayor and his cohorts, since they have no national interests and since national ideological considerations are subordinated to local, practical political needs.

Indeed, the standard practice of the local organization is to support the president, be he Democratic or Republican, on matters of national policy generally. On great national and international issues such as the cold war, nuclear weapons, Vietnam, and national tax, economic, and labor policies, the normal tendency of the locally oriented Democratic politicians is to support the president. There is a kind of implicit understanding that political leaders should tend to their own bailiwick, that leadership at another level should be supported, and that, since it is the president's task to oversee the national and international interests of the nation, such matters are within his prerogatives and beyond the province of other politicians, even those from the other party.

This subordination of national interests to local interests carries over into the electoral process too. Even the presidential election is not necessarily a primary concern of the local politicians. In 1960, for example, when Chairman Daley led the Illinois Democratic delegation to the Democratic National Convention in Los Angeles, the party leaders were interested in a candidate for president who could help them carry the local offices in Cook County, particularly the office of state's attorney. The party had lost that office in 1956 to a renegade Polish Democrat, Benjamin Adamowski, who had given the organization considerable trouble during the four years he had served as a Republican state's attorney. At the convention in Los Angeles, a native son of Illinois, Adlai Stevenson, who had run twice for the presidency, was the candidate of the independent and liberal Democrats from Illinois. They sent thousands of telegrams to Mayor Daley, asking him to support Stevenson for the presidential nomination. But Daley ignored the telegrams and supported John

Fitzgerald Kennedy, not because Kennedy was considered the best-qualified candidate for the presidency but, rather, because a Kennedy candidacy would better serve the interests of the Democratic organization of Cook County. Given the fact that the Chicago archdiocese is the largest Roman Catholic archdiocese in North America, the organization could use an Irish Catholic at the top of the ticket to help beat Adamowski, a Polish Catholic, in Cook County. Kennedy provided the necessary qualifications. The strategy worked. Kennedy helped carry the city of Chicago by over 400,000 votes (although he carried the state by only 8000 votes), and Adamowski was beaten in Cook County by 25,000 votes.°

This was the roadblock that Senator Eugene McCarthy ran into in his quest for support from the Democratic organization of Cook County for the presidential nomination in 1968. The party leaders knew that McCarthy could win. But the answer to the question "Could he do us any good?" was not clear-cut. In fact, McCarthy's candidacy presented the Cook County Democrats with a situation in which he would probably not do the party any good if he won, but indeed would probably do the organization in Chicago and Cook County considerable harm, even though he met the local test of being an Irish Catholic. The party leaders recognized that, if McCarthy were to become the Democratic presidential candidate in 1968, thousands of college students would descend upon the city and begin working precincts on behalf of McCarthy but not for the local Democratic party. In fact, they could be quite sure that the same college students who would be working for McCarthy would at the same time be working against the machine.

Who needs such a candidate? Better to go with Hubert Humphrey, even if he lost, than to go with Eugene McCarthy, even if he could win. If Humphrey lost and Nixon were elected president of the United States for the next four years, the local organization could survive that much better than a McCarthy victory. For a McCarthy victory could also mean the channeling of federal funds into local community organizations in cities like Chicago, bypassing the local organization and building up countervailing political

---

° A local joke which made the rounds was that Robert Kennedy called Daley on election night at midnight, inquiring, "How many votes do we have in Cook County?" to which Daley allegedly responded, "How many do you need?"

power centers which would be inimical to the interests of the local organization. It was primarily for that reason that Mayor Daley made his close-to-the-vest approach to Senator Edward Kennedy to encourage him to declare publicly his candidacy for the presidential nomination in 1968. With Kennedy at the top of the ticket, the organization was assured a victory for the county offices and a presidential candidate they could live with and deal with if he won. But, since Kennedy would not declare himself in advance of a pledge of Daley's support, the mayor and the other party leaders opted for Humphrey, knowing he might lose the presidency. (Daley's innate political caution inhibited him from openly supporting Kennedy and possibly backing the wrong horse if Kennedy did not run or failed to gather enough support to secure the nomination.) That, however, was still preferable to the possible implications of a McCarthy candidacy and victory.

The same standards have been applied to candidates slated for other national offices such as United States senator or congressman from Illinois. The party is always willing to slate candidates such as Paul Douglas or Adlai Stevenson III for the Senate, and several liberal congressmen from the city such as Sidney Yates or Abner Mikva for the House of Representatives. They serve to pacify the liberal, anti-machine Democrats in the city, particularly in the districts they represent, and they help deliver some of the liberal vote in the city and county for the rest of the ticket. Not that these men sell themselves or their ideals and principles to the party. The party does not require that they compromise their principles significantly and has little interest in what these men do in Washington, as long as they represent the party's interests in the national capital. This understanding leaves liberal reform Democrats free to pursue their political ideologies and ambitions at a national, and sometimes even a state, level while giving the party ticket a liberal leavening flavor to compensate for the more conservative, machine-type politicians slated for the local offices in which the party is really interested.

However, leadership posts in both the congressional and state delegations are reserved for safe, more conservatively oriented members of the party's inner circle. When liberal, Jewish Congressman Sidney Yates had succeeded to the leadership of the Illinois Democratic congressional delegation by virtue of seniority, experience, and ability, he was slated for the United States Senate seat against incumbent Republican Senator Everett McKinley Dirksen in 1962. In a race similar to William Clark's in 1968, in which Yates ran well downstate but not as well as he should have in Cook County, the machine's home territory, Yates lost to Dirksen by only 140,000 votes. Two years later, after an interim appointment to the United Nations, Yates was given his old seat in the House of Representatives, but he had lost his seniority and his post as head of the Illinois Democratic delegation. That post went to Congressman Dan Rostenkowski, a ward committeeman and a member of the party's inner circle. Rostenkowski, one of Mayor Daley's favorite younger city Democrats, has held the post since 1962, while Yates has faded into semi obscurity.

A similar situation has traditionally existed in the Cook County Democratic delegation to the Illinois General Assembly. In both the state senate and house of representatives the traditionally Democratic minority leadership posts are held by more conservatively oriented legislators who are close to the party's inner circle, who are subservient to the Cook County organization's interests, and who can work well with the downstate Democratic politicians who collaborate with the Cook County machine. The liberals, on the other hand, are either frozen out or consigned to minor posts by the party hierarchy. In 1971, when the Democrats had a majority in the state senate for the first time in the twentieth century, the party leadership was confronted with a revolt of black legislators led by liberal black Senator Richard Newhouse who demanded more power for the black bloc in the Illinois Democratic delegation. Daley flew to Springfield and designated as president pro tem of the senate, State Senator Cecil Partee, a longtime, conservatively oriented black legislator who was closely identified with the party's inner circle. The liberal blacks who had led the revolt achieved their aim of greater black power, but that power was given to the more conservative, machine-oriented blacks.

The dynamics of the relationships between the Cook County Democratic organization and the state of Illinois, the nation, and the Democratic party at both the state and national levels are clear. The interests of the state, the nation, and of the Democratic party at both levels are always subordinated to the interests of the Democratic organization of Cook County. This is not to say that the members of the local organization have no interest whatsoever in state or national affairs, or in the Democratic party at the state and national levels. But such interest or concern, if it does exist, is secondary to local interests in the value system of the local politicians.

The basic foundation on which the local Democratic party is built has far-reaching consequences for any liberal Democrat who has political aspirations. He is, by definition, practically barred from achieving major local office in Chicago and Cook County. He may be sent to Springfield or Washington to represent a district or the state and the party at those levels. But he must be willing to support local party interests and candidates, and pursue the party's interests at the state and national levels when issues affect the local interests of the party.

In most cases, this requirement does not inhibit a liberal Democrat from taking a liberal position and pursuing a liberal political philosophy at the state and national levels. For, on most issues at these levels, the local party does not have a position, and a liberal senator, congressman, or state legislator is left free to pursue his own interests and ambitions. Since most liberal, issue-oriented Democrats prefer to pursue issues at the state or national levels, the relationship between liberal Democratic state representatives, congressmen, and United States senators, and the local Democratic politicians can be worked out on the basis of an arrangement which suits the interests and ambitions of both the liberal Democrats and the local politicians.

✤ 6 ✤

The Machine and the Political Opposition

In the political system within which the machine operates, potential opposition to the machine can come from two possible sources outside the Democratic party—from the opposition Republican party or from independent political movements. To maintain its existence, the machine must be able to deal with, co-opt, or overcome all attempts made to reform or defeat the machine which emanate from either of these sources. How does the machine deal with these opposition elements within the political system?

The Loyal Opposition: The Republicans in Chicago

American politics is conducted within the framework of two major factors—the two party tradition and local control and dominance of those two parties. In a country in which the parties are broad-based coalitions of diverse groups, making their appeal to all segments of the electorate and operating within a framework which makes it almost impossible for a third party to achieve major status, a majority party need only concern itself with one other major party. In a nation of fifty states, and fifty Republican and fifty Democratic parties in each of those states, the rules of the political game are set by the realities of American political life, which for the past forty years have included the Democratic party's national dominance and overwhelming control of most of the major cities of the country.

In a nation in which there are approximately three registered Democrats for every two registered Republicans and in which approximately 44 percent of the population identify themselves as Democrats, while only 23 percent of the population identify themselves as Republicans, any local Democratic party would normally have an advantage over any local Republican party. Furthermore, the migration of ethnic Catholics, Jews, and blacks into the major cities of this country insured the domination of those cities by local Democratic parties, for it is among these groups in our population that one finds the heaviest percentage of Democratic voters. According to a 1970 Gallup poll, approximately 39 percent of white Protestant voters in this country identify themselves as Democrats and an approximately equal percentage identify themselves as Republicans. But approximately 60 percent of the Catholics, 72 percent of the Jews, and 80 percent of the blacks identify themselves as Democrats. The normal Republican vote in any of the major cities in any election is about 40 percent of the electorate, while the normal Democratic vote is approximately 60 percent. Consequently, any local Republican party in any major city in the United States operates under two built-in disadvantages, the national dominance of the Democratic party in the country, and overwhelming support for the Democratic party among those groups in our population which inhabit the major cities. Analysis of the situation of the local Republican party in any major American city must begin with the recognition of these elementary facts. These facts are particularly significant in attempting to evaluate the role of the Republican party in Chicago, a city of approximately 1,750,000 Catholics, 1,300,000 blacks, and 125,000 Jews.

The Dynamics of Republicanism in Illinois. The Republican party in Chicago and Cook County operates under still another disadvantage. The Democratic party has held unbroken control for over forty years of the mayor's office in Chicago, the Chicago City Council, the bureaucracy in the city, and the local judiciary, and has also dominated county government during most of that time.

An effective political party needs five things: offices, jobs, money, workers, and votes. Offices beget jobs and money; jobs and money beget workers; workers beget votes; and votes beget offices. In Chicago and Cook County, Democratic control of practically all major offices insures that the Republican party will have difficulty generating workers, voters, and money. Chicago's 3148 precincts are covered by approximately 30,000 Democratic jobholders, while at least two-thirds of the precincts in the city are not covered by Republican workers. Without workers to cover the precincts, the Republican party cannot get its message across to the voters of the city. Without the voters, the Republican party cannot gain the offices. Without offices, the party cannot get jobs and money. And, without jobs and money, the party cannot get workers. Consequently, an election between Republicans and Democrats in Chicago is like a race between a dray horse and a thoroughbred.

The predicament of the Republican party in Chicago is exacerbated by its relationship to the Republican party in the suburbs and downstate. Unlike the statewide Democratic party in Illinois, which is normally controlled and disciplined by the highly centralized, efficient Cook County organization, the Republican party in Illinois is fragmented into Chicago Republicans, suburban Republicans, and downstate Republicans. The power centers of the Republican party in Illinois are in the suburbs of Cook County and in the downstate counties. Without massive help from those two outside power centers, the Republican party in Chicago cannot seriously challenge the Democratic organization in the city. Since the Republican party in the city of Chicago does not have enough jobs to recruit an effective precinct organization and raise money in the city, workers and money must be brought into the city from Republican power centers in the suburbs and downstate. But since Republicans in the suburbs and in most downstate counties hold enough offices at the municipal, county, and statewide levels to take care of their local workers, they have little interest in assisting their city colleagues in getting the jobs and money they need in order to get the votes for the offices they need.

Consequently, Republicans in Chicago find themselves in an analogous situation to suburban and downstate Democrats vis-à-vis the Chicago Democratic machine. If the Democratic and Republican parties in Illinois were truly statewide parties, Chicago Democrats would assist suburban and downstate Democrats in building a strong statewide Democratic party, and suburban and downstate Republicans would assist Chicago Republicans in building a strong statewide Republican party. But there are no statewide parties. There is a local Democratic party in Chicago, interested almost exclusively in its own perquisites. There are weak suburban and downstate Democratic parties in which the Chicago organization has practically no interest. And, on the other side of the political fence, there are strong Republican parties in downstate Illinois and suburban Cook County, and a weak Republican party in Chicago in which the strong downstate and suburban Republican parties also have no interest. In fact, suburban township Republican committeemen, who normally should assume the chairmanship of the county central committee, usually refuse to do so. Accepting the chairmanship of a countywide central committee would involve a suburban committeeman in the problems of the Republican party in the city and expose him to criticism by his constituents in his suburban township who have no interest in the problems of the city.

Left to their own devices in the city, most Republican ward committeemen accept their status as junior partners in a political system, take whatever crumbs the Democratic ward committeemen offer them in their wards, make little effort to turn out the vote in the city, and often collaborate with their Democratic counterparts in elections. Of the fifty Republican ward committeemen in the city of Chicago, probably not more than a dozen have legitimate ward organizations, offer more than token opposition to the Democratic party in their wards, and get enough patronage and perquisites for themselves so that they can maintain more than a facade for the Republican party in their wards. Indeed, some of the Republican ward committeemen in the strongest Democratic wards hold office as committeemen by virtue of Democratic voters in the ward. This is made possible in wards in Chicago where the Democratic vote total is so high, and the Republican vote total so low, that large numbers of Democratic workers and their friends can register as Republicans and overwhelm any legitimate Republican candidate in a party primary in the ward.

The Nonexistent Committeemen. A list of the fifty Republican ward committeemen in Chicago is a catalogue of unknowns and nonentities. Any attempt to get in touch with most of them to secure information about their ward organizations is an exercise in frustration and futility. Some of them do not have ward offices, others do not have listed telephone numbers, either at home or at their ward headquarters, some are either out of town or unavailable at all times, and others refuse to answer questions or make comments on any matter pertaining to their wards.

"Where do you find the Republican committeeman in the 42nd Ward?" I asked several City Hall acquaintances one day at lunch in Chicago, after a student researcher who had attempted to get in contact with the Republican 42nd Ward committeeman told me that it was impossible to reach him. "In George Dunne's office," replied the two Democratic politicians.

"Are you kidding?" Charles J. DeSimone, Jr., the Republican candidate for alderman in Tom Keane's 31st Ward, told a *Sun-Times* reporter on February 22, 1971, when asked about his chances of beating Alderman Keane in the forthcoming aldermanic election. "I am running because there are two groups—the Republican and the Democratic—and I am a good Republican," said DeSimone. "Keane has been a good alderman."

Four years earlier, in the 1967 aldermanic elections, *Chicago Daily News* columnist Mike Royko interviewed the Republican candidate for alderman in Mayor Richard J. Daley's 11th Ward, a seventy-seven-year-old retired milkman named Steve Mankowski. "My committeeman, John Wall, comes in and says to me, 'Steve, I've got good news for you,'" Mankowski told Royko. "I said, 'What kind of good news?' He said, 'The Cook County Central Committee had a meeting, and they have decided that they want you to run for alderman again.' I said, 'Well, what's the good news?'"

In 1969, a student researcher, attempting to find 11th Ward Republican headquarters, described her experiences: "The outside doors to the headquarters are boarded up, which initially tends to discourage a possible visit. There are two alternative entrances, however, if one is perseverant enough to discover them; one behind the pin-setting machine in the bowling alley, and another through a tavern and series of mysterious hallways. The only way one can get in touch with the Republican committeeman is a personal visit to the headquarters on Tuesday or Thursday nights, as there is no phone in the headquarters, and he keeps his home number unpublished." Next to the Republican ward headquarters, located in a building owned by the committeeman, is a bowling alley and a tavern. As a further precaution to protect the headquarters from being found by inquisitive constituents, the committeeman had the lettering "11th Ward Republican Organization" removed from the office window. "I think it scared the people away from the bowling alleys over his headquarters," said the researcher.

On election night, in November 1964, an acquaintance of mine was in the headquarters of one of the black Republican ward committeemen on Chicago's South Side when a telephone call came to the Republican committeeman from Democratic Congressman and 2nd Ward Committeeman William Dawson, the black Democratic political boss of the South Side, who congratulated the Republican committeeman on the poor showing he had made in his ward. In Chicago's 1st Ward, a student researcher living in the ward was amazed to discover that his barber was being slated as Republican candidate for state senator from the ward. "How come you're running for state senator?" the student asked his barber. "They asked me!" said the barber. "What have I got to lose?"

The experiences of a group of student researchers attempting to gather information about the Republican ward organizations in Chicago in the late 1960s and early 1970s reads like a twentieth-century Alice-in-Wonderland hegira. In the aldermanic election in the 1st Ward in 1967, the Democratic candidate ran unopposed and received 9628 of the 10,308 votes cast in the election. This figure could have been higher, according to the student researcher, who lived in the ward, but the ward organization through its precinct captains had many of its people vote Republican to give the semblance of an opposition party in the ward. "There ain't none," responded a long-time resident of the 2nd Ward when asked how many Republican precinct captains there were in the ward. "On several occasions," wrote a student researcher, "I attempted to secure an interview with the Republican committeeman in the 3rd Ward, but was not successful. Each time, he claimed to be very busy. This was rather hard to believe, considering the fact that the regular Democratic organization controlled 90 percent of the electorate. After several attempts to secure an interview with the Republican committeeman, or any Republican for that matter, I abandoned the idea."

"The fact that the Democratic organization is the only real political organization operating within the ward is blatantly obvious once one tries to reach the Republicans," wrote a student researcher about his experiences in the 12th Ward on Chicago's southwest side. "After three weeks of phoning ward headquarters without any results, one tends to doubt the existence of a Republican organization in the 12th Ward. No office hours are posted on the door and the photographs of key Republicans scattered in the window are yellowed. The total appearance gives the impression that no one has come near the place in ages." "The Republicans rely mainly on TV and the big newspapers to help them," wrote another student researcher about the 12th Ward. "Their office used to be near my house, but they went out of business and moved. I went to their new address and found a For Sale sign in the window." "The Republican ward committeeman [in the 12th Ward] is approaching 80 years old and is going blind," wrote another student researcher. "He is not a well man and consequently is unable to play an active part in ward politics. The Republican Party has no permanent ward office as the Democrats do. The Republican County Central Committee headquarters gave a number for reaching the Republican committeeman, but no one ever answered. There seems to be a problem of contacting the Republican Party in the ward. Whenever the word 'precinct captain' was mentioned to an individual, the person never asked which one, it was taken for granted that he meant the Democratic one."

"In our Congressional District [the 13th Ward on Chicago's southwest side], there has been virtually no campaign," wrote another student researcher. "I can tell you who the Democratic candidate is because he is the incumbent—William Murphy. There might not even be a Republican candidate. There are no billboards, advertising, debates, or precinct captains working in their behalf. It is almost as if they agreed not to bother spending all that money to campaign. Maybe the Democrats ran both candidates." In another southwest side ward, the 18th Ward, "The Democrats controlled the ward from the time of the Roosevelt administration until 1962," wrote a student researcher. "Today, on the local level, the Republicans control the ward, although they act as if they don't. And the Democrats don't, but they act as if they do. For example, the office of the headquarters of the 18th Ward Republican organization, a small unobtrusive office located in a small unobtrusive building, is located on 79th and Damen. One has to squint in order to read the sign which says, '18th Ward Republican Organization.' The people in the office are business-like and polite to visitors, slightly cynical toward Democrats, and faintly worried, if not downright bitter, about the influx of Negroes into the eastern part of the ward. The office of the 18th Ward Democratic Organization is located on 81st Street and Ashland Avenue. The office is approximately ½ block long. The sign which says '18th Ward Democratic Organization' is two feet high and extends across the entire front of the building. People inside are generally loud, relaxed, open and optimistic. They give one the impression that they are confident that Republican control can't last forever. They are generally optimistic about the influx of Negroes into the ward."

In the 19th Ward, on Chicago's far South Side, which usually goes Republican in state and national elections but always goes Democratic in the aldermanic election, the Republican committee-man told a student researcher that, "he can only handle only minor requests for service because he does not have the connections within the city or county government to help the people." Although he does not like doing so, the committeeman must refer most requests for service to the Democratic alderman. "All in all," wrote the student researcher, "the 19th Ward is a Republican ward largely because of the socio-economic factors of the inhabitants. Yet the Republican Party itself is a loose, nebulous organization, weakened by factions within itself and lack of patronage. The only election that the Republicans seem to lose in the ward is for alderman."

In the 21st Ward, on Chicago's South Side, "I had a difficult time contacting the Republican committeeman, and eventually had to reach him by phone," wrote a student researcher. "No one, even good Republicans, seemed to know where the ward office was located, and then there was a problem that the Republican committeeman wasn't there very often."

Back on Chicago's west side, in the 24th Ward, a researcher attempting to find Republican headquarters was given an address in the ward which turned out to be in the middle of a lagoon in Douglas Park. Another researcher, finding it impossible to get in touch with the elected Republican ward committeeman in the 24th Ward, finally reached the acting Republican committeeman ap-pointed by the Republican county central committee, a former

Democratic precinct captain. His office was housed in a former dry cleaning store on Roosevelt Road. "The coatrack and counter are still there," wrote the researcher, "and there are no desks. The office had been moved to the new address on Roosevelt Road because a few months before, the former headquarters was hit by a fire bomb which destroyed the building in which the headquarters was housed."

In Alderman Vito Marzullo's neighboring 25th Ward, the Republican headquarters at 2157 W. Cermak Rd. is usually locked, and there is normally no sign of life. In contrast, Marzullo's headquarters at 2530 South Blue Island Avenue is a beehive of activity on Tuesday and Thursday nights, when the alderman receives his constituents and services their needs. And, unlike many aldermen, Marzullo is always available to constituents or inquiring reporters at his aldermanic office in City Hall every morning of the week. The elected Republican committeeman in Marzullo's ward, who won his post one year with a smashing landslide victory of 1134 to 4, was dumped by the Republican county central committee. There was some suspicion that his landslide victory was promoted by some of Democratic Committeeman Marzullo's precinct workers. The committeeman was also unable to carry his precinct in a Republican primary for the organization gubernatorial candidate in 1964, Charles Percy. He lost the precinct almost 2 to 1 to Lar ("American First") Daly, a comic political character, who is a perennial candidate for public office in Illinois.

In Democratic Committeeman Bernard Neistein's 29th Ward on Chicago's west side, a student researcher had no more luck in getting in contact with the acting Republican committeeman appointed by the county central committee than he did in getting in contact with the elected Republican ward committeeman. The regular Republican committeeman, according to the student researcher, "attends a good many wakes. Thus it is very hard to see him. When you call his office and inform his secretary that you are a student studying the ward, it seems that he has just left to attend a wake. When you visit the regular Republican headquarters in the ward (which is located in a basement apartment on a residential side-street), it seems that the committeeman was unavoidably called away to a wake. The acting Republican committeeman seems no more anxious to talk with a student studying the ward. Countless messages to his home seem to get misplaced, although someone is always anxious to take another one. A telephone call to the other Republican headquarters in the ward is met with the reply that the acting committeeman is presently engaged in a conference, but he will call back when he is finished. When he doesn't call back, another telephone call to the headquarters gets the reply, 'Sorry, but the acting committeeman has not come in yet.'"

In the 30th Ward, a student gathering information on the ward went to the Regular Republican Organization headquarters. "I stopped in at their office one night before the election. The office was an old storefront equipped with rows of folding chairs and an old wooden table. I couldn't tell if the walls were painted or not, they were literally covered with political posters. I went up to the gentleman who looked like he was running the operation and asked if it would be possible to meet the ward committeeman. The man told me that the committeeman was not present on that night, and we exchanged phone numbers. He told me I would be contacted. I waited several weeks in vain and then tried calling them. I called twice a day for a week without any result and drove past several nights in a row without seeing any lights on anyplace. It's my opinion that there was a highly localized earthquake under the office and that the interior and its occupants were swallowed up, never to be seen again."

In Committeeman Tom Keane's 31st Ward, on Chicago's northwest side, a student researcher living in the ward described his experiences. "Republicans are generally resigned to the fact that this is a Democratic ward. Their precinct captains visit only the voters who they know are Republicans and do not attempt to convert anyone. We have lived in the same house in this ward for 18 years and have never ever seen a Republican precinct captain. Furthermore, the 31st Ward regular Republican ward organization has its office only a few blocks from our house, yet I have never even seen the door open. The only way I know that anyone goes in there is that a few months before elections, some Republican posters are put on the windows inside the office." According to another researcher in the 31st Ward, "As to Republican opposition, there is none. The Republicans do maintain an office near the intersection of Grand Avenue and Damen, but the place is always locked and barred. Upon calling the Republican County Central

Committee headquarters, an inquirer is politely told that a representative will meet you at the Grand Avenue office at 7 P.M. When the inquirer arrives there, he finds little has changed and the office is still locked. After several attempts it is advisable to abandon the project completely. A Republican precinct captain gave me this advice concerning Republicans in the 31st Ward. 'It is inadvisable to make waves in Thomas Keane's personal ward.' This captain has a part-time job with the Board of Education. He candidly informs you that he obtained the job through the help of one of Thomas Keane's aides." Another researcher in the 31st Ward "was rather disappointed in trying to find out about the Republican organization in the ward. I called up the Republican Central Committee to find out who their committeeman was and where his office was located in order to go and talk to him. They told me the committeeman was Mr. ———, and he did not have an office but worked out of his home. They also gave me his home phone number which turned out to be someone else's phone number. It wasn't until I found out from a Democratic precinct captain that the Republicans do have an office at 3901 W. Grand Avenue that I was able to dial their number. However, that did not help me as no one would answer though I phoned frequently trying to contact someone there. From this and other reasons which will come up later in my paper, I feel I can confidently say that the Republican organization in the 31st Ward is a very weak and ineffective political group." The situation in the 31st Ward under Committeeman Keane's all-pervasive leadership goes back a long time. According to the *Chicago Daily News*, in the 1950s, when the then Republican Committeeman Charles Gross of the 31st Ward was murdered in a shotgun slaying on the street, an investigation into Mr. Gross' status revealed that he had been loaned money by Democratic Committeeman Keane and had been on a city payroll under Keane's sponsorship.

This is not to say that all Republican ward committeemen in Chicago collaborate with their Democratic counterparts or make no effort to win elections for their party in the city. There are the John Waners, the Timothy Sheehans, the John Hoellens, and the Allen Freemans. But a considerable percentage of the Republican ward committeemen have sold out, given up, or collaborated with the Democratic machine either out of recognition of the hopelessness of the situation or out of pecuniary and political self-interest.

In recent years, the Republican leadership of the party in the state and in Cook County have occasionally attempted to improve the party's electoral prospects in the city of Chicago by appointing acting committeemen in some of the wards to work with the party leadership and by ignoring the duly elected committeemen in those wards. Former Republican county chairmen Hayes Robertson and Edmund Kucharski, former Governor Richard Ogilvie, Attorney General William Scott, and Senator Charles Percy have all made some effort in the past to develop a better working Republican organization in Chicago by by-passing some of the collaborationist committeemen and by working with acting committeemen in those wards. But their efforts have been relatively ineffective, most of the elected collaborationist Republican committeemen have hung on, and even some of the acting committeemen have been co-opted by the Democrats.°

The Rationale of Collaboration. Why do so many Republican ward committeemen cooperate with the Democratic machine in Chicago? The answer to that question probably lies in a variety of reasons. In some cases, the Republican committeemen are professional politicians in politics for almost purely personal economic and political advantage. They have little interest in their party, its philosophy, or its prospects. It is a way to make a living, the work isn't too hard, the demands are not great, and collaborating with the Democrats is a form of social security, since the Democratic machine will probably be in office for the foreseeable future. For others, there is a pragmatic recognition of the facts of political life in their wards. Without jobs, money, and workers, the best they can

---

° During the 1970 campaign, I was at a cocktail party for a major Democratic candidate for office, talking to the ward secretary from Alderman Vito Marzullo's ward. A short distance away, Alderman Marzullo was engaged in earnest conversation with an individual, holding the man by the shoulder and lecturing him. "Who's the alderman talking to?" I asked the ward secretary. "Oh, that's the newly appointed acting Republican committeeman in our ward," said the ward secretary.

Two student researchers, who interviewed the acting Republican 1st Ward committeeman, were told by that official that "the progress made in the past twenty-six months is nothing short of miraculous." "What was miraculous," wrote the students in their term paper, "was that we were finally able to see him. We sat in the outer lobby of his office for over an hour, while a rather faded picture of George Washington glared down on us. Finally, through a glass door we heard that dedicated knight of Republican politics whisper, 'Are those damn kids still here?' Because he couldn't leave without passing us, he finally invited us in."

hope for is to make a legitimate effort and bring in as good a vote as they can. But they can get a smattering of patronage jobs from their own party, a medium-level job for themselves, an opportunity to hold a title in the Republican party, and whatever other prerogatives go with a title. For mediocre men with limited goals in life, the payoff, small as it is, is sufficient.

There are others, however, who face the facts of political life in another way. Recognizing the long-term domination of the city by the majority Democratic party, and cognizant of the unwillingness of their Republican cohorts in the suburbs and downstate to help them in their wards, they also recognize that the best way in which they can serve their constituents as well as their own interests is to work with the majority party. A Republican committeeman who works well with his Democratic counterpart can get help from the Democrats in getting elected committeeman and can also get help in getting elected as state representative or alderman. (In Illinois, each legislative district sends three representatives to the lower house of the state legislature. The cumulative voting system, under which each voter has three votes which he can cast for one person, makes it possible and, indeed, probable for a minority party always to elect one legislator from each district in the state, regardless of the number of voters from the other party in that district.) A number of Chicago's Republican ward committeemen hold safe seats in the state legislature with Democratic help. A Republican committeeman could possibly also get a fairly lucrative appointive position somewhere in the city or county bureaucracy in an office safe from scrutiny from his constituents or the media. In such a position, he can be a big fish in a little pond. He can serve his constituents, open the proper doors to the bureaucracy for them, and give himself job security and sufficient financial rewards to satisfy both his ego and economic needs.

A Republican committeeman in the 7th Ward told a student researcher in 1966 that "there is an extremely friendly and helpful relationship between the parties in the ward. They give each other tickets for various events and help each other in nonpolitical capacities."

The ostensibly Republican 7th Ward alderman, who was known as a "Republicrat," rarely had opposition when he ran for re-election and was even endorsed by the Democratic organization in the ward. When he was faced with a strong challenge from an independent candidate in 1971, the Democratic majority in the city council altered the boundaries of his ward to give him more ethnic Catholics on the south end and to give the black voters on the north end to Alderman Leon Despres of the 5th Ward, the most outspoken and capable independent Democratic alderman in the city council.

The Republican alderman usually voted with the Democratic majority in the city council, was elected chairman of an important committee by the Democratic majority and was finally, as a reward for his faithful service, put on the circuit court bench as a judge by Mayor Daley. The alderman did provide excellent service to his constituents, especially on the south end of the ward. Excellent maintenance of beaches, new sewers and street lights, widening of main streets, better garbage pick up, and aid to area schools were provided by the city as compensation for his cooperation with the Democratic party.

The Republican alderman typifies the Republican politicians in the city who operate like their Democratic counterparts, have access to the proper authorities through the proper channels, and have their own social security system without having publicly to compromise themselves and join the other party. Another was the late state representative, Clem Graver, a Republican politician from Chicago's west side, whose operations were described by writer John Bartlow Martin in the *Saturday Evening Post* on December 19, 1953:

Son of poor parents, Graver has been on the public pay roll since 1926. He usually had a job paying over $300 a month. Why?

"I was the outstanding precinct captain in Cook County and I could have practically any job I wanted," he has said. "I am still the Number One precinct captain of Cook County." His precinct was in a laborers' region just south of the old ghetto. "Till I took over, it used to be solid Democratic," Graver has said. "I beat Franklin D. Roosevelt in my precinct. I got 498 for Dewey one year. Roosevelt got 6." (The 6 were cast by Democratic poll officials.)

What is the secret of Graver's success? It is simple. He works for his people all the time. He has said, "You've got to take care of the people. You're running around all night for them. You've got to get up at two, three in the morning and drive people to the hospital. You've got to get people jobs. This," he said one day in May, "is my busy season. People want to get the kids' tonsils out before the polio season, I have 150 to 200 kids got to get their tonsils out every year; their folks can't afford a private doctor and I got to get them in the county hospital. I take care of 1000 people myself every year, Christmas baskets. You gotta make all their affairs, four or five Legion posts you gotta go along with them on their dances; some months I average four weddings a week I go to. The people I've buried personally in my ward! Poor people are very grateful. Some of them homes you go into, they've got my picture hanging over the bed with the crucifix—that's how much they think of me. The people in my district don't care what I do here"—meaning in the Legislature—"just as long as I don't forget them there."

Newspapers have criticized Graver. Like many river-ward politicians, he was thought to have syndicate connections. He usually opposed reform. Graver has said, "What do my people care about what the newspapers say about me?" And, "They don't write about when you take 1000 kids to the Shrine circus."

Every Thursday night during the session when Graver returned from Springfield he spent the evening in his ward headquarters, formerly a shoemaker's shop at 18th and Halsted Streets. In the window a brilliant green-and-red-and-blue neon sign, 21ST WARD REGULAR REPUBLICAN ORGANIZATION flashed over pictures of Representative Graver, President Eisenhower and Vice-President Nixon.

On a Thursday night in June, Graver's outer office was filled with supplicants. In a tiny inner office, bare and suffocatingly hot, its only window painted black, Graver sat at a desk, two precinct captains hovering at his shoulder or ushering in the people—men with traffic tickets, a woman who had a cataract over one eye, a man who wanted to avoid jury duty, a man who wanted to get his tax bill reduced, a man who wanted a relative paroled from the state penitentiary.

Graver kept piling their documents on his desk—"the slips," he called them. The phone rang almost constantly. On the wall were scribbled the telephone numbers of the county hospital, district police station, and someone named Spike. More people kept coming—a woman who wanted to get her daughter into a school for crippled children, a precinct captain who was feuding with a rival, a Negro who complained that forty-three children were living in one tenement flat, a Mexican who said he'd been cheated by a used-car dealer.

To everyone, Graver said, "I'll straighten that out." After more than two hours, the waiting room was empty. Graver said, "It's like that every Thursday night."*

* Graver disappeared on June 11, 1953. He was kidnapped by three men and has not been heard from or seen since that day.

Electoral Patterns. Graver's showing in his precinct in national elections was an example of another interesting relationship among professional politicians in Chicago. A collaborating Republican ward committeeman can be allowed to make a decent showing for his party in national or state elections which are not significant to the Democratic organization in the city. But he had better not offer serious opposition or electoral trouble for the Democratic party in local elections which are important to the party. An analysis of the election returns in Chicago reveals some interesting statistics when one compares election returns in the wards in national, state, and local elections. Wards that go two or three to one Democratic in national elections sometimes go ten or fifteen to one Democratic in local elections. Wards that go three to two or almost break even in national elections go three or four or five to one Democratic in local elections.* It may well be that a Democratic organization which is interested primarily in gaining, retaining, and reaping the rewards of local office, and which co-opts its opposition in order to achieve its goal, would be willing to allow that opposition to make a respectable showing in national and state elections in which the local organization has little interest. Thus, the interest of both parties to the partnership are served. The Democratic organization gets its help at the level in which it is really interested, and the Republican politician can make a respectable showing for his party at the level in which the Democratic organization is least interested.

The task of a collaborating Republican ward committeeman in Chicago is made easier by the scheduling of local elections in the city and county. The mayoral election is scheduled in April of odd-numbered years, two and one-half years after national presidential and major statewide elections are scheduled, one and one-half years before the next national and major statewide election, and five months after the elections for most major county offices. Thus, the election schedule effectively separates the mayoral election in Chicago from national, state, or even countywide political trends which might be dangerous to a Democratic mayoral candidate running in Chicago. The only other candidates on the

---

* In the 19th Ward, for example, the Republicans carry the ward in national and state elections, but a Democratic alderman is always elected, sometimes by majorities as high as two to one.

ballot are the aldermanic candidates who have not received a majority in the aldermanic election in February of that same year.

The scheduling of the mayoral primary and the aldermanic elections in February of the odd-numbered years serves several political purposes. First, it is in the worst month of the year insofar as Chicago's weather is concerned, at the end of a long winter, at a time when most people are unwilling to go outside for any purpose whatsoever. This insures a small turnout in both the mayoral primary and the aldermanic elections by those voters who are not controlled by, indebted to, or subservient to the machine's precinct workers. But the Democratic machine turns out a massive vote for its mayoral candidate in the primary and, consequently, for the machine's candidates in the ostensibly nonpartisan aldermanic elections, while the Republican party, without an effective precinct organization in the city, cannot turn out much of a vote for its mayoral candidate in its primary or for its candidates in the aldermanic elections.

Combining the partisan mayoral primary with the ostensibly nonpartisan aldermanic election has another effect on potential voters in the city. If they come into a precinct polling place and ask for a Republican primary ballot, such requests can be duly noted by the Democratic precinct captains in those polling places. One result of this situation is that not only does the Democratic mayoral candidate usually get a massive primary vote while his Republican opponent gets a light primary vote, but the aldermanic elections are significantly influenced by the massive Democratic primary turnout for the mayoral nomination. Under state election law, the candidate who gets a majority of the total number of votes cast in the aldermanic election in each ward is elected to the city council, and a run-off election in April for aldermanic seats takes place only if no candidate gets the majority in the February election. Thus, the fusing of the mayoral primary with the aldermanic election always insures the election of a heavy Democratic majority to the city council. A further objective of the massive Democratic turnout in its mayoral primary is to demonstrate to the electorate and to potential sources of campaign funds that the Republican nominee has a very small following, while the Democratic nominee for mayor has massive support. These are some of the reasons why the Democratic high command cranks up the machine and turns it loose full force in the February primaries.

An analysis of the February primary and April electoral votes for the mayoralty in the two parties reveals some interesting statistics. In the 1955 mayoral primary, the year in which Mayor Daley was first elected to office, there were 746,015 votes in the Democratic primary in February, while in the Republican primary the total was only 122,473 votes. In the mayoral election in April, the total Democratic vote was 708,660, 38,000 less than the primary vote. But the Republican electoral vote multiplied almost $4\frac{1}{2}$ times to 581,461 in the April election.

The importance of separating the city mayoral and aldermanic elections from national elections is indicated by the number of voters who voted in national elections in the city in comparison to the number of voters who voted in the mayoral and aldermanic elections. In the 1952 presidential election, over 550,000 more people voted in Chicago than voted in the 1955 mayoral election. In the 1956 presidential election, 589,926 more people voted than were to vote in the 1959 mayoral election, and, in 1963, 460,641 fewer people voted in the mayoral election than had voted in the 1960 presidential election. Finally, in Daley's great victory in 1967, a mayoral election in which Daley carried all 50 wards in Chicago, there were 324,436 fewer votes than were cast in the 1968 presidential election.

The Democratic organization's control of most of the major county offices is safeguarded by scheduling elections for those offices, with two exceptions, in the even-numbered years in which the presidency of the United States and major statewide offices are not up for election. The county board presidency, the county assessor, the county treasurer, the county clerk, and the county superintendent of schools are all elected in those even-numbered years. The only significant county offices which are scheduled for presidential and important statewide election years are state's attorney and clerk of the circuit court. Thus, practically all the important offices in which the Democratic organization is interested are also safeguarded from potentially dangerous national or state-wide political trends.

Potentially dangerous voter revolts in the city are guarded against by scheduling bond referendums in primary elections in which the machine can turn out the vote, and by undertaking tax increases, massive new spending programs which might be unpopular with the taxpayers, and needed repairs on expressways and streets, which might aggravate motorists and public transportation commuters, immediately after elections.

At the precinct level, in precincts having a shortage of Republican captains and workers, Democratic precinct captains sometimes recruit ostensibly Republican voters to serve as Republican election judges. Since under state law, each precinct must have a total of five election judges, three Democratic and two Republican or two Democratic and three Republican judges in alternate precincts, the Democratic organization sometimes gives the Republican party a lift by supplying Republican as well as Democratic election judges. Needless to say, these worthies are not overzealous in checking credentials, in guarding against illegal voter assistance, and in taking the tally.

Control of the county clerk's office and the board of election commissioners also gives the Democratic party a decided advantage over the Republican party in the city and county. Polling places can be moved or made inaccessible, places on the voting machine or the ballot can be allocated on the basis of the candidate's affiliation with the party leadership, and voting machines can be supplied to Democratic ward organizations several weeks before the election so that they can teach their voters how to use the machine on election day without assistance.*

This is not to say that the Democratic organization in Chicago wins elections by stealing votes, coercing voters, or violating election laws. While it is true that there are precincts in which all of these things take place at one time or another, it is also true that

---

* A Republican friend of mine was in the ward headquarters of one of the best solid Democratic black wards on Chicago's South Side two weeks before an election. In the ward headquarters, two voting machines were being used by Democratic precinct captains to instruct their voters on how to use the machines at the polling place on election day. My Republican friend got in line, took his turn behind the curtain in front of the voting machine, and pulled the lever for a straight Republican ballot. A precinct captain popped his head through the curtain, stared at the machine, turned to the Republican, and said, "Is that how you does it? That's not how we does it here!" In the 1964 election, the one in which this incident took place, the ward delivered approximately 35,000 votes for President Lyndon Johnson to approximately 1,000 votes for Republican presidential candidate Barry Goldwater, and approximately 34,000 votes for Democratic Governor Otto Kerner to approximately 2,000 votes for Republican gubernatorial candidate Charles Percy.

some Republicans in downstate Illinois and even in some suburban areas of Cook County are doing exactly the same things that the Democratic organization in Chicago is doing before, during, and after an election. In DuPage County, the strongest Republican county in Illinois, directly west of Cook County, Republican election officials have been notorious for their behavior on election day. Voter registrations are not properly checked, ballot boxes are taken home to be counted, peculiar vote totals show up on election night, and vote tallies are held until Republican election officials get some idea of what kind of vote is needed in DuPage County. Indeed, it has been alleged by some that, in parts of downstate Illinois, farmers vote without leaving their fields, and that trees, chickens, and stones all vote. °

The Democratic party in Chicago does not win massive electoral victories by vote stealing and coercion. While some of these things do go on in some precincts, the party's strength is based for the most part on three things: service to the voter; hard work; and sharp tactics. The seasoned professionals in the Democratic organization, from the precinct level up to the county chairman, know every trick in the book, take advantage of every opportunity, do their homework, and play for keeps. If politics is the art of the possible, Democratic politicians in Chicago leave no stone unturned in demonstrating that all kinds of things are possible if only one applies oneself with dedication, ingenuity, and intestinal fortitude to the task at hand.

Intraparty Relationships. The problems of the Republican party in Chicago are compounded by the relationship of the ward

---

° On election night, in the 1964 gubernatorial election between incumbent Otto Kerner and challenger Charles Percy, I was in a suite rented by the Kerner campaign staff in the Conrad Hilton hotel in Chicago to receive the election returns. On the board, the tally coming from all across the state of Illinois indicated that Kerner was running a solid 190,000 to 200,000 votes ahead of Percy. But by 11 P.M. Percy had not yet conceded, one reason being that DuPage County had not yet reported. However, six of Chicago's key wards had not reported either. By 11:30 P.M. the Republicans in DuPage gave up and began to turn in their vote returns. Shortly afterward, the six Chicago wards began reporting. In 1966, when millionaire Michael Butler ran for the state senate from DuPage County, he sent out a first-class mailing to all registered Republicans in DuPage County. Almost 20 percent of the letters came back to the Butler campaign headquarters, indicating that those registered Republicans had died or moved. Several years before, the Republican-dominated Illinois General Assembly had passed a law requiring re-registration of all voters in Democratic Cook County but not in the Republican counties of downstate Illinois.

committeemen to two other potential sources of power for the party, Republican officeholders in the city and county, and potential financial contributors to the party. When a Republican in Chicago wins a city or county office, he has usually done it without much help from the party organization. Since he is not indebted to that organization, the perquisites of office—jobs, contacts, and money—which come under his control are distributed by him personally, not through the party organization. Relationships are thus established between ambitious officeholders and patronage-hungry ward committeemen, not between the committeemen and the county central committee. To get patronage, a Republican ward committeeman must deal with the individual Republican officeholder, rather than with the party organization. The officeholders, for their part, are interested in their own personal fortunes, not in the party's situation in Chicago. Consequently, Republican control of city or county offices generally fragments the party into contending splinter groups, vying with each other for a better place in the political sun.

The contrast with the Democratic party is obvious. On the Republican side is a weak, fragmented minority party, dominated by ambitious, self-serving individuals. On the other side of the political fence is a highly centralized, tightly disciplined organization, which forces every officeholder and member of the organization to subordinate his personal needs and interests to the overall interests of the organization. In such a milieu, the wonder is not that so many Republican ward committeemen in Chicago collaborate with the Democratic organization, but rather that any of them pursue an independent policy and maintain an effective ward organization.

The situation of the Republican party in Chicago and Cook County is aggravated by another factor. It is a fact of life in Chicago, and indeed, in America, that the major support for the Republican party from within the electorate comes from middle-class and upper-middle-class people in our society, while the major support for the Democratic party in cities like Chicago, and in the country, comes from the working classes and lower-middle classes. This has a profound effect on the relationship of the professional politicians in both parties to their constituents. A heavy percentage of Republican voters do not need or want patronage jobs. They have been brought up in the Anglo-Saxon-Protestant folklore of rugged individualism and self-reliance, of social and familial traditions of individual initiative and effort, of a separation of authority between church and state, between the various organs of the state, and between the state and voluntary organizations and individuals. These traditions manifest themselves politically in a primary concern with limiting the role of government and politics in order to protect the freedom of the individual.

The Democratic party, in contrast, is dominated much more by its Catholic, Jewish, and black elements. The Catholics and the Jews have long traditions of familial and religious collective responsibility in dealing with problems. They come mostly from countries in which the tendency to turn to the state for remedial action is traditional. They are striving, together with the blacks, for equality more than for freedom in American society. There is consequently a greater willingness among these groups to accept the use of governmental and political power to get what they want from American society.

On the local level in cities like Chicago, these attitudes lead to a rejection of participation in politics on the part of those groups in the city and county whose natural affiliation is with the Republican party. But the Democratic electorate, rooted in the working-class and lower-middle-class elements in the city, not only accepts but actively promotes the use of the political process to secure the things they want in life.

Since many of the jobs and prerogatives which are the rewards of participation in politics in cities like Chicago are beneath the aspiration levels of many Republican voters, it is difficult for Republican politicians to recruit their constituency to work in political organizations. But the opposite is true in the Democratic party. For those elements in our society who are beginning to climb the ladder of American life, many of the rewards which politicians have to offer in exchange for labor in the vineyards of the precincts are respectable, desirable, and worthwhile. In other words, Democrats as a group need the jobs and favors which politicians can dispense, but most Republicans do not. Consequently, Democratic politicians have a much more fertile field to plow in seeking help for their organizations than their Republican counterparts.

Republican politicians seeking help for their organizations can usually get such help from one of two possible sources. First, they can try to compete with the Democratic party in offering rewards and perquisites to people interested in participating in politics for those reasons. But since they are at a significant disadvantage in cities like Chicago in competing with their Democratic counterparts in offering those rewards, they usually get the leavings. Who in his right mind would seek out a Republican politician in Chicago for a job, a favor, or a connection?

The only other potential source of help for a Republican politician are those rare and unusual individuals who are willing to participate in the drudgery of political work without monetary compensation or political rewards. Whereas it is sometimes possible to recruit such people for short periods of time prior to an election, it is almost impossible to recruit them to work precincts year around, to canvass voters, to distribute literature, and to raise money for the ward organizations. This kind of voluntary effort must be measured against the day-to-day, year-round contact of Democratic workers with their constituents in the precincts. The problem of recruiting volunteer help is further complicated by the fact that most volunteer amateur politicians involve themselves only in campaigns which have some significant ideological or philosophical thrust. Those campaigns normally involve national elections and candidates for national office, who are ideologically oriented and have enough charisma to attract to their personal campaigns volunteers who do not normally work for political parties, but for individual candidates, and who are of little use to ward organization politicians.

Few candidates for local offices, however, have charisma, are ideologically oriented, or can attract volunteers to their campaigns. Most campaigns for local offices are not run on the basis of issues and ideology but, rather, on the basis of personal contact, service to constituents, and strict attention to the mechanical details of good precinct work. Since these things interest volunteer workers the least, few Republican ward committeemen can ever recruit signif icant volunteer help in their wards.

There is one source, however, from which the Republican party in Chicago and Cook County can recruit volunteer help, the Young Republican organization. Unlike the Democratic party in Chicago, the Republican party in the city has a somewhat active Young

Republican organization. Indeed, the YRs (as they are known in the trade), have served as a political training ground for some of the most important Republican leaders at the county and state levels.

In Chicago, the YRs provide about one-third of the Republican precinct captains, and some Republican ward organizations call on the YRs to help in local campaigns. However, a built-in conflict exists between the YR leadership and the Republican ward committeemen. Like most professional politicians, Republican ward committeemen are suspicious of and generally hostile to amateurs attempting to infiltrate their ward organizations. They recognize, too, that the most professionally oriented among the YRs have political ambitions which may involve dumping the old Republican ward leadership and replacing it with people from the YR organization in the ward. So, while the Republican party in Chicago relies upon the YRs to supply a significant percentage of the precinct captains in elections, the organization is unwilling to allow the YRs to become too strong and has consistently sought to keep them in a position of subordination to the regular organization. Young Republican leaders are usually slated for city and county offices which they have little chance to win. So, while it is true that a pool of volunteer precinct help is available to the Republican party in Chicago in the Young Republican organization, it is also true that the professionals in the Republican organizations try to keep the YRs under control and on the periphery of party power. That policy effectively restricts the use of the major source of precinct workers for the party.

There is one other possible source of assistance to the Republican party in Chicago whose potential has been neutralized by a combination of Democratic co-optation and Republican ineffectiveness—the potential financial contributors to the party. Since the Republican party controls few offices in the county, and practically none in the city, it does not have access to the governmental sources of money which any party needs in order to maintain an efficient organization. Consequently, the Republican party in Chicago must rely on contributions from private sources. Normally, one would expect that bankers, businessmen, and those who have inherited wealth would support the Republican party. This is generally true at the national level of American politics, where Republican bankers, businessmen, and the wealthy usually support their party financially. It does not follow, however, that those same individuals are willing to support the Republican party at the local level in cities like Chicago. For bankers and businessmen, like all other individuals in a community, need services and favors from government. Since the Republican party in Chicago and Cook County does not control the government, the party cannot provide the services and favors that the bankers and businessmen need in the city and county. And, conversely, since the Democratic party usually controls all major offices in the city and county, that party can provide the favors and services the businessmen and bankers need.

It is a fact of political life in Chicago and Cook County that, while most businessmen and bankers in the city are Republicans at the state and national levels, they are not Republicans locally. Like the poor, the working class, and the middle class, the economic aristocracy in the city subordinates its ideological and political aspirations to its economic needs. This is true at both the city and ward levels. At the city and county levels, Republican bankers and businessmen support the Cook County organization with contributions, buy tables for the $100-a-plate dinners, endorse Mayor Daley for re-election, support Democratic candidates for city and county offices, serve on city committees appointed by Mayor Daley, and cooperate with the party both politically and economically. At the ward level, banks, major corporations, public utility firms, and many smaller industrial companies cooperate with Democratic ward committeemen. In return, the ward committeemen provide help in zoning, police and fire protection, leniency in inspections, and tax reductions. At the citywide level, the organization provides the same kinds of services for the giant corporations and banks in the Loop.

"Nobody's independent," Alderman Vito Marzullo told *Chicago Daily News* reporter Lois Wille in 1967. "Nobody in the world. In my ward I've got Ryerson Steel Company, and the Ryerson family is the biggest Republicans there is. But you know what? Every year they make a $300 contribution to my organization. What do I care if they're Republicans? They need service and favors, the same as everybody else in my ward." *

---

* "Dear Alderman Marzullo," wrote an executive officer of a major public institution in Marzullo's ward in a letter the alderman showed me. "First, let me congratulate you on your

Because of these relationships between businessmen, bankers, and civic leaders, and the Democratic organization, the major potential private financial support available to the Republican party in Chicago and Cook County is effectively shut off, and the party is left in a financial situation in which it cannot get money from control of government offices, and does not get money from those private financial sources from which the local party should normally benefit. Occasionally, the party will find a financial angel like multi-millionaire insurance tycoon W. Clement Stone, who seems to be willing to spend some of his private fortune on improving the prospects of the local Republican party. But, while Republican politicians generally are willing to take money from whatever source they can, most of them do not share in the good things distributed by people like Mr. Stone. Private contributors like Mr. Stone do not give money to local party organizations. They make their contributions to individual candidates in whom they happen to have a particular interest, and much of the money goes, not to the ward organizations, but to high-priced, high-powered advertising, and to television and mass-media campaigns in behalf of the candidates. In such a situation, it is generally safer for a collaborating Republican ward committeeman to continue his relationship with the Democratic organization than to trade that safe relationship for a risky one with a nonprofessional contributor to the party who has little interest in his local situation.

In summary, the Republican party in Chicago and Cook County has been the minority party for forty years because of a combination of factors—the strength of the Democratic party in the nation, as well as in the city; the ethnic, religious, and racial makeup of Chicago's population; the local party's inability to win elections without outside support from the suburban and downstate Republi-

---

re-election as Alderman of the 25th Ward. I can say this because you are one of the few full-time Aldermen whose capability for caring for needs of your constituents as well as for the city as a whole have been so well recognized that you have no opposition in the coming elections.

"About three years ago, you were kind enough to introduce an ordinance providing for a Residential Planned Development (Institutional) which covered our property between ——— and ———. We also own property south of ——— and plan to make use of same for parking purposes . . . .

"The block south of ——— is zoned 'residential' and I wonder whether you would consider an ordinance adding these areas to our Planned Development Program."

cans, which has not been forthcoming; the lack of financial support from normally Republican supporters; the inability to recruit workers without gaining and holding city and county offices; the caliber of professional Republican politicians in the city and county; and the efficiency and effectiveness of the local Democratic machine in getting out its own vote and in co-opting local Republicans.

However, even if one recognizes the sorry state of the Republican party in Chicago and the dominance of the political life of the city and county by the local Democratic machine, another question must be raised and answered. How badly do the people who actually control the Republican party in Chicago and Cook County really fare in Dick Daley's town?

Not badly at all. Republican bankers profit handsomely from the deposit of public funds, the purchase of municipal bonds, and the financing of huge construction projects. Republican State Street merchants benefit nicely from the construction of expressways, parking lots, and improved transit facilities which bring customers to their doors. Republican hotel owners are thankful for the many conventions brought to the city by Chicago's zealous mayor, and for the availability of entertainment facilities for pleasure-seeking conventioneers on the fringes of the Loop. Republican real estate tycoons sleep better at night dreaming of the zoning changes and favorable tax assessments they might be able to ask for. Republican construction firm executives can calculate earnings more hopefully after examining their contracts for expressways, new office buildings, and residential complexes. Republican newspaper publishers can affirm their dedication to a free press while they accept city and county advertising contracts, favorable tax assessments, and the illegal use of the boulevards by their delivery trucks that speed to get all the news that is fit to print to Chicagoland's citizenry. Republican churchmen can offer prayers in thanks for contributions and services rendered to their flocks by the politicians. Republican public utility and steel company board chairmen can issue better reports to their stockholders when regulatory pollution ordinances are not passed or are loosely enforced. Republican university trustees can balance their budgets better after totaling up the tax dollars they save as tax-exempt charitable institutions on their extensive real estate holdings in the city.

This is not to say that all these relationships are bad for the city and the community at large. A thriving city needs construction, investment, a good business climate, and a favorable tax rate. But, in the order of priorities, and in the expenditure of funds, Chicago's Republican economic aristocracy benefits immensely from its relationship to Chicago's Democratic machine, in contrast to the pathetic, small-change practices of Republican politicians in the city. And, of course, while the poor and the powerless do get some goods and services from the trickle-down politics of Chicago's Democratic political, and Republican economic, ruling class, the system benefits those at the top immeasurably more than those at the bottom. It was ever thus in all societies, including those which preach proletarian equality for all while they practice aristocratic inequality for some.

It may well be that the relationship between the Irish Catholic Democratic political rulers and the Anglo-Saxon-Protestant Republican economic overlords of Chicago is typical of the structure of all societies in which political and economic power is juxtaposed in the interests of those who hold that power. And the Irish have advanced their economic and social status significantly in comparison with their situation in the past on the old sod in their homeland, where they were not allowed to share in the good things that the possession of power confers by their Anglo-Saxon English oppressors.

In Chicago, where party labels are relatively meaningless and serve as a facade behind which the real business of the community is conducted by the power seekers and holders, the realities of "Who Governs?" are that the ostensible public differences between politicians and persons of power in both parties are subordinate to their private interests. As for the shibboleth that the Republican party in Chicago should really strive to capture political control of the city in the interests of its constituents, the myth can be laid to rest and given a decent burial. As *Chicago Daily News* City Hall reporter Jay McMullen once headlined a column, "With Mayor Dick Daley, Who Needs a 'Republican'?"

The Independents

Although former Alderman Mathias ("Paddy") Bauler may have been right when he said in 1955 that "Chicago ain't ready for reform," the Democratic machine in Chicago has been periodically challenged by liberal, independent Democrats who have striven mightily to force the machine to mend its ways and serve what they consider to be the public interest of the citizenry of the city. The goals of the independents vary from "seeking to make democracy work and to improve the quality of life in our society" by implementing a "program for good government and progressive legislation through political action," to defeating the mayor and "firing as many of his patronage employees as is legally possible." But all the independent political movements in Chicago have been unified in the belief that reform is not only desirable but possible. "The real test of our experiment," according to a 1970 newsletter of the Independent Precinct Organization, the newest reform group in Chicago, "is whether we can persist and bring about not only occasional victories but complete reform in Chicago politics." The task may be difficult, and the obstacles many, but virtue will triumph in the end. Reforming politics in Chicago "is a feat we cannot accomplish alone, but we can be a catalyst in something of a model if we have the guts and intelligence to fight until we win an enduring victory."

Are these hopes and aspirations realistic in Chicago? What are the prospects for bringing about reform or destruction of the machine through independent political action? What kinds of people participate in such movements? What kinds of tactics do they employ to bring about their objectives? And, finally, how does the machine deal with such challenges to its power from the true believers in the efficacy of the good society?

The independent political reform movements in Chicago fall into two broad categories, those which believe that the machine can be reformed from within the party and those which believe that they must remain outside the local Democratic party because it cannot be captured from within, only destroyed from without. Their tactics vary from organizing to elect independent candidates to local offices and defeat the machine's candidates, to endorsing and publicizing the qualifications of political candidates, to researching and publicizing issues in order to educate the citizenry of the city so that they can participate more meaningfully in the political process. They garner support, from time to time, from the newspapers, civic-minded businessmen, reform-oriented religious leaders, and, occasionally, from the moribund Republican party in Chicago. But their political effectiveness is stringently limited by the lack of any mass popular support from the citizenry of the city.

While the independent political organizations may have diverse objectives and different tactics, they operate from the basis of a limited, homogeneous membership, and have little rapport with most of the population of the city. Their members generally fit the mold that political scientist James Q. Wilson described in his study of independent Democratic political movements, *The Amateur Democrat.* "For the most part," wrote Wilson, "they are young, well-educated professional people, including a large number of women. In style of life, they are distinctly middle- and upper-middle-class; in mood and outlook, they are products of the generation which came of age after the Second World War and particularly after the Korean conflict; in political beliefs, they are almost entirely among the liberals of the left. They bring to politics a concern for ideas and ideals. . . . Because the amateur is attracted to politics by principles, there is some overlap between those who are interested in politics of principle and those who are, in a broad sense, intellectuals. But the overlap between the world of intellectuals and the world of club politics is not great, for although many amateur politicians, particularly in the Democratic Party, are intellectual 'consumers,' few are intellectual 'producers.' . . . There is . . . a striking shortage of intellectual producers such as creative scholars, artists, and writers. Few university professors of stature are found active in club politics, and serious writers are usually active in politics, if at all, at a different level." The active membership of such groups, as Wilson also points out, is generally recruited from two groups in the population—middle-class professional Jews and civic-minded white Anglo-Saxon Protestants. Few Catholics and blacks are attracted to active participation in such movements.

The political independents are also separated from the great mass of the population by their philosophy of politics and of the role of government in society. Since they are generally middle class and community-minded, they reject a politics of material rewards for individuals in proportion to their contributions to the political parties and believe that special concessions to private groups violates the principles of good government. In cities like Chicago, liberal Jews and white Protestants are a distinct minority in a population which is predominantly black, Latin, and ethnic Catholic. The anti-white feelings of a considerable percentage of the black community in Chicago, the political ineffectiveness of the Latins, and the clannishness of the ethnic Catholics who are generally suspicious of middle class, intellectual white Protestants and Jews, make it difficult for the independent political movements to make any contact with the mass of the population. The ethnic Catholics and Latins are conservatively oriented politically, are uncomfortable with middle-class intellectualism, and are conditioned to membership in family, ethnic, and religious organizations rather than in communitywide or citywide civic-minded groups. And the welfare poor and working-class blacks, Latins, and ethnic Catholics are also oriented toward a politics of clout and favoritism in a city in which they constitute a majority of the population, and in which politicians are cognizant of the need to pacify their demands.

Consequently, the independents have been able to successfully challenge the machine only in those wards in the city in which a substantial proportion of the population fits the mold described by Professor Wilson. Thus, the 5th Ward on Chicago's South Side, in which the University of Chicago is located, has traditionally sent a liberal, reform Democratic white alderman to the city council, since the ward has a plethora of "intellectual consumers" who are attracted to residency in the ward because of its proximity to the university. But no other South Side, southeast side, or southwest side ward has sent a liberal, white alderman to the council in recent history. And, while several liberal black aldermen have been elected from several South Side black wards in recent years, theirs were generally victories of black candidates who were not opposed by capable, well-known black machine-oriented candidates. Had the machine had the foresight to find and groom capable black machine candidates in those racially changing wards, those liberal black aldermen might not be sitting in the Chicago City Council today. In black wards, where capable black politicians have been groomed, the machine has had little trouble in fending off challenges from liberal, independent black candidates.*

* There have been some ripples of black, Latin, and ethnic Catholic independent movements, with some local, limited success, but no indications of much impact on the city's traditional political patterns.

In the last few years, the independents have had some limited success in challenging the machine on Chicago's North Side. In 1971 Alderman William Singer of the 43rd Ward and Alderman Dick Simpson of the 44th Ward mounted successful campaigns and defeated machine-sponsored candidates for the city council in their wards, but their victories were due to a fortuitous concatenation of circumstances in their wards which aided them in successfully challenging and defeating the machine.

Both wards are located on Chicago's mid-North Side, fronting on Lake Michigan, and are composed of a heterogeneous population mix which is peculiar to that area of the city. The eastern ends of both wards are made up of high-rise apartments, flanked by substantial four-plus-one apartment developments just west of the lakefront, buttressed by the Old Town, New Town, and Lincoln Park neighborhoods, with deteriorating housing and some slum areas in the western ends of the wards. The high-rise apartment buildings have attracted a substantial number of middle-class and upper-middle-class, fairly well-educated "intellectual consumers" to the area. The four-plus-one apartment developments, which are mainly cheaply built studio and one-bedroom apartments, have attracted a substantial number of young, well-educated, single men and women, and young marrieds just beginning to climb the economic and social ladder.

The Old Town, New Town, and Lincoln Park areas have also attracted a substantial number of "intellectual consumers," radicals, hippie types, and liberal middle-class business and professional people who are making their last stand in the city. The area has a high percentage of liberal Jews and white, middle-class Protestants, and a low percentage of small-homeowning, neighborhood-oriented ethnic Catholics. Both wards had aging Democratic ward commit-teemen, who were formerly powerhouse members of the organiza-tion but who had become increasingly ineffective. In both wards, the local Democratic organizations underestimated the strength of the liberal independents, overestimated the strength of their own organizations in their changing wards, and slated weak candidates who had no appeal to the burgeoning middle-class, liberal popula-tion in the eastern end of the wards. The independents were highly organized, imbued with an *esprit de corps*, and financially solvent. In essence, the independents created countervailing machines in those two wards which confronted declining, aging Democratic organizations which were losing touch with the changing population of their wards. In both wards, the independents were thus able to at least match and even surpass the machine in both quantity and quality of workers, supporters, and voters.

The great hope of the independents is that they can use the experiences and tactics which were successful in these two wards, build a citywide independent organization ward by ward, and capture control of the city council and, eventually, of the mayor's office. But an objective appraisal of those hopes indicates that while there is some possibility of creating strong, independent political movements in three or four other North Side wards, there is little chance that it can be done in most of the city.

Even in the other three or four North Side wards which are comparable to the 43rd and 44th wards, where high-rise and four-plus-one apartments are being built, countervailing population pressures are developing from the black, Spanish-speaking, and southern-white elements of Chicago's population who are moving into Chicago's North Side wards in force. And the machine, cognizant of the inadequacies of the aging ward committeemen in those wards, has replaced them with young, hardworking, committeemen of a moderately liberal political persuasion, who are more attuned to the middle-class, better-educated residents of the high-rises and four-plus-ones.

There is another disadvantage under which the liberal, independent movements in Chicago operate in attempting to overthrow the Democratic machine. Since they do not have patronage and, indeed, are opposed to patronage, they must rely on volunteer help. Political volunteers are usually young, idealistic, and excited by the prospect of participating in a political campaign aimed at overthrowing the machine. But young people age, idealism gives way to pragmatism, and the excitement of the first political campaign evaporates in the realization that political precinct work the second and third times around is not exciting and rewarding but dull and frustrating. Young idealists get married, have children, assume greater personal responsibilities, become more deeply involved in their own careers as they move up the economic scale, and become less community-oriented as they become more self- and family-oriented. It is difficult for young wives with children to do precinct work, or young husbands with growing families and greater career responsibilities to spend evenings and weekends educating unwilling and recalcitrant citizens to fight the good fight for civic reform. And, when the children reach school age, it is time to make the move to the suburbs for schools, a backyard, and an easier way of life.

Consequently, a volunteer political organization, unable and unwilling to compensate its members with monetary rewards or career opportunities, must constantly replace its original constituents with new volunteer workers. If the neighborhood remains stable and signs of urban blight do not appear, there is some hope for attracting new, young idealists into the organization to replace those who move on to greener pastures. But as the neighborhoods west of the lake deteriorate, and the ubiquitous four-plus-ones become the slums of the future as the young marrieds move out, it is likely that the percentage of the middle-class, well-educated segment of the population of these neighborhoods will decline, and the percentage of lower-class, uneducated people will increase, even in those North Side neighborhoods where there are strong, independent movements today. If the machine adapts to the changing population, maintains the strength of the regular organization by patronage and discipline, and pacifies the steadily growing lower-class populations of these areas, it can probably outlast the independents and keep the virus from spreading to the rest of the city.

The independents' hopes of building an alliance with liberal, independent black and Spanish-speaking leadership in the black and Spanish-speaking wards are inhibited by a built-in dilemma. The reforms they propose—the abolition of patronage, putting city services on a nonpartisan basis, eliminating favoritism and clout, and blunting the power of the political machine—have little appeal to the blacks and Spanish speaking who are now politically coming into their own. What the independents are asking the blacks and Spanish speaking to do is to give up the prerogatives that go with political power, at a time when political power is passing into their hands. If the blacks and the Spanish-speaking population accept that approach to politics and government, it would be demonstrating a concern for the commonweal and the public interest which has never been characteristic of people in their situation. As black state representative Harold Washington of Chicago's South Side declared on February 14, 1975, in announcing that he supported Mayor Daley for re-election, "it would set back black political empowerment seven or eight or more years if Alderman William Singer defeats Daley on February 25th [in the mayoral primary election]." According to Washington, while he wanted corrections made in the patronage system, he did not want it to be abolished. "It helped other ethnic groups," Washington told black *Chicago Tribune* columnist Vernon Jarrett. "Why should it be denied use by my people?"

The independents' program for the future of politics and government in Chicago runs counter to the interests of those segments of the population which are now coming into their own in the city. Their program reflects the outlook and philosophy of middle-class, well-educated, professional people who are predominantly of Jewish and white Anglo-Saxon-Protestant origin which may well fit the needs of the burgeoning suburbs of Cook County. But it does not coincide with either the aspirations or the interests of the poor and working-class blacks, the Spanish speaking, and the ethnic Catholics who inhabit the city of Chicago.

The machine has had little need to concern itself with the threat from the political independent movements in Chicago. Working from the base of its political and governmental power, its patronage army, and its ability to pacify the aspirations and needs of the bulk of the population of the city, the machine has generally been able to ignore the independent movements in Chicago. When it has been seriously threatened on occasion by those movements, the machine has either co-opted the leadership, adopted some of the goals of the movement and disarmed its potential appeal to the electorate, or relied on its entrenched power to fend off any serious challenge. Thus, the Paul Douglases, the Adlai Stevenson IIIs, and the Paul Simons, have been granted power and position within the organization. The Abner Mikvas, the Anthony Scarianos, the Robert Manns, the Leon Depreses, and the William Singers have been tolerated, if not embraced. The William Clarks have been punished, the Dan Walkers have been ostracized, and the Dick Simpsons have been rejected. The machine is comfortable in its relationships with the independents, knowing its strength, capable of adapting to the changing city, and secure in its conviction that it can outlast the opposition.

❧ 7 ❧

Government and the Machine

The most dangerous threat to the Chicago machine's existence is the power of government to curtail or eliminate the activities of the machine by legislation and regulation. Imperative to the machine's continued existence and prosperity is the ability to fend off, control, or block such regulation by governmental agencies at the three levels of American government—federal, state, and local. How does the machine deal with the threat to its power from Washington, Springfield, or City Hall?

Dealing with Washington

In the American federal system, local communities like the city of Chicago are creatures of state government, are directly regulated by state government, and have few direct legal and political relationships with the federal government in Washington. However, most big cities depend on federal subsidies for schools, welfare, improvement of transportation facilities, urban renewal, and other vital services which local communities must provide to their citizenry. Although local communities must meet federal standards to qualify for those funds, direct federal-local relationships of a regulatory nature are minimal as long as the local community meets federal administrative guidelines. Since the United States Constitution is practically silent on political parties and political processes in the United States, the role of the federal government in regulating local political activities is also minimal. Local political parties are free to pursue their objectives and conduct their business with little supervision or control from Washington, except for the federal government's investigatory and prosecutive powers.

One possible danger stems from the legislative power of Congress. Either house of Congress may delve into the intricacies of local politics in communities like Chicago by using the investigatory powers of its standing or special committees, which can hold public hearings in a local community, take testimony, publicize the conduct of local officials to the media, and recommend remedial action by Congress in matters in which federal funds are involved. However, a powerful local party usually has little to fear from congressional committees. With seven staunch Democratic congressmen from the city representing the local machine's interest in Washington, with one Democratic senator in the United States Senate and the possibility of good relationships with a Republican senator from the state like the late Senator Everett Dirksen, with solid Democratic control of both houses of Congress for the past forty years, and with a powerful influence on potential Democratic presidential candidates in Congress because of Illinois' importance in national presidential elections, the Chicago machine has had little trouble in keeping congressional investigations into local political situations to a minimum.

A second source of possible federal involvement in local politics is the executive branch of government. Administrative agencies like the Department of Justice with its prosecutive powers and the Internal Revenue Service with its investigatory powers are the major potential sources of trouble from within the administrative bureaucracy in Washington. Other executive agencies such as the departments of Housing and Urban Development, Health, Education and Welfare, and Transportation, which disburse federal funds to local communities under guidelines set by Congress, can also affect the fortunes of local politicians. The key to dealing with these agencies and keeping them from involving themselves in local political situations is a good relationship with the president of the United States. Since executive agencies in the federal administrative bureaucracy operate under his direct authority and control, a word to the wise in those agencies from the president will usually suffice to discourage them from delving too deeply into local political situations.

The Democratic organization of Cook County has a powerful weapon at its disposal in dealing with a Democratic president or a Democratic presidential aspirant—its ability to deliver or not to deliver the state of Illinois for a Democratic candidate in national elections. Since Illinois is one of the critical, bellwether states in presidential elections, it behooves a Democratic president or presidential candidate to maintain good relationships with that organization. The same rule of thumb applies to all potential Democratic presidential aspirants. "Daley's the ball game," the late Senator Robert F. Kennedy told a reporter at a press conference, when asked about the importance of the Democratic organization in Chicago with regard to Kennedy's campaign for the presidential nomination in 1968.* In numerous cases in recent years Democratic presidents have dampened down the ardor of bureaucrats in agencies such as HEW and HUD, when those bureaucrats were excessively eager in applying the standards set by Congress for granting subsidies to the city of Chicago.

When a Republican president occupies the White House and Republican appointees direct the major federal executive departments, the problem is somewhat more complex for the local Democratic organization. However, a *modus vivendi* can be worked out between pragmatic men on both sides of the political fence. The local organization can deliver a block of Democratic votes in Congress on matters which are important to the president but not significant to the local party. Mayor Daley can offer public support for the president's national programs and help to mobilize public opinion in his community for those programs. Thus, when President Richard Nixon proclaimed the ninety-day wage-price freeze in 1971, Mayor Daley declared, "I would hope and urge everyone would cooperate. I hope it is not made a political issue. It is far more important than politics. . . . The President is to be congratulated on his courage and determination and willingness to try to do

---

* When Kennedy came to see Daley to solicit his advice as to what he should do to secure the Democratic presidential nomination in 1968, Daley is supposed to have replied, looking askance at Kennedy's shaggy, long haired appearance, "Get a haircut!"

something to stop the running inflation in this country and particularly to stop the international speculation which has been taking too much advantage of the dollar. We've got to start to protect ourselves at home and do the things that will make a better society." The president, according to the mayor, had consulted with "some of the great minds of the country." Also, when the Pentagon Papers were published, Mayor Daley supported President Nixon's position. In a press conference, Daley said that publishing the secret Pentagon Papers "should be called into question." Insofar as the war in Indochina was concerned, the mayor said that "President Nixon was doing the best he could to get the United States out of Indochina."

It might also be possible, in a presidential election year, for the local Democratic organization to concentrate its efforts on the local offices and let the chips fall where they may for the Democratic presidential candidate. In return, for his part, á Republican president could keep a tight rein on Republican bureaucrats in the federal administrative agencies who might want to disburse federal funds to community organizations opposed to the Democratic organization in the city, or who might want to cut off federal funds to Chicago's schools unless they proceeded more rapidly to integrate the school system, and on investigative personnel in the Department of Justice and the Internal Revenue Service who are too eager to look into local matters.

Potential threats from federal law enforcement agencies can best be dealt with when a Democratic president occupies the White House by having the senior Democratic senator from Illinois recommend a Democratic lawyer with good relationships to the Democratic organization of Cook County for the position of United States Attorney for the Northern District of Illinois, and by maintaining good professional, political relationships with the occupant of the White House and his attorney general. Thus, competent, capable attorneys such as Otto Kerner, Edward Hanrahan, and Thomas Foran, with good reputations and backgrounds but also cognizant of the interests of the Democratic party of Cook County, are usually selected for that office. Since Mayor Daley would normally be consulted by the senior Democratic senator from Illinois about such an appointment, it would be almost impossible for someone hostile to the Democratic organization of Cook County to be selected for that position.

When a Republican president occupies the White House, the problem is somewhat more complicated. Normally, however, good relationships with a senior Republican senator from Illinois, such as the late Senator Everett McKinley Dirksen, will suffice to ensure the appointment of a Republican United States Attorney for Northern Illinois who can build a respectable record in the office without seriously inhibiting the business of the Democratic machine. When such an arrangement breaks down, serious consequences can result for the Democratic organization of Cook County. With the death of Senator Dirksen in 1970, and Senator Charles Percy's emergence as the senior Republican Senator from Illinois, the Democratic Cook County organization found itself in a potentially dangerous situation vis-à-vis the federal prosecuting authorities in the state of Illinois. In 1972, the local Democratic party faced a Republican president, Richard Nixon, who was determined to win re-election at all costs, who was aware of the importance of the state of Illinois in national presidential elections, and who was convinced that the presidency was stolen from him in 1960 by the Democratic organization of Cook County. Nixon's appointment of a hard-driving, ambitious, capable young lawyer, James R. Thompson, as United States Attorney for Northern Illinois, marked the beginning of an intensive drive on the part of the Republican-controlled Department of Justice to break the power of the Daley organization in Cook County. The conviction under federal statutes of a former governor, a former state director of revenue, an incumbent county clerk of Cook County, and several aldermen, with more indictments and prosecutions indicated in the foreseeable future, provided a dramatic demonstration of what could happen to the local Democratic organization's interests when confronted with a hostile Republican president, attorney general, and local United States attorney.

From time to time, the Cook County Democratic organization has had to deal with threats to its interests emanating from orders handed down by federal district court judges involving federal funds for the city of Chicago which are essential to the city's fiscal stability. Since 1970, Judge Richard Austin, who was nominated to the federal district court by former Senator Paul Douglas with

Daley's approval, has been trying, without success, to force the Chicago Housing Authority to build public housing in white areas of the city. The Authority, which is controlled by men close to the local party leadership, and the Chicago City Council have, to date, successfully pursued a policy of noncompliance with Judge Austin's attempts to force the city to alter its long-established policy of concentrating public housing projects in black areas in deference to the hostility of Chicago's ethnic white citizens to any attempt to integrate the city's neighborhoods with such projects. In 1975 a local federal district court judge ordered the city to throw out a list of candidates who passed a Chicago Civil Service Commission examination for the police department on the grounds that the examination was unfair to blacks and Latins, and another judge in Washington, D.C. ordered nineteen million dollars in federal revenue-sharing funds withheld from Chicago until the city complied with the federal court's order to give a new examination.

But, in summary, it is fair to say that, while opportunities exist for federal regulation, investigation, and possible prosecution of local politicians by the federal government, the instances in which such action is taken are rare indeed. Over the past forty years, the local Democratic organization in Cook County has demonstrated a willingness and ability to come to terms with or fight off such federal activity by using its political clout within the national Democratic party and by cooperating with the national Republican leadership when necessary.

Dealing with Springfield

The greatest potential legal danger to the machine is the power of the state government in Springfield. Since the city of Chicago, like all municipalities in the state of Illinois, has no inherent powers of its own, except for the home-rule powers granted by the state constitution, and has only those powers granted to it by the state, the governmental powers and political institutions of the city can be altered or emasculated by the state legislature. And, since Illinois often has a Republican governor and a Republican-controlled legislature, the massive legal powers which the state exercises over the city are sometimes in "enemy" hands.

The basic services which the government of the city must

provide to its citizenry must be maintained at a decent level if the Democratic hold on the city is to be maintained. Order must be guaranteed, taxes kept at an acceptable level, decent public transportation supplied, an adequate school system maintained, and satisfactory sanitation and recreational facilities provided. If the state legislature does not provide sufficient aid or delegate adequate power to the city, or approve the disbursement of sufficient federal funds for these programs to the city, there is always the danger of a citizen revolt aimed at throwing the machine out of office.

The state government in Springfield has always had the power, too, to alter, by state law or constitutional amendment, the format of the governments of the city of Chicago and Cook County. The legal powers of the mayor can be restricted, the composition of the city council can be altered, or the powers of administrative offices can be diminished. Changes can be made in the electoral laws governing the dates of local elections or legal qualifications for getting on the ballot. Control of the election machinery by the Democratic-dominated county clerk of Cook County and Board of Election Commissioners of the City of Chicago can be restricted or withdrawn.

Specific steps like taking the control over the city's budget from the mayor and giving it back to the city council would significantly reduce the power of the mayor. Changing the ward system in Chicago and the composition of the city council from a body of fifty aldermen representing fifty wards to an elective body of approximately fifteen aldermen elected at large from the city would reduce the power of the aldermen and, more important, of the ward committeemen in providing patronage and services to their constituents in the wards. Scheduling the mayoralty and aldermanic elections to coincide with national presidential elections would significantly improve the chances of the Republican party for capturing the mayoralty and a majority of seats on the Chicago City Council. Reducing the requirements for getting on the ballot for ward committeeman would make it easier to challenge incumbent Democratic committeemen. In other words, the state government in Springfield, which is often dominated by the Republican party, has usually had the power to alter the financial, political, and governmental systems under which the machine in Chicago must operate.

The most important legal step the state government in Springfield could take to reduce the power of the Democratic machine in Chicago would be to make a simple change in the civil service law governing the city's employees. Under state law, almost all city and county positions in Chicago and Cook County are required to be filled through civil service procedures. Legal qualifications, examinations, and hiring and promotion are ostensibly governed by the merit system. However, there is one loophole in the state civil service law governing employees in Chicago and Cook County. Whenever a qualified employee cannot be found for a position in the city or county, the administrator in a department can hire a temporary employee on a 120-day appointment. If, at the end of the 120-day period, the administrator still has not found a qualified employee for the position, he can renew the 120-day appointment. This provision is at the heart of the patronage system in Chicago and Cook County. If the city and county civil service commissions do not give examinations, or if they set up qualifications which are too difficult for prospective employees to meet, it is difficult to find qualified employees who meet the requirements for permanent employment under the state civil service law. Under these conditions, temporary employees can be appointed to city and county positions for 120-day periods renewable for many years.

This is not to say that many temporary employees are not well qualified for the city and county positions they hold, or that they do not perform adequately on their jobs. Indeed, there is a great deal of truth to Alderman Vito Marzullo's assertion that "the qualities which make a man a good precinct captain make him a good employee." It is generally true that people who are capable of doing good precinct work are capable of doing good work on a city or county job, too. It is also true, of course, that mediocre precinct workers generally make mediocre employees, and that a number of low-level positions in the city and county bureaucracy are filled by inefficient people. But many top-level administrative and middle-level supervisory positions are staffed by fairly competent people who are the best precinct captains in the ward organizations and who also have the ability to do a decent job for the city and county.

Nor is this to say that the patronage system is superior to a merit system in local government but, rather, that merit employment has its inadequacies, too, and that civil service personnel blanketed into positions in the bureaucracy may not be more efficient than patronage employees who are required to demonstrate political efficiency in the precincts and at least some competence on their government jobs. A fairly high percentage of the patronage employees in the city and county who hold responsible administrative positions are probably as competent as most civil service personnel holding comparable positions in other levels of government. If the criterion for evaluating the performance of most of the upper-level patronage employees is performance on their jobs, not how they got their jobs, many of them would rate as high as their civil service system counterparts in government. And, given the salaries and kind of work available in the lower levels of the city and county bureaucracies, civil service examinations for most of those positions would probably not attract people of higher caliber than those who staff those positions through the patronage system.

However, whatever the merits of civil service versus patronage in evaluating employee efficiency, such considerations are not the determining factors in the state legislature's unwillingness to abolish the 120-day temporary employment exemption to the state civil service law or to alter the electoral laws and governmental and political systems in Chicago and Cook County. The reasons for the unwillingness of a Republican-controlled state government in Springfield to use its legal and legislative powers to cripple or restrict the power of the Democratic machine in Chicago must be sought in the interstices of political relationships between pragmatic politicians in both the Republican and Democratic parties in Illinois.

The accepted political theory of the relationship between the two major parties in this country is that they are two opposing parties holding differential theories of government and offering the electorate a choice between alternative programs and competing candidates, of varying outlooks and abilities, for public office. In theory, the American body politic is fragmented between Republicans and Democrats, liberals and conservatives, or, as Madison put it in *The Federalist Papers*, between "those who hold and those who are without property." The contest in American politics is supposedly between the "ins" and the "outs," the "ins" seeking to retain the perquisites and powers of public office, and the "outs" seeking to displace them so that they can enjoy those perquisites and powers.

How well does the reality of politics and political relationships in Illinois fit this theory? Why don't the Republican "ins" in Springfield help the Republican "outs" in Chicago to throw the Democratic "ins" out of office? Why don't the Democratic "ins" in Chicago help the Democratic "outs" in the suburban areas of Cook County to throw the Republican "ins" out of office? Why don't the Republican "ins" in the suburban areas of Cook County help the Republican "outs" in Chicago to throw the Democratic "ins" out of office? And why don't the Democratic "ins" in Chicago help the Democratic "outs" in downstate Illinois help to throw the Republican "ins" out of office?

The answer must lie in the fallacy of the assumption that the divisions in our politics are between Republicans and Democrats, liberals and conservatives, poor and rich, and "ins" and "outs." The real divisions in American politics may well be between the "ins" of both parties, who band together against the "outs" of both parties. Further, the more binding relationships in American politics in cities like Chicago and in states like Illinois may well be between the professionals in both political parties and directed at retaining control of the perquisites of politics for professionals in both parties against the assaults by nonprofessionals in both parties on the inner citadels of power held by the professionals.

The possibility of a political relationship of collusion and cooperation of professional politicians at the local levels of American politics is directly related to the nature and character of the American party system. While it may be true that a two-party system operates in the United States at the national level, one-party systems operate at the local levels of our politics in thousands of cities and counties across the country. Since practically all the big cities in this country are solidly Democratic, and practically all of the suburban communities and rural areas of the country are solidly Republican, most local offices and legislative and congressional districts are safe for one party or the other. In fact, the only genuine political contests for public office in American politics normally take place at the national level for the presidency and at the state level for statewide offices.

Contests for statewide offices in big industrial states like Illinois, Pennsylvania, Ohio, New York, and California are often photofinish horseraces between the vote totals of the urban-industrial complex and the rural hinterland of the state. In Illinois, for example, a political rule of thumb in a statewide or national election is that the Democratic party must come out of Cook County with a majority of at least 250,000 votes to carry the state in a statewide election, since the Republican party normally carries downstate Illinois outside Cook County by a majority of at least 200,000 votes. To carry Cook County safely, the Democratic party must come out of the city of Chicago with a minimum of 350,000 votes over the Republicans, since the Republicans will normally carry the suburbs of Cook County by approximately 150,000 votes.

In theory, in states like Illinois, statewide elections are contests between the interests of the urban-industrial complex and the rural, small-town areas of the state, and those conflicting interests are the issues in a statewide campaign between the two major political parties. But the practical interests of professional politicians and public officeholders do not necessarily coincide with the theoretical interests of the voting public. The practical interests of professional politicians and public officeholders are to gain office, retain office, and reap the perquisites of office. In pursuit of those goals, professional politicians in both parties have a common interest in fending off the efforts of the nonprofessionals in both parties. Since nonprofessionals generally seek to reform political and governmental practices, and to reduce or eliminate the kinds of perquisites that professionals are interested in, the professionals in both parties have a much greater common interest with each other than they have with the nonprofessionals in their own parties.

The key to understanding the relationship between the professional Republican politicians who normally control the state government of Illinois and the professional Democratic politicians who control the city of Chicago and Cook County can be found in this pragmatic assessment of their interests by the professionals in both parties. Their interests and perquisites must be safeguarded, not so much from the professionals in the other party as from the nonprofessionals in both parties. It is safer, more sensible, and more beneficial to deal with each other as ostensible enemies but nominal allies. A facade of public conflict must be maintained, but a network of private cooperation can protect their interests and perquisites from the real enemy, the nonprofessionals.

In Illinois, Republican control of the state government in Springfield and Democratic control of Cook County and Chicago provide a milieu within which the interests of the professionals in both parties can be met. Since Cook County, with its 5.5 million people, is one-half the state of Illinois, there are sufficient perquisites to satisfy the needs of Democratic politicians in Chicago and Cook County. There are sufficient city and county jobs to take care of the needs of the faithful, enough governmental contracts to be let, enough offices to satisfy those whose ambitions run in that direction, and enough opportunities to satisfy the economic pecuniary and political power drives of those who belong to the club. The state government in Springfield, with sufficient patronage, government contracts, and state offices in Springfield, and the local offices throughout the other 101 counties in Illinois provide the wherewithal to pacify the needs of Republican politicians in Illinois outside of the city of Chicago.

This is not to say that there is a binding contract between Democratic professionals in Chicago and Republican professionals in downstate Illinois to stay out of each other's bailiwicks and totally surrender public offices and their prerogatives in their respective fiefdoms to the other side. They can contest with each other for those offices and prerogatives, but they must close ranks with each other, in their common interest, against the would-be reformers in both parties who would deprive them of the prerogatives of office.

Above all, the legal and political rules and relationships under which the game is played must be kept flexible enough so that the professionals in both parties can earn a living, enjoy the limelight, and live the good life without fear of control or retribution by the sovereign electorate, which must be kept in ignorance of the realities of the political process. If the voters ever come to understand those realities, they might rise up in wrath and smite the professionals with the latent, unused power vested in them by the democratic process. For, when the ignorant masses shake off their traditional apathy, no one can predict what the consequences might be. An aroused, irrational electorate, whose normal proclivity is to throw all the rascals out of office and substitute a new group of rascals, is a threat to the professionals in both parties. The basic assumptions of the uninformed electorate about their rulers are that they are all thieves, that those who are in office are inevitably corrupt, and that, while those one puts in office to replace them will also be corrupt, it will take them some time to attain the level of corruption that the current crop of officeholders have already achieved.

Professional politicians, who must make a living in politics, instinctively understand both the inherent prejudices of their constituents and the potential danger to their livelihoods which lies in those prejudices and the latent power of the voters. They know, too, that contemporary American politics has not changed much from the system described by Henry L. Mencken a half-century ago in his *Notes on Democracy*. Analyzing the basic similarities between direct and representative democracies in 1926, Mencken wrote:

Under both forms the sovereign mob must employ agents to execute its will, and in either case the agents may have ideas of their own, based upon interests of their own, and the means at hand to do and get what they will. Moreover, their very position gives them a power of influencing the electors that is far above that of any ordinary citizen: they become politicians *ex officio*, and usually end by selling such influence as remains after they have used all they need for their own ends. Worse, both forms of democracy encounter the difficulty that the generality of citizens, no matter how assiduously they may be instructed, remain congenitally unable to comprehend many of the problems before them, or to consider all of those they do comprehend in an unbiased and intelligent manner. Thus it is often impossible to ascertain their views in advance of action, or even, in many cases, to determine their conclusions *post hoc* . . . . The great masses of Americans of today, though they are theoretically competent to decide all the larger matters of national policy, and have certain immutable principles, of almost religious authority, to guide them, actually look for leading to professional politicians, who are influenced in turn by small but competent and determined minorities, with special knowledge and special interests . . . .

The American people, true enough, are sheep. Worse, they are donkeys. Yet worse, to borrow from their own dialect, they are goats. They are thus constantly bamboozled and exploited by small minorities of their own number, by determined and ambitious individuals, and even by exterior groups . . . . But all the while they have the means in their hands to halt the obscenity whenever it becomes intolerable, and now and then, raised transiently to a sort of intelligence, they do put a stop to it.

The tolerance which professional politicians in both political parties have for each other stems from a pragmatic recognition of their common interests, from an awareness of the common danger to them from the electorate, and from an instinctive understanding of the danger of reform for all of them. Republican politicians in Springfield and Democratic politicians in Chicago and Cook County know that if a reform wave gets going there is no telling from what quarters it will pick up support or in what direction it will move. Once the door is open to reform, newspapers, ministers, educators, political independents, civic organizations, and various and sundry other nonprofessional entities in the body politic are likely to be stirred up. If personnel practices are reformed in Chicago and Cook County, there may be a demand for the abolition of patronage in Springfield. If legal protection of incumbent politicians in Chicago is reduced by changing election laws, downstate Republican county chairmen may be the next target of reformers. If the Chicago City Council is reduced to a manageable size and if safe constituencies are threatened, the zealous advocates of more efficient and less costly government might ask why state legislative districts need three representatives and try to reduce their number from 177 to 59, thus denying 118 dedicated and deserving public servants the opportunity of serving their constituents, their districts, their state, and possibly even their own interests.

Better to let sleeping dogs lie, especially since the sleeping dogs on the other side of the political fence are really of the same genre as one's own people. "Don't make no waves!" In fact, don't make no ripples, either! For ripples might become waves, waves might rock the boat, and all those aboard the boat, whatever their political beliefs, might be cast into the water.

The City Government and the Machine

The most interesting and important relationship of the machine to government is the link between the machine and the government of the city of Chicago. Since the city government is the agency which is most closely tied to the machine, which is closest to the people of the city, which is most susceptible to influence by reform and opposition elements in the body politic, and which must provide the essential services the citizenry demands in order for the machine to remain in office, it is imperative for the machine's survival to maintain a tight control of that government. The four organs of government which must be kept under control are the city council, the courts, the bureaucracy, and the office of the mayor.

In legal theory, the city council should formulate policy, the courts must administer justice, the bureaucracy must provide necessary services, and the mayor must execute the ordinances passed by the city council. However, since the primary interests of the machine are its own perpetuation and the retention and expansion of perquisites, the political interests of the machine do not necessarily coincide with the legal theory of the city's body politic. To maintain its existence, the machine must be sure that the policies legislated by the city council do not interfere with the machine's purposes, that the local courts do not use their judicial powers to interdict or inhibit the machine's prerogatives, that the bureaucracy serves the interests of the machine as well as the interests of the community, and that the executive power in the city is neutralized or utilized for the machine's benefit.

The key to understanding political-governmental relationships in Chicago can be found in the dynamics of a one-party political system which must operate in a democratic rather than a totalitarian milieu. The closest analogy to the relationship of the machine to the city government is the relationship of the Communist party in the Soviet Union to the Soviet government. But since the city of Chicago is not a totalitarian state, the machine must operate with different techniques than does its one-party counterpart in the Soviet Union. While there are similarities in the political-governmental relationships in the two systems, there are also significant differences. The machine's leaders in Chicago cannot use the secret police, the army, detention camps, and exile to Siberia to deal with the opposition. They cannot openly censor the press, the mass media, and the instruments of communication in the city. Instead, they must use the techniques of adaptation, co-optation, superior political skill, and the clandestine use of force to deal with the political opposition.*

---

* A friend of mine, who has been active in Republican politics in Chicago for a number of years and has dealt with the machine's leaders, has been a political consultant to the Central Intelligence Agency, advising foreign governments on how to deal with opposition Communist parties in those countries. He has also lectured to CIA personnel in Washington

However, there are significant similarities in the operation of the two systems. In both systems there is a one-party rule, with no opposition permitted in the Soviet Union, it is true, and political opposition permitted legally in Chicago. But the Democratic party in Chicago is so strong vis-à-vis its Republican and independent oppositions that it can operate essentially in the same way that a party can in a one-party totalitarian system. The machine has political power infinitely superior to that of its opposition, almost total control of the governmental apparatus of the city, powerful influence over all elements that make up the body politic, and control of most of the perquisites and rewards which are normally distributed to participants and would-be participants in the political process. But the retention of power, which is the primary objective of the machine's leaders, is considerably more difficult for Democratic politicians in Chicago than for their Communist counterparts in the Soviet Union, and in some ways requires a higher degree of political skills and techniques than is necessary in a totalitarian one-party system.

How does the machine deal with and control the organs of local government which can affect its power and perquisites in the city? How does it neutralize or utilize the city council, the courts, the bureaucracy, and the executive branch of city government?

The City Council. Chicago's city council, while ostensibly a legislative body, is in reality a ratifying assembly. It could be described as Chicago's Supreme Soviet, and, indeed, its procedures and actions have sometimes been compared to that body by some of its most severe, reform-oriented critics. The council is the largest municipal legislative body in the United States, made up of fifty aldermen, one from each ward, elected for a term of four years on an ostensibly nonpartisan basis, in the February mayoral primary of that year. The council has been reduced in size, if not in quality, from its high-water mark of seventy aldermen, two from each of the city's thirty-five wards, before the statutory changes of 1921 and 1935 which created the present system.

---

on the psychology and strategy of Communist politicians. When asked how he had developed insights into the psychology of politicians in foreign countries where he had never been active politically or resided, he responded, "I have been dealing with these kinds of guys in City Hall in Chicago for forty years."

The council has always had its fair share of Plunkitt of Tammany Hall characters who "seen their opportunities and seized them," the most famous in the past being the two 1st Ward aldermen, Hinky Dink Kenna and Bathhouse John Coughlin. (Hinky Dink's and Bathhouse John's careers are chronicled in Lloyd Wendt and Herman Kogan's *Bosses in Lusty Chicago*.) According to reform journalist William T. Stead, author of *If Christ Came to Chicago*, a corporation lawyer declared in 1894, "There are 68 aldermen in the City Council, and 66 of them can be bought; this I know because I have bought them myself." Two years later, the quality of Chicago's representation had improved somewhat, according to political scientist Charles E. Merriam, who, in his book *Chicago: A More Intimate View of Urban Politics*, wrote that "a preliminary investigation showed that of the 68 aldermen there were only six who were suspected of being honest. There was no doubt about the others."

The reputation of the aldermen at that time occasionally stimulated a counterreaction on the part of the aroused citizenry. "In 1897," according to Merriam, "when the proposal to extend the franchises of the traction companies was pending, and it seemed probable that such an ordinance would pass, notwithstanding the general opposition, extraordinary measures were taken by the aroused citizens. A number of patriots attended the council and sat in the gallery in silent protest. Their indignation was emphasized by ropes that were dangled from the gallery over the heads of the aldermen in a menacing fashion." *

The contemporary council has its fair share of colorful characters, too. The star, of course, is the mayor himself, Richard J. Daley, who acts as presiding officer at all council meetings. Despite a parliamentary prohibition on engaging in debate with members on the floor from the chair, and a personal declaration that *"Robert's Rules of Order* is the greatest book ever written," the mayor frequently departs from his role as chairman, makes long speeches, engages in debate with opposition aldermen, castigates their

* Such a gesture would be impossible in the physical confines of the contemporary Chicago City Council. The present day leadership of the council is protected from close physical proximity to interested spectators by the layout of the council chambers. Interested citizens must sit in a row of seats in the rear of the council chamber on the main floor, or if they are in the gallery above the heads of the aldermen, they are separated from the proceedings below by a glass retaining wall.

behavior and motives, cuts off their microphones when he thinks they have spoken too long, and occasionally explodes in a display of Irish temper when offended by some remark or action of one of the opposition aldermen. The mayor was ably assisted by the number-two man in the Democratic organization, Alderman Tom Keane of the 31st Ward, who was also chairman of the council's powerful Finance Committee and was the mayor's floor leader. Keane, a brilliant lawyer, parliamentarian, and politician, cut down the opposition with pungent, gravel-voiced sallies and remarks. Before the mayor, and behind his floor leader, in serried ranks, sat approximately forty minions of the machine, ready to spring into action at a call from the chair, or to vote down the disloyal opposition who did not share their concern for the city's welfare and future. In their ranks were found the mayor's own alderman, Michael Bilandic, tough alley fighters like Edward Vrdolyak and Vito Marzullo, some of the younger, better-educated new organization representatives, and the silent sheep-like mass of the faithful, waiting to cast their votes on signal from former floor leader Keane. (When Keane was forced to give up his seat in 1974, after being convicted of mail fraud in federal court, Bilandic succeeded him as Finance Committee chairman and floor leader.)

Some of the most colorful characters in the council's more recent history were the late Alderman Krska, whose sole function in the council seemed to be to stand up occasionally and shout, "God Bless Mayor Daley!" and Mathias ("Paddy") Bauler, the long-time alderman from the Near North Side's 43rd Ward. Bauler, who met his constituents at his tavern on North Avenue, where he sat behind the bar wearing a top hat, once shot a police lieutenant in his tavern. "He swore at me and called me a fat Dutch pig," said Alderman Bauler, explaining why he had drawn his gun in a battle reminiscent of the scenes in *High Noon*. Bauler sometimes entertained the council by engaging in a wrestling match with himself on the council floor, rolling around the floor locked in a series of holds, while his colleagues howled in laughter. Bauler was also the most traveled alderman in Chicago's history. He would fly to Hong Kong to buy shirts, to Paris for lunch, or to Germany for a beerfest. Every year, in his last few years in office in the 1960s, Alderman Bauler would run an art show in the rear of his ward headquarters next door to the saloon on North Avenue. With paintings hung on the

walls, and free refreshments served by some of Bauler's precinct
captains dressed in Chinese gowns imported from Hong Kong for
the occasion, the affair was usually the most colorful, if not the most
artistic, event of the year.

Aldermanic elections in contemporary Chicago are not as
interesting and exciting as they were fifty years ago. In 1921, the
home of Alderman Johnny Powers, one of the local ward bosses, was
bombed. Powers, who was involved in a political feud with Mike
D'Andrea, the president of the Unione Sicialana, charged D'Andrea
with the responsibility for the bombing. When D'Andrea announced his nonpartisan candidacy against Powers for Powers'
aldermanic seat, D'Andrea's headquarters, the home of one of
D'Andrea's lieutenants, and a hall where D'Andrea's supporters
were holding a rally were all bombed. Alderman James Bowler, who
was replaced by Alderman Vito Marzullo when he went to Congress
and who supported Powers, declared, "Conditions in the 19th Ward
are terrible. Gunmen are patrolling the streets. I have received
threats that I was to be 'bumped off' or kidnapped. Alderman
Powers' house is guarded day and night. Our men have been met,
threatened and slugged. Gunmen and cutthroats have been imported from New York and Buffalo for this campaign of intimida-
tion. Owners of halls have been threatened with death or the
destruction of their buildings if they rent their places to us. It is
worse than the Middle Ages." After D'Andrea was defeated in the
aldermanic election, two of Powers' supporters were killed. Within
two months, D'Andrea was murdered, and two of his closest friends,
who had sworn to avenge his death, were also murdered.

The bombings, the gunplay, and some of the comedy are gone
from the contemporary city council scene, but some traces of the
old atmosphere still remain. "Nineteen sixty-seven," according to
Chicago Daily News columnist Mike Royko, "was a good year in the
Chicago City Council. Only 4% of the aldermen were shot." That
was the year that Alderman Ben Lewis of the 24th Ward was found
in his ward headquarters the night after his re-election, his hands
handcuffed behind his back, and a bullet hole through his head. It
was also the year in which Alderman Leon Despres, the reform
alderman from the University of Chicago's 5th Ward, was shot in
the leg in a holdup attempt in his ward.

On the floor of the council, administration stalwarts occasionally insult their opponents in an atmosphere reminiscent of the good old days. When Alderman Seymour Simon of the 40th Ward rose to speak, Mayor Daley often asked Simon, a former fair-haired boy in the organization who was booted out and who became a member of the opposition, why he didn't get a hair cut. Floor leader Keane also often insulted Simon and other members of the opposition.* When a Picasso statue was erected in front of the Civic Center in the Loop, Alderman John Hoellen, a Republican from the 47th Ward, objected to the city's spending money for the Picasso work, saying that nobody knew what the Picasso creation was. Alderman Keane responded, "It's a baboon, and its name is John Hoellen." † When independent, reform Alderman Dick Simpson of the 44th Ward, who teaches political science at the University of Illinois, Chicago Circle Campus, attacked one of the administration's proposals on the floor, Alderman Vito Marzullo, another administration stalwart, told Alderman Simpson, "You couldn't teach a dog in my ward."

In the council, interspersed among the overwhelming majority of the faithful, were one Republican and a few independent aldermen who pushed for civic reform, and who consistently opposed the Daley administration's positions. The small band of independents was led by veteran reform Alderman Leon Despres, who was elected to the council in the same year that Richard J. Daley was elected mayor of Chicago, and who had consistently fought the good fight since 1955. Despres, who retired from the council in 1975, is intelligent, articulate, and dedicated. He knew the odds but also understood the realities of how a minority can apply pressure against an overwhelming majority in a legislative body like the Chicago City Council. Supported by young, liberal independents like William Singer and Dick Simpson, liberal black aldermen like William Cousins and Anna Langford, former organi-

---

* In 1972, after months of attempting to get an alley cleaned in his ward, and getting no satisfaction from the city bureaucracy, Simon finally called the *Chicago Daily News* Public Service Department "Beeline." A call from Beeline to the bureaucracy finally resulted in a pledge to come and clean the alley in Simon's ward. The incident indicates the manner in which the organization sometimes deals with the opposition.

† Hoellen told an interviewer that, after fifteen years in the City Council, he still had no office space in City Hall, no legislative assistants, and "not even a place to hang my hat." Black independent Alderman Sammy Rayner used the public washrooms in City Hall for months until one day Alderman Despres noticed him going in and showed him the private washrooms reserved for the aldermen.

zation supporter Seymour Simon, and often by Republicans like John Hoellen, Despres led a band that made a valiant, often futile, but occasionally successful fight against the leaders of the Daley organization.

The minority opposition has developed some ingenious tactics for influencing legislation in the council and public policy in the city. According to Republican Alderman John Hoellen, "The mission of the opposition is to talk to the city." In fulfilling that mission, the opposition aldermen are aided by the support and coverage of the mass media. Attacks on administration proposals in the council always make a good film clip on the ten P.M. news on the television channels. A speech on the council floor that attacks the mayor's budget or exposes the activities of patronage payrollers is always good for a front-page headline in Chicago's three major daily newspapers. The opposition can also perform a watchdog role as the Democratic organization's legislative proposals are presented in the council. "We'd all fall asleep if they weren't there," according to an administration stalwart. "They keep us alert. There are things we'd like to do but can't because of the opposition aldermen."

The opposition aldermen can have some effect on public policy in the city in another way, too. Legislation which they propose, which is always buried by the Democratic administration but then receives public support through the intervention of the media, is often adopted by the administration as its own. According to Alderman Despres, "The appearance of being defeated on votes is misleading, because independent aldermen with a long-term view can push proposals to successful enactment. Very often, the victorious enactment occurs after the administration gracefully accepts defeat, reintroduces the independent alderman's measure as an original administration measure, and passes it."

However, despite the opposition's use of exposure, delay, harassment, and initiation of legislation, the facts of political life in the Chicago City Council are that the Democratic organization maintains a tight hold on the legislative branch of city government. Given the overwhelming majority that the organization has in the council, the amount of work an independent or opposition Republican alderman has to put in to stay abreast of the administration's policies, the amount of time an independent or opposition Republican alderman must devote to servicing his constituents in his ward without a great deal of cooperation from the city administration, and the low salaries paid Chicago's aldermen, the machine moves normally towards its legislative objectives in the city council, annoyed sometimes, delayed occasionally, and frustrated infrequently by the tactics of the opposition, but secure in its majority and its ability to outlast the opposition. Since (until 1975, when it was raised to $17,000) the aldermanic salary of $8,000 a year did not provide a decent standard of living for an honest opposition alderman, since he does not have access to the perquisites and prerogatives which membership in the organization can bring to a city legislator, and since the organization normally can effectively block any further political ambitions that opposition aldermen may have, few independent aldermen remain in the city council for any length of time. Despres, of course, was the exception, but he paid for his independence by being totally barred from becoming a congressman, a state legislator, or a judge.

The formal legislative procedures of the city council also operate to promote the Democratic organization's objectives and to inhibit effective action by the minority opposition. The council normally meets only once or twice a month, at the call of the mayor. Much of the time at the infrequent meetings is spent eulogizing Democratic politicians who have died and to passing resolutions praising some organization or individual for service to the community. Sometimes, as the morning wears on, as many as twenty aldermen will eulogize one of their departed comrades. Ordinances introduced by aldermen are referred to appropriate committees, and, of course, all ordinances introduced by opposition or independent aldermen are buried in the committees. Whenever an opposition alderman attempts to get a piece of legislation which he has introduced sent to a committee which he considers favorable to the legislation, several of the administration aldermen call out the names of other committees, and the legislation is then sent to the Committee on Committees and Rules for burial. In the all-powerful Finance Committee, legislation which the administration considers inimical to its interests is sent to the Subcommittee on Miscellaneous Matters, sometimes referred to as the Mish-Mash Committee, where it is given a decent burial.

The manner in which Alderman Keane conducted a committee meeting was described by the *Chicago Tribune* on April 15, 1955:

Ald. Keane (31st) arrived 11 minutes late for a meeting Tuesday morning of the council committee on traffic and public safety, of which he is chairman. The committee had a sizeable agenda, 286 items in all to consider.

Ald. Keane took up the first item. For the record, he dictated to the committee secretary that Ald. A moved and Ald. B seconded its approval, and then, without calling for a vote, he declared the motion passed. Neither mover nor seconder had opened his mouth. He followed the same procedure on six more proposals, again without a word from the aldermen whose names appeared in the record. Then he put 107 items into one bundle for passage, and 172 more into another for rejection, again without a voice other than his own having been heard.

Having disposed of this mountain of details in exactly ten minutes, Ald. Keane walked out. The aldermen he had quoted so freely, without either their concurrence or their protest, sat around looking stupid.

Most likely they are.

Watching a meeting of the Chicago City Council is like watching a symphony orchestra performing a work under the direction of a skilled conductor, assisted by an equally skilled concertmaster. When matters came up for debate on the council floor, Mayor Richard J. Daley would recognize Alderman Thomas Keane, who set the tone for the administration's position. Then a black alderman, usually Alderman Wilson Frost; an Italian alderman, usually Alderman Vito Marzullo; a Polish alderman; and one of the younger, better-educated administration stalwarts would be called upon to speak in support of the administration's position. After the groundwork was laid and a consensus built in this manner, Daley would allow one or two of the opposition aldermen to speak against the measure. Two or three administration stalwarts would be recognized to respond and attack the opposition's position. The virtuoso and solo performances by the star performers were fitted into the script by the maestro on the podium, Mayor Daley. Then, finally, the vote would be taken, with concertmaster Alderman Keane signaling the proper stance on the matter before the council. It was all cut and dried, but it was good entertainment, and the administration's steamroller moved on after having flattened the opposition once again.

In summary, the Chicago City Council has not been a legislative body in the parliamentary sense, but rather a ratifying assembly

which is closer in spirit and procedure to its counterpart in the
Soviet Union, the Supreme Soviet. And the relationship between
the Democratic machine in Chicago and the Chicago City Council
is more analogous to the relationship between the Communist party
hierarchy in the Soviet Union and the Soviet government, than it is
to the normal relationships of political parties to governmental
agencies in a democratic political system. Since the Democratic
organization has maintained an overwhelming majority in the city
council, as well as uninterrupted control of the mayor's office, the
judiciary, and the administrative bureaucracy in the city for over
forty years, and since Chicago operates under a one-party system,
governmental legislative, executive, judicial, and administrative
powers are often subordinated to the needs and interests of the local
Democratic party as well as the citizenry of the city.

The formal legal structure of the city government is weak,
decentralized, and lacking in any real power. The political organization of the Democratic party is well organized, powerful, authoritar-
ian, and highly centralized. In such a milieu, the party controls the
governmental apparatus and often uses that apparatus for its own
partisan political objectives. In many cases, those interests and
objectives coincide with the interests of the citizenry, but, when
they do not, the political preferences of the party take preference
over the interests of the ward constituencies of the elected
representatives, the aldermen, and the general citizenry.

The Courts. "This is a [judicial] system which exalts a political
party above all else. This is a system that sets political obeisance
above justice in our courts. This is a system that makes honorable
men puppets of political patrons." * Thus did Republican Archibald
J. Carey, Jr., an opponent of the Democratic machine of Cook
County, describe the court system in Cook County in 1963. Two
years later, critic Carey switched parties and was elected to the
Cook County Circuit Court as a Democrat.

How true are Judge Carey's allegations about the subservience
of the judiciary to the Democratic political machine in Cook
County? If the Democratic party does use the judicial system in

---

* Quoted in Joseph Karaganis, "Who's on the Bench? In Cook County, It's Usually a
Politician," *Chicago Sun-Times* II (September 7, 1969), p. 1.

Chicago and Cook County for its own purposes, what tactics and mechanisms does the party use to influence and control it? To answer these questions, it is necessary to examine the structure of the courts, the process of judicial selection, the backgrounds of the members of the bench, and the administration of the court system of the city and county.

Cook County's and Chicago's courts, as in all states, are an integral part of the state judicial system. Under the 1970 Illinois Constitution, the state is divided into five judicial districts, with the First Judicial District encompassing Cook County, and the remainder of the state divided into four judicial districts of substantially equal population. Cook County elects three of the seven state supreme court justices, and twelve of the twenty-four appellate court judges. At the circuit court level in the First Judicial District, the state constitution provides that the city of Chicago and its suburbs shall be separate units for the selection of circuit judges, with at least twelve judges elected at large from the suburbs outside Chicago, and at least thirty-six judges elected at large from the city. Under the constitution, also, each circuit court shall have associate judges appointed by the circuit judges, with the provision that in Cook County at least one-fourth the associate judges shall be appointed from and reside outside the city of Chicago. Supreme court and appellate court judges serve terms of ten years, while circuit judges serve six years and associate judges serve four years.

All elected judges are nominated in primaries and elected in general elections. Supreme court and appellate court judges must stand for re-election at the end of their terms of office. Sitting circuit court judges in Cook County who wish to remain on the bench must file a declaration of candidacy to succeed themselves with the Office of the Secretary of State. The secretary of state then certifies the judge's candidacy to the election officials of the county. Sitting circuit court judges then are presented to the voters of the county on the judicial retention ballot, a ballot in which the voters have the option of voting "yes" or "no" on whether a sitting circuit court judge shall remain in office. In other words, once elected to the Circuit Court of Cook County, a sitting judge does not run against an opponent for re-election but, rather, runs against his own record. This procedure practically insures a permanent seat on the bench for any sitting circuit court judge, since few voters have any

knowledge of his background, record, judicial conduct, or capabil
ity. Since the judicial retention ballot was instituted, only one sitting
circuit court judge has ever been rejected by the electorate. And,
during his term of office, a sitting judge can be removed, suspended,
censured, reprimanded, or retired only by a court's commission
consisting of one supreme court judge, two appellate court judges,
and two circuit court judges.

The Circuit Court of Cook County is divided into two
departments, County and Municipal. The Municipal Department,
which hears minor cases, is staffed by associate judges and
magistrates who are appointed by the circuit court. The County
Department of the circuit court, which hears major cases, is divided
into seven functional divisions law, probate, family, divorce,
criminal, county, and chancery. Each of these divisions is headed by
a presiding judge. The circuit judges and associate judges also elect
one circuit court judge as chief judge of the circuit court, who acts
as chief administrative officer, assigning judges to divisions, duties to
court personnel, and the time and place of court sessions.

How does a lawyer become a judge of the Circuit Court of Cook
County? Without question the surest and safest road to a seat on the
bench is through the party organization. Before the 1970 Illinois
Constitution was adopted, judicial candidates were nominated by
party conventions in each of the state's five judicial districts. That
meant that the judicial candidates in Cook County were nominated
in conventions controlled by the county central committees of the
two parties. And, since the Democratic party has carried Cook
County for most county offices in most elections for the past forty
years, nomination by the Democratic Cook County party convention was tantamount to election to the judiciary. Occasionally, in
the past, when there was a chance that the Republican party might
elect some judges to the circuit court, the leadership of the two
parties would get together to form a coalition slate of judges, slating
just enough Republicans and Democrats to fill every seat on the
bench. In other words, the candidates slated for the judiciary were
all elected without opposition. Since the Republican party in Cook
County has had difficulty in electing Republicans to the bench
under their own power (between 1923 and 1953 no Republican had
won a contested judicial election in Cook County), the Republican
party was normally happy to accept the crumbs from the table and

secure a few judicial posts for deserving Republican lawyers. Under County Chairman Daley's leadership, the Democratic party has also occasionally co-opted outstanding Republican candidates for the bench by offering them places on the Democratic slate. In 1962, when there was considerable newspaper and civic pressure for judicial reform, Chairman Daley persuaded six blue-ribbon Republicans, who had been slated by the Republican party as candidates for the circuit court, to switch over and run as Democrats. All six accepted Daley's offer and were elected to the bench in the fall election.

While judicial candidates for the circuit court must be nominated in primaries under the new 1970 Illinois Constitution, the change in the selection process from a judicial convention to a primary has not significantly altered the control of the process of judicial nomination by the Democratic party hierarchy. The county central committee's slatemakers control the primary elections as easily as they did the judicial nominating conventions, and the process of judicial nomination and election has remained essentially unchanged.

Selection of a judicial ticket by the party's slatemakers is an exercise in balancing political, geographic, racial, religious, and ethnic considerations. Judicial nominations are allocated to the various ward organizations in proportion to the effectiveness of the organization's efforts on the party's behalf, the power of the committeeman, and the need of the slatemakers to balance the ticket ethnically, racially, and religiously. Once a judgeship is allocated to a ward organization, it normally remains the property of that organization, with the committeeman's having the prerogative of selecting a judicial candidate to replace one who has died, retired, or moved to a higher court. Thus, each ward, particularly the powerful wards, are given adequate representation on the circuit court bench to represent and look after the interests of the ward.

Having a judge on the bench from his ward organization gives the committeeman and his precinct captains a channel of communication with, and access to, the county judicial system which can be used on behalf of the ward's constituents. Conversely, a sitting judge's continuing interest in the local ward organization's problems and affairs serves to buttress the image of the committeeman with his organization and provides a degree of respectability and prestige for that organization and the committeeman. Many sitting judges continue to attend ward organization meetings and ward fund-raising affairs, lauding the committeeman to the organization from the podium and demonstrating to the faithful that it is possible to achieve high office through laboring in the vineyards of the precinct. The relationship can be a two-way street. For an ambitious judge who would like an assignment to the chancery division housed in the Civic Center rather than to the criminal courts housed in the out-of-the-way building at 26th and California on Chicago's southwest side, or who would like to be considered for an appellate court or a federal judicial appointment, the continuing support of a powerful committeeman and efficient ward organization can be of great value.

An examination of the backgrounds of the judges who serve on the Circuit Court of Cook County indicates the efficacy of the political route to the judiciary. Of eighty judges elected to the position of circuit court or associate circuit court judge from 1960 to 1968, at least seventy-three were active in ward or township organizations, with many of them holding official posts such as precinct captain, president of a ward or township organization, secretary to a committeeman, or even committeeman of a ward or township organization. The extent of the political backgrounds of most of the members of the judiciary of the Circuit Court of Cook County was spelled out by attorney Joseph Karaganis in an article which appeared in the *Chicago Sun-Times* on September 7, 1969. Karaganis' research documented the political backgrounds of the circuit court judges and associate judges elected to the Cook County bench between 1962 and 1968.

The surest route to a seat on the circuit court bench is through long and faithful service in one of the three major legal offices which are responsible for the prosecution of crime in Chicago and Cook County—the United States Attorney's Office for Northern Illinois, which handles prosecutions for federal offenses in Cook County; the State's Attorney's Office of Cook County, which handles prosecutions for violations of state law in Cook County; and the Corporation Counsel's Office of the City of Chicago, which handles the prosecution of violations of municipal ordinances.

Democratic attorneys who have political connections or backing and who serve as United States Attorney for Northern Illinois, state's attorney of Cook County, or corporation counsel of the city of Chicago have a clear path to a seat on the bench. According to Karaganis, of the seven Democratic United States attorneys in the last forty years, three became federal judges, one died in office, one became the state's attorney, and two retired to private practice. All the men who served as state's attorney of Cook County since 1933 were rewarded with seats on the bench, except for two incumbents in that office. (One of those was Edward Hanrahan, who had a falling out with the organization after his defeat for re-election as state's attorney in 1972, and notified the party that he was not interested in a seat on the bench.) And, according to Karaganis, more than half the circuit court judges in Chicago have served in at least one of the three offices as assistant corporation counsels, assistant state's attorneys, or assistant United States attorneys.

In these offices an ambitious young lawyer with aspirations for a judgeship can prove his loyalty and dedication to the party by serving an apprenticeship for long years as an assistant state's attorney or assistant corporation counsel, maintaining his membership in a ward organization, delivering his precinct for the party, and giving free legal services to the constituents of his ward committeeman. As an assistant state's attorney or assistant corporation counsel, he can also serve as a link between the ward's constituents who become embroiled with the law and the city and county judicial systems. This is not to say that he need take or give bribes in such situations, but he can offer advice, make contact, and suggest the proper way to negotiate settlements of pending cases.

Through this process of apprenticeship and service, the party protects itself from anti-organization activities by members of the judiciary by testing their party loyalty and political *realpolitik* over many years of service before they are slated for the bench. And, while it is difficult to remove a circuit or municipal court judge from the bench, he can be influenced or disciplined by making his tenure on the bench unpleasant and arduous. He can be given the most tedious work, be transferred regularly from one court to another, be exiled to the boondocks of the criminal court at 26th and California, be assigned a heavy work load, and be barred from any future advancement to a higher court. Strict control of the sitting judges in the various divisions of the circuit court is also insured by making sure that all chief judges of these divisions are men of unquestioned loyalty and party responsibility.

The party requirement of long service in the vineyards of the state's attorney's and corporation counsel's offices also makes for a situation in which circuit court judges are usually men who are fairly well up in years before they are rewarded with a seat on the bench. According to the *Daily News* of June 3, 1970, more than half the twenty-three Cook County circuit court full judges who were seeking retention in the November election would be seventy years old or older before their next term of office expired in 1976. "If these judges are returned to the bench, as expected," according to *Daily News* writer Larry Green, "the Circuit Court would bolster its reputation as one of the most exclusive senior citizen clubs in the Chicago area." Of the twenty-three judges running on the retention ballot, only three would be under sixty at the end of the term in 1976. The average age for full judges running for retention would be sixty-eight years at the end of their terms, while the average age of associate judges would be seventy-one.

Nationality, race, and religion are also important factors in dispensing judgeships to the party faithful. For the party's slatemakers, the judicial ticket, as well as the regular county ticket, should be properly balanced to take into account the ethnic, racial, and religious makeup of the city and the county. As with all the other important county offices, however, the Irish play a predominant role in the judiciary. In 1970, at least twenty-five of sixty-six circuit court judges were Irish, six of the twelve appellate court judges in Cook County were Irish, one of the three Illinois Supreme Court justices was Irish, and three out of ten of the members of the United States Court of Appeals for the Seventh Circuit were Irish. Once the Irish have received their fair share of the judicial ticket, the rest of the slate is normally made up of a balance of the other ethnic, racial, and religious groups in Chicago and Cook County, with a significant percentage of Poles and Jews on the ticket. (These two ethnic groups receive substantial quotas on the judicial ticket because the Poles constitute the largest ethnic group in the city, and Jewish lawyers make up a considerable proportion of the legal profession in the city and county.) The black breakthrough to the circuit court bench came about fifteen years ago when Judge Wendell Green was put on the bench. Since then, an ever-increasing number of blacks has been awarded seats on the circuit court. Chicago's Latins went unrepresented in the judiciary until the Democratic organization determined that there were a sufficient number of Spanish-speaking citizens in Chicago to warrant having a judge. When that time arrived, Judge David Cerda, an American of Mexican origin, was chosen for the circuit court bench, and his wife, Maria, a Puerto Rican, was put on the Chicago Board of Education by Mayor Daley.

A law degree from the proper law school is also of great value in being elevated to the Circuit Court of Cook County, with DePaul and Loyola, the two Catholic law schools in Chicago, being the major sources for the county judiciary. In 1970, of ninety-four circuit court judges, thirty-four had gone to DePaul, twelve to Loyola, eleven to John Marshall, fourteen to Kent, eight to the University of Chicago, eight to Northwestern, six to Harvard, and one to Yale. In other words, more than one-third the circuit court judges had attended DePaul Law School, Daley's old law school, and almost one-half the judges had gone to either Loyola or DePaul. John Marshall and Kent, two law schools attended normally by part-time students, people working full time, or college graduates who are unable to get into the best law schools, ranked second behind the Catholic law schools. Chicago, Northwestern, Harvard, and Yale, four of the most prestigious law schools in the country, together provided only about one-fourth the judges on the circuit court bench in 1970.

Since a judgeship is one of the choicest political plums that the party has to dispense, and since those chosen for such a high office are practically guaranteed a lifetime position free from direct control by the party, the party leadership allocates judgeships normally only to those who have proved their party loyalty through service and longevity. There are, however, some exceptions to the rule. Occasionally, an attorney with an outstanding civic record can be slated for the bench, even if he has not been a party regular, in order to pacify the newspapers and reform elements in the community. The party is sometimes willing to slate a wealthy attorney whose lifelong ambition is to cap his career with a seat on the circuit court. He might be slated, provided he is willing to make a substantial financial contribution to the party's coffers. In fact, according to reliable sources, candidates slated for the circuit court may be required to make a substantial financial contribution to the party in partial payment for the favor bestowed on them by the party. This has been true, not only for candidates for the circuit court, but also for some who have sought a place on the federal bench in Illinois in both the Democratic and Republican parties.

The party's control of the judicial branch of local government is buttressed by maintaining a strong party control of the prosecuting authorities in the city and county, and good relationships with law enforcement officials and the legal profession. The two key offices that the party must control are the corporation counsel's office and the state's attorney's office. Since the corporation counsel is appointed by the mayor, and since the Democratic party has maintained control of the mayor's office since 1931, the party has had no trouble in maintaining control of that office. However, since the state's attorney is a county official, elected on a countywide basis, in which a heavy suburban vote, added to the Republican vote in the city, can elect a Republican to that office, it behooves the party to slate candidates for state's attorney with great care and consideration for their reliability and electability. The office of state's attorney is particularly important, not only because he is the attorney for all the other county officeholders, but also because he has control of the county grand jury and can press indictments or suppress prosecution on all matters of state law. Since most of the activities of party politicians fall under the purview of state rather than federal law, control of the state's attorney's office will normally suffice to protect the party's interests and activities from potentially dangerous regulation by the state of Illinois.

Because of its keen interest in the state's attorney's office, and great care in selecting and supporting Democratic candidates for that office, the party has maintained control of the state's attorney's office in Cook County for most of the past forty years, too, losing the office only twice in that period. In 1956, Benjamin Adamowski, a renegade Polish Democrat, who had switched to the Republican party, managed to capture the state's attorney's office, riding in on his popularity with the massive Polish constituency in Chicago and on President Eisenhower's coattails in the presidential election of that year. After four years of continuous trouble with Adamowski, the party's major objective in the 1960 election was to recapture the state's attorney's office. In pursuit of that goal, the party slated a blue-ribbon candidate, Daniel Ward, who was dean of the De Paul

University Law School and who also had the advantage of being an Irish Catholic. And, to insure a heavy Democratic vote among the city's massive Catholic population, Mayor Daley strongly supported John F. Kennedy for the presidential nomination at the Los Angeles convention in 1960. Daley was not so much interested in electing Kennedy as president, as he was in using the Kennedy name and the Kennedy religion at the top of the ticket to help him win the state's attorney's office back in Cook County. The strategy worked, since Kennedy carried the city of Chicago heavily, and Dan Ward defeated Adamowski by 25,000 votes in the county. It was still a close shave, however, since a Democratic candidate normally can carry the county by 150,000 to 200,000 votes.

The only other time that the Democrats have lost the state's attorney's office was in 1972. After slating the incumbent Democratic state's attorney, Edward Hanrahan, who had been indicted and brought to trial for hiding evidence in connection with a state's attorney police raid on the Black Panther headquarters in Chicago, the party leaders decided to back away from Hanrahan after being pressured by reform Democrats, black leaders, newspapers, and the leading candidates on the state ticket who told the mayor that Hanrahan had become a major handicap to the party that year. After being dumped by the party, Hanrahan contested the party's choice, Raymond K. Berg, in the primary and defeated Berg. However, massive defections of black Democratic voters, and liberal Democrats in the city and suburbs, led to Hanrahan's defeat and the election of a Republican reform candidate, Bernard Carey.

However, even in times of travail, when a Republican holds the state's attorney's office, the party can normally fend off too much pressure from a Republican state's attorney by utilizing its influence in the courts and fighting a delaying action in the hope of surviving the four-year Republican term without too much damage to the party's position and image. And, since the budget of the Cook County state's attorney's office is determined by the Cook County Board of Commissioners, which always has a two-to-one Democratic majority, and normally has a Democratic president, a Republican state's attorney who becomes too ambitious and troublesome can also be hamstrung by having the funds for his office and staff assistance reduced.

The Democratic party's control of the judiciary in Cook County and Chicago is buttressed by the party's control of other governmental offices which are a part of or which deal with and support the court system. All the personnel who service the circuit court are under the direct control of either of the presiding judges of the circuit court, who are all Democrats, or of other normally Democratic county or city functionaries such as the clerk of the circuit court and the sheriff of Cook County. Thus, process servers, bailiffs, and clerks who service the court and deal with the attorneys and citizens who are involved in litigation in the circuit court are almost all Democratic precinct captains or connected in some way with the Democratic ward organizations in the city. An additional link is thus provided between the ward and township committeemen of the Democratic party of Cook County and the administrative apparatus of the circuit court through the relationship of the ward committeemen and the ward organizations to the personnel of the court. That relationship can be utilized in many ways—guidance, assistance, expertise, and service. Like most agencies of the city and county government, the relationship is one of cooperation, guidance, and understanding between the ward organizations and the city and county agencies, utilizing the informal processes of the political system to unravel the threads of the inner fabric of the city and county governments and to unlock the right doors to the proper agencies in order to better service the interests of the citizenry which holds in its hands the ultimate fate of the political organization.

Finally, a working relationship with the legal profession itself in the city and county can help to fend off any serious outside challenge to the Democratic organization's control of the court system in Cook County and Chicago. Thus, the Chicago Bar Association is consulted on the slating of candidates for the bench; prestigious law firms are awarded legal business; influential attorneys can be utilized and rewarded; and the legal profession in the county and city can be dealt with, if not as an ally, at least not as an enemy, and hopefully as a tolerant, participating observer of the local political and legal scene.

Thus, the Democratic party's control of the judicial branch of county and city government is maintained through an amalgam of careful screening of potential candidates for the bench through long years of service to the party; through a consideration of the ethnic, racial, religious, geographic, and economic forces within the community; through a system of rewarding or punishing those who aspire to a judicial post; through a network of informal contacts between the political organization and the court system itself; through a tight control of the key prosecutive offices in the county and city; and through a working relationship with the legal profession itself.

⚜ *8* ⚜

Whither the Machine?

The Daley machine is the last of the big city machines in the United States. It has survived trends and forces in the urban areas of this country which have brought down the great political machines in most other major municipalities. It has not only survived but has adapted itself to changing circumstances, refined its techniques, and, indeed, increased its power and influence in the city of Chicago. Although political prophecy is the ultimate irrationality of the study of politics, I believe it is necessary to try to make some reasoned judgment about the future of the Chicago machine. History, as evolutionary description of events, is useful primarily for an understanding of the past. Political science, as analysis of the present, is valuable mostly for the scholar and teacher. But political prognosis, as a guide to the future, can serve the layman, the scholar, and the professional politician in their attempts to deal with and resolve the problems of society. As Winston Churchill once put it, "We study the past so that we can understand the present and try to predict the future."

Since the future of the urban areas in the United States is inextricably bound up with two major developments—the influx of blacks and other minority groups into our cities and the exodus of the white middle class and working class to the suburbs—this concluding chapter focuses on the possible impact of those two forces on the future of the Daley machine, both in Chicago and in the Chicago metropolitan area.

The Daley machine is more than a city machine. It is also a metropolitan-area machine whose tentacles reach into the government of Cook County. The future of the machine is bound up with developments, not only in the city, but also in Chicago's suburbs. In other words, since much of the strength of the Chicago machine is based on its control of the government of Cook County, the changing patterns of life and politics in the suburban areas of Cook County are sure to affect the machine's future as a viable political organization. And the massive growth of the black and Spanish-speaking segments of Chicago's population will critically affect the machine's situation within the city's limits. It is the purpose of this chapter, then, to analyze the machine's prospects in the city and the county in the light of the great population changes which are taking place in Chicago and its suburbs.

The Machine and the Suburbs[*]

Chicago's suburbs, like the city, are undergoing radical change. The black migration into Chicago has stimulated a massive exodus of white middle-class and working-class citizens. While the black population of the city increased between 1950 and 1970 from approximately 400,000 to 1,300,000, the total city population dropped from 3,620,962 to 3,366,957. In the same period, the population of the suburban area of Cook County increased from 987,830 to 2,106,713. The face of the suburban area of Cook County is being altered in two major ways: first, many new development suburbs have sprung up where farmers' fields once graced the landscape; second, the old, established, close-in suburban cities and villages are undergoing a transformation.

The First Migration. Chicago's working- and lower-middle-class, ethnic, heavily Catholic, white population has been leaving the city for new tract development suburbs. New, fairly homogeneous population centers are being established by the fleeing working- and lower-middle-class white Democrats from the city. Contrary to popular mythology, these fleeing Democrats are not becoming Republicans in their new communities. Isolated from surrounding established towns, in close proximity physically to other emigrant

[*] Much of the material in this section appeared in Milton Rakove, *The Changing Patterns of Suburban Politics in Cook County, Illinois* (Chicago: Loyola University Press, 1965) and is reproduced here, with minor changes, by permission of the Center for Research in Urban Government.

Democrats like themselves, and relatively untouched by established Republican-dominated suburban organizations, most of the former city Democrats are retaining their traditional affiliation with the national Democratic party.

However, on local issues they have tended to become relatively nonpartisan, as homeowners and taxpayers, without regard to any formal party affiliation or doctrine. Traditional Democratic New Deal liberalism or Republican hostility to welfare-state measures and governmental activity in a broad range of programs are both relatively meaningless to these new suburbanites. Their primary concerns are administrative, not political, matters at the local level. Taxes, sanitation, flood control, schools, zoning, and property values occupy whatever time they have to devote to public affairs. Appeals to their civic-mindedness on an ideological basis fall on deaf ears. They are practical, pragmatic, self-centered, narrowly oriented and concerned, and nonideological politically insofar as local problems and issues are concerned. As for the city which they left, the county of which they are a part, the state which spawned them legally, and the nation which guides their ultimate destinies—those are matters of relatively little concern in comparison to their immediate local problems. Their major interests are to make sure that blacks do not follow them into their new communities, and to keep their taxes down, even if it means unsatisfactory, inadequate local services and facilities.

These are not New England town-meeting communities governed by Anglo-Saxon ideas of what the good society should be. They are, rather, made up of first- and second-generation Eastern and Southern Europeans, influenced by their peasant and proletarian backgrounds, and dominated by still-retained prejudices and fears of the strangers beyond the fence.

In contrast, the old established cities and villages of Chicago's suburban hinterland are undergoing a significant political transformation. These communities are attracting upper-middle-class city Democrats who come in search of good schools, safe streets, clean government, and all the other trappings of the middle class American dream. Most of these new suburbanites are the newly arrived middle class in America. Their fathers were laborers, small businessmen, and skilled tradesmen. They are doctors, lawyers, teachers, corporation junior executives, and successful businessmen.

Their wives are college graduates, and their children are born to the upper-middle class. The Catholics and Jews among them have assimilated as much as possible to the dominant Protestant middle-class values of white America, in the pattern described by Will Herberg in *Protestant, Catholic, Jew*. They have not left their faiths, but they have adapted socially, culturally, and often politically to what they believe are American traditions.

Unlike the city emigrants to the new development suburbs, they have retained their Democratic liberalism, applied it to local community problems, and combined it with their new-found Anglo-Saxon-Protestant concepts of conservative, anti-machine, nonpartisan, well-run local government. They are hybrids, fusing the old with the new, the untried with the true, that which they are with that which they would like to be. They are Ortega y Gasset's revolting twentieth-century masses who pursue culture, politics, recreation, and community life with a passion not seen in their newly discovered conservative communities for many years.

They have left the city behind, but most of them work there, have attachments there, and are concerned with its problems, unlike the old settlers in their new communities. They will probably never go back, but they think they might. In the meantime, they are in the process of urbanizing their new communities, even while they are adapting to them. They are a disturbing force in these old communities, partially adaptive, partially disruptive, accepting the values but challenging them at the same time. They are in the process of creating a new, more partisan politics in the once tranquil, administratively oriented, nonpartisan Republican-establishment suburbia of Chicago. They are Democrats who have half-adopted some of the better tenets of Republicanism and are forcing their neighbor Republicans to rethink and reevaluate their own party principles and their communal values. These suburban communities are the opposite of the new development suburbs, where politics is negligible and administration is all important. In the old suburban communities, nonpartisan administrative matters are becoming increasingly political and intertwined with county, state, and national political directions and ideologies.

The Suburbs in the '70s. A generation after the beginnings of the great migration from the city, the truth has begun to sink in on the emigres. They can never go back. The city they once knew is gone. The neighborhoods they once lived in have changed. The cultural life and recreational facilities they once thought they could take advantage of are too hard to get to, are too costly, and have lost their appeal after twenty years. The houses for sale are too old, the condominiums too expensive, the rents too high, the streets and transportation facilities too unsafe, the shopping areas too unappealing, and the politics too tough in a city striving to maintain a balance between the old ethnic groups and the rapidly growing black and Latin populations.

What to do now is the question plaguing many of the original city emigres. Since you can't go back, you either stay put or go farther out. To stay put means an older house, now too large for the two of you who are left, greater upkeep to maintain the property, taxes for schools in which you no longer have any children, and the distinct possibility that your property may decline in value as the older suburban communities begin to show the signs of deterioration and develop the problems that originally drove the emigres from the city. To go farther out means trying to sell the house in a deteriorating real estate market. It means pulling up stakes and going, not to the once-familiar old neighborhood in the city, but to a new community farther from your job, socially difficult to break into anew, and probably higher taxes for new schools and other services you don't need any more.

Over the past decade many of the old, established suburban communities, and some of the immediate postwar development suburbs, have become middle-aged municipalities which differ in degree but not very much in kind from the old neighborhoods in the city. What has happened over the past twenty-five years is that the emigres moved the city as they once knew it to the suburbs and urbanized those areas so that they resemble the city of a generation or so ago. However, what is lacking in these communities is the sense of neighborhood that existed in the city. Chicago was never a city in the sense of being a community with which its citizens could identify. It was a city of neighborhoods based on ethnic, religious, and racial identification among people with the same backgrounds, cultures, and interests. In other words, Chicago was a geographic expression, a city made up of a number of separate communities. The older suburbs are cities without any neighborhoods and, in

most instances, without any sense of community at the neighborhood level. They are too large and too fragmented among their
disparate elements to be a community, and too small to encompass
separate, identifiable localities with a strong sense of neighborhood.
As a consequence, many of the people who moved to these
communities in the past twenty-five years find themselves in a new
city or village where they cannot identify with either a neighborhood or a city as a basic community. They are in limbo, living once
again in the city they once left, with many of its attendant problems
but without belonging to or identifying with that city or with any
neighborhood.

The New Migration. A generation after the original mass
migration from the city to the suburbs, Chicago's hinterland is
experiencing a second wave of migrants different from those who
left the city in the post-World War II era. A major segment of this
second wave of migrants is made up of the children born in the
postwar baby boom who are now reaching their maturity. The
progeny of working-class and lower-middle-class parents have
inundated the colleges and universities, have become much more
white collar and professional than their parents, and have raised
their sights socially, culturally, and economically considerably above
the aspirations of their forebears. This whole generation of young
people is earmarked for suburban living by instincts, interests, and
aspirations.

The pattern of living for the twenty- to thirty-year-olds in this
group is already clear. When they graduate from college they do not
go back to the small towns, the old city neighborhoods, or the older
suburban communities from which they came. They move into
apartments in the city in neighborhoods like New Town, Lincoln
Park, Rogers Park, or other such communities, which still have
reasonable rents in older apartment buildings, or into the slums of
the future, the ubiquitous four-plus-ones.

Then the hunt begins for a mate. Once married, these young
couples usually take an apartment in one of these neighborhoods or
else in the close-in suburban communities like Evanston or Oak
Park, near enough to the city for both working partners to
commute, cheap enough to fit the budget, and convenient enough

to the social and cultural activities of the city and its close environs which attract their generation.

But then the first child appears. From that day on, the move to the suburbs is inevitable and inexorable. Where are the adequate parks and playgrounds, safe streets and sidewalks, green grass and yards for these young families? Not in the city. Who needs or can afford the cultural advantages the city offers, now that the family has expanded? And, most important of all, where will the children go to school?

Where to go in search of a house? Not in Evanston, Oak Park, Forest Park, Elmwood Park, or Cicero and Berwyn. They are too old and too much like the city, the houses are too big or too archaic, the natives are from another generation. Not to Winnetka, Glencoe, Olympia Fields, or Flossmoor. They are too expensive, too conservative, and status oriented. Not even so much any more to Skokie, Oak Lawn, Westchester, or South Holland. They were settled by another generation, and, while not aging or deteriorating yet, they are not new enough and are showing signs of developing urban problems. Where does a young couple with a limited income but decent prospects and a small family with plans for more children find a new house on a fair-size lot at a decent price in an area safe from too much urbanization and possible deterioration? Way out in Schaumburg, Palatine, LaGrange Park, Palos Heights, and even in DuPage and Lake counties.

One of the hallmarks of the suburban explosion of the late '60s and early '70s is the great leap outward of the new generation of young marrieds. They are not only leaving the city but are leapfrogging all the old, middle-aged, and fairly new suburbs. They are divorcing themselves from the city permanently and will never go back. Nor will they move inward later to the older suburbs. If they relocate again, they will go farther out, not closer in.

A second group now leaving the city is the small but valiant band of diehards in the areas of the city threatened by the rapidly expanding black ghettoes on the South Side and the far west side. Residents of South Shore, Chatham, Austin, and similar neighborhoods are heading out to Northbrook, Glenview, Elmhurst, Hinsdale, Oak Brook, and other fairly expensive upper-middle-class communities.

The exodus of both of these groups, the young marrieds and the diehards, pales in comparison with a potentially explosive situation which could trigger a mass exodus from the city and radically alter the population balance in Chicago between approximately 1,500,000 whites, 1,300,000 blacks, and 500,000 Latins. That situation is bound up with the dangerously critical financial condition of the Roman Catholic parochial schools in the city. The city of Chicago encompasses the largest Roman Catholic archdiocese in North America, containing nearly 1,750,000 Catholics, most of them working-class or lower-middle-class Poles, Italians, Irish, Bohemians, and Lithuanians. These people make up the bulk of the white citizenry of the city. They have remained in the city primarily because their jobs are located there, and secondarily because they could not afford to move to the suburbs (or at least they thought so). They have remained in the city, too, despite the massive expansion of the black and Latin populations, because they were able to send their children to the Catholic parochial schools, as most Catholic parents do as a matter of religious obligation, and for moral and disciplinary training.

The critical condition of the Roman Catholic parochial schools in Chicago has been generally ignored by downstaters and suburbanites, who are predominantly white and Protestant, on the comforting assumption that even if the parochial schools in Chicago go under, it will be of no concern to them. For all that will happen, they believe, will be a massive inundation of the public schools in Chicago by Catholic children, and that will be a problem only for Mayor Richard J. Daley and the Chicago Board of Education.

That comforting head-in-the-sand juxtaposition of downstaters and suburbanites bids fair to be as invalid as most of the myths on which our enlightened citizenry have been weaned politically. For the fact of this matter may well be that, if the parochial schools in Chicago close, it will not be the city's public schools but, rather, suburban public schools which will be flooded by Catholic children. A fair assumption is that many Catholic parents in Chicago will pick up and leave for the suburbs and their supposedly more desirable public school systems rather than send their children to the Chicago public schools.

They will be encouraged to make the move to the suburbs, too, by the declining importance of the other two factors that have kept them in the city—job opportunities and the cost of suburban housing. The most rapidly expanding industrial growth in the Chicago metropolitan area is in the suburbs, particularly in the northwestern suburban areas. And in the suburban areas, particularly in the far communities, is the rapid expansion of multiple-dwelling units, apartment buildings, and townhouses which will make it possible for working-class city dwellers to make the move to new jobs and apartments at reasonable rents where the children can go to what they think are better schools, far from the city and its attendant problems. The Chicago metropolitan area thus may well be on the verge of a new mass exodus from the city that will make the last twenty-year flood of emigres seem like a trickle, and of a suburban population expansion which will radically alter the old myth of a suburbia of space, green grass, bucolic comfort, and every man a middle-class king in his trouble-free suburban castle.

If the projected population trends for the 1970s in Chicago's suburban ring hold true, these trends will also significantly alter the relationship of the suburbs to both the city of Chicago and the state of Illinois. The growth of the suburban ring, stretching not only into the far reaches of Cook County, but also into DuPage, Kane, Will, Lake, and McHenry, and even into Porter and Lake counties in Indiana, is creating a conglomerate population and urbanized area that is becoming the most important segment of the state of Illinois socially, culturally, economically, and politically. The population of that urban sprawl will be better educated, more economically prosperous, more sophisticated politically, and more demanding than the population of Chicago or downstate Illinois.

We are probably witnessing a major shift in political power in Illinois from the two traditional power centers of the state, Chicago and downstate, to a new entity, the suburban ring of Chicago. That area will have few interests in common with the city, and even fewer interests in common with downstate. It will have numerous problems, some of which can as yet barely be discerned. It will have much of the wealth, the population, and the political power of the state, and it will almost certainly use that power to bend state government and state public policy to its interests.

The New Suburban Politics. What are the emerging patterns of politics in the suburban areas? In the older, settled, well-established suburban cities and villages, the emerging pattern is somewhat different than that in the new development suburban communities. The older communities have always been dominated by a moderately conservative, middle-class, white-collar Republican population. Local governments have traditionally been well run. Schools are good, streets are clean, lawns are neat, police departments are generally incorruptible, zoning ordinances are strictly enforced, budgets are meticulously scrutinized, tax increases are carefully weighed, parks are maintained, and nonpartisan government is expected from the safely Republican administration. In other words, concern for good local administration is accepted as a way of life and a natural concomitant of responsible Republican conduct and philosophy.

The Democratic immigrants moving into the older suburbs have not disturbed the status quo. In fact, they not only support the basic policies of their local governments but are willing and anxious to push them further. Since they moved to these communities for better schools, safer streets, and better recreational facilities for their children, they work harder for school bond issues, parks, and enforcement of zoning regulations than do some of the old settlers whose children have grown up and who do not need the parks and schools as much as the new immigrants.

Any differences about these administrative matters are usually differences in degree rather than in kind. Indeed, there is a remarkable consensus and homogeneity of opinion between the old settlers and the new immigrants. The *noblesse oblige* of the natives and the aspirations of the immigrants have served as a mortar to bind the two groups together in a common effort to keep the community clean, desirable, prosperous, progressive and middle class. In such a milieu, the bare-knuckle political conflicts over administrative matters, which characterize the tract-development suburbs, are mostly nonexistent. Politics is much more genteel, tolerant, and hopefully nonpartisan.

Thus, in contrast to the development communities, where politics is geared essentially to administrative matters, those same administrative problems are, to a considerable extent, removed from the political arena in the old, middle-class suburban communities. However, another significant political development is evolving in these older suburban communities. Ideology is rearing its ugly head in the once homogeneous, administratively oriented communities in both the Democratic and Republican parties. This ideological trend can be attributed basically to two factors, one affecting the Democratic party and the other affecting the Republican party in these communities.

The Democratic Party. Most of the former city Democrats have been Democrats all their lives because of heritage and tradition. They are liberal, anti-machine, generally anti-Daley, and anti-patronage. Their wives are college graduates who majored in subjects like political science, history, sociology, or psychology and have moved past the *Kinder, Küche,* and *Kirche* existence of their mothers, just as their husbands have graduated from the skilled-worker, small-businessman vocations of their fathers. The wives, as much as and sometimes even more than their husbands, are dedicated political activists who, in some cases, have more time than do their husbands to devote to politics.

Neither husbands nor wives are content to live with the ideological status quo in their communities. They need an outlet for their liberalism. They are issue-oriented as well as concerned with good schools, more parks, and clean streets. These administrative matters do not provide a sufficient outlet for their political drives. They are also interested in civil rights, breaking down restrictive housing and employment barriers in their communities, medical care, labor legislation, welfare, and all the other legacies of their New Deal antecedents. At this level they break with their old-settler, Anglo-Saxon-Protestant Republican neighbors. They either attempt to drive the local Democratic organizations to adopt their liberal programs or else set out to capture control of them to further that purpose.

For these Democratic liberals, the old suburban shibboleths propounded by the native Republicans are meaningless or irrelevant. Rugged individualism, private initiative and enterprise, fear of government domination, hostility to federal assistance, and the other traditional tenets are rejected. For the Democratic immigrants, federal aid for schools, public transportation, recreational facilities, civil rights, and metropolitan development are regarded as both necessary and proper. Since most of these problems are local in nature, as well as universal in character, the intertwining of political ideology with local administrative policy is inevitable.

Thus, in contrast to the evolving pattern of Democratic politics in the development suburban communities, where administrative matters are all-important and ideology is almost irrelevant, the internal politics of the Democratic party in the old suburbs is becoming increasingly ideological. In these suburban communities the local Democratic organization and voters can be depended on to support national candidates of their party who profess the traditional liberalism of the party. But they will not go down the line for local, county, or even statewide Democratic candidates who are not attuned to their ideological orientation. Their political activity with regard to such candidates takes the form of lukewarm activity, withholding support, or outright opposition.

The consequences of this development are threefold: First, while the national Democratic party can safely depend on these voters for support for presidential and senatorial candidates, the state and county Democratic parties cannot be assured of that same support for local candidates. Second, since the local candidates cannot rely on any real support from the local organizations, they are forced to rely on amateur volunteers and expend a great deal of time, effort, and money attempting to organize the communities. Such activity on the part of a candidate is usually met by hostility or opposition from the local organization whose territory is being invaded and whose control may be threatened. Third, as the Democratic population of these communities increases in number and power, the Cook County and statewide Democratic organizations will have to pay more attention to the type of candidates they run for county and state offices. Those candidates will have to be less organization-oriented and more ideologically oriented.

Further, because of the geographic concentration of these ideologically oriented Democrats in certain districts or wards of their communities, they can sometimes elect local aldermen to the city council. They then gain a public voice, greater influence in the local Democratic organization, and greater power in determining the choice of legislative, congressional, and county candidates from their districts.

The Republican Party. The increased importance of ideology in the Republican party in the older suburban communities has somewhat different roots than the Democratic ideological orientation. It is, in part, a response to the challenge of the newly arrived Democratic liberals in the suburban communities. The liberalism of the activist Democrats is stimulating a counter conservative reaction among what had been an ideologically fairly quiescent Republican population. As long as there was no serious challenge to the status quo in these communities, there was no need to concern oneself with ideological matters. It was ever thus throughout history. No ruling aristocracy has ever sullied its hands in the political arena unless and until its prerogatives were threatened close to home.

So it is in the old Republican suburbs. Equal opportunity for blacks, tolerance of Jews, and acceptance of Catholics were proper and respectable as long as blacks lived in the South or on Chicago's South Side, Jews stayed on the west side or in Rogers Park, and the Catholics who moved in were the Irish aristocracy who had been in America so long that they could be partially accepted into the ruling class. These people could be tolerated in the community as long as they were not too numerous and did not disturb the status quo. But the Democratic liberals want not only to support a march in Montgomery, Alabama; they also want to march in Fountain Square in Evanston. They want not only to provide public housing in Chicago but also to eliminate restrictive housing covenants in Kenilworth. They want not only better schools in Chicago but also a greater voice in school policy in Glencoe, Oak Park, and Wilmette. The Republicans in these suburbs are being split into four factions over what response to make to the challenge to the status quo in their communities.

There are those Republicans who are totally unaware of the phenomenon. Since they continue to move in their own traditional circles, they are not aware that any problem exists. They rarely participate actively in politics or look at election statistics. They mingle socially, culturally, and politically only with other Republicans who don't participate actively in politics, either, except occasionally to bemoan the loss of county, state, and national elections. And there is always some solace in the fact that the local municipal government and the congressional representative are still Republican.

There are other Republicans who are becoming vaguely aware of the new development, are slightly disturbed by it, but are somewhat baffled as to what to do about it. They do not know how to deal with the situation, and they do not understand the attitudes and aspirations of the new immigrants. In this group are the English, Scotch, Dutch, German, Scandinavian Anglo-Saxon Protestants from Northern and Western Europe who are quiet, polite, and unemotional. They find it difficult, if not impossible, to mix socially or politically with the Eastern and Southern Europeans and Jews who are less polite and more gregarious, emotional, and voluble.

This is not to say that the attitude of the old settlers in these communities is a manifestation of anti-Semitism, anti-Catholicism, or racism in most cases. It reflects, rather, a different pattern of social behavior than that of the incoming immigrants. For, not only do the Anglo-Saxon-Protestant natives fail to speak to the new immigrants, they hardly ever speak to each other or mingle socially, except in a superficial, formal manner. A new arrival in one of these communities finds himself confronted with "a blind audience of closed doors." The doors are closed not only to him but usually to the other native residents of the community as well.

There is also a deeper, much more profound difference in social attitude and behavior between the two groups which affects their political orientation. Among the Anglo-Saxon-Protestant Northern and Western European Republicans are social and familial traditions of individual initiative and effort, of self-reliance and independence, of fragmentation of authority between church and state, between the various organs of the state, and between the state and voluntary organizations. These traditions manifest themselves politically in a primary concern with limiting government in order to protect the freedom of the individual. The Democratic Catholics and Jews have strong traditions of familial and religious collective responsibility in dealing with problems. They come mostly from countries in which the tendency to turn to the state for remedial action is traditional. They are striving for equality more than for freedom in a new society. There is consequently a much greater willingness to accept the growth of governmental power as necessary, and even desirable, to give them the equality for which they are striving.

This attitude has grown even more prevalent as these minorities, including blacks, have become cognizant of two of the basic dynamics of the American political system—the power of determined and united minorities to inhibit or block majority action inimical to their interests by using government to protect themselves from majority oppression, and the ability of such minorities to use government to achieve their own objectives.

In other words, the basic social and political aspirations of these two segments of our population are different, and their attitudes toward government reflect these differences. The blacks realize that government can be used to force integration in schools, equality of employment opportunity, and access to restaurants and hotels. The Jews recognize that government can be used to block the majority from requiring their children to recite Christian prayers in school. The Catholics recognize that the principle of the separation of church and state, enforced by government, gives them equal status under law. They seek, then, not a reduction in the power of government, but rather an expansion of that power, as does the Democratic party. Since the Republican party stands for a reduction of governmental power, it has little to offer these people.

Many of the Republicans in this second group, dimly perceiving what is happening, realize that the proposed changes in the status quo will affect their position in American society. Recognizing that government is the instrument through which alterations in the status quo are being made, they are demanding a reduction in the powers of government and a return to a society in which decisions are made by private individuals or voluntary organizations, with government being used to enforce those decisions. If these people represented a substantial majority of the Republicans in the suburbs, they could conceivably reverse the current of the contemporary American political mainstream.

This, however, is not the case. The Republicans in the suburbs include not only the two groups described above but also two other distinct viewpoints. One of these viewpoints is expressed by a substantial segment of the suburban white Anglo-Saxon Protestants whose religious, moral, and intellectual background and training drives them to support or participate in the efforts of the Catholic-Jewish-black immigrants to achieve an equal place in American society. They do this, not on the ground that they have something to gain themselves, but, rather, on the old fashioned ground that it is right and in accordance with the principles of the American society which they built and which they cherish. Because of their sympathy with the aspirations of the minorities, they are driven to support some Democratic candidates and policies and to oppose some candidates and policies of the Republican party.

Without the active or tacit support of this third Republican group, the existing division of American society between the ethnic, religious, and racial minorities on the one hand and the white Protestants on the other would be much deeper than it is. The Catholics, Jews, and blacks would then be confronted with a difficult, if not impossible, task in achieving equality in American life and in their ultimate objective, the eradication of their status as hyphenated Americans and the acceptance and assimilation as just plain Americans.

There is a fourth group of Republicans who are aware of the problem and look upon the efforts of the minority groups as a threat to their very existence. They are determined to go to any length to keep the minority groups in their proper place in American society, which is to say, in a subordinate position. This group constitutes a small but extremely vocal minority of suburban Republicans.

Here can be found the right-wing fringe of the American political spectrum. The stark truth of the matter is that many of these people welcome the exclusion of Catholics, Jews, and blacks from the Republican party, have no desire to change the existing situation, and would rather continue to be members of a losing but pure, untainted party than try to become a majority party by contaminating their ranks with what are for them the undesirable elements of American society. These aggressive, ideologically oriented, right-wing conservatives are determined to force their Republican neighbors in the suburban communities to make a choice, to stand up and be counted, or else be counted out of the local Republican organizations.

The right-wing conservatives have learned the lesson of American politics. They are infiltrating the local organizations, working precincts, distributing literature, holding meetings, and running for local offices. Where they gain influence on or capture control of a local organization, the ideologically moderate Republicans are offered the alternatives of adjusting to and accepting the true faith of unreconstructed conservatism or of abdicating the political arena. Or, they can overcome the habits and predilections of a lifetime of moderate Republicanism and move half-heartedly and unwillingly into the Democratic party.

The old, administratively oriented, nonideological character of Republican politics is disintegrating in the establishment suburbs. It will no longer suffice for the local Republican professional politicians to pay lip service to conservatism at the national level while ignoring ideology in local matters. The interrelationship of local and national politics on an ideological level is paramount for the right-wing conservatives. Even more than their Democratic liberal counterparts, they call to account all candidates of their party at any level on an ideological basis.

These developments in both the Democratic and Republican parties are slowly changing the traditional character of politics in the suburbs. Administrative efficiency on the part of elected officials is still demanded. Fidelity to the principle of nonpartisan school, park, and zoning boards is still required. Bond issues for local improvements are sometimes still supported. Personal adherence to the code of middle-class homogeneity and respectability is still observed. But the barely audible murmur of ideological controversy is slowly rising in volume and may, in time, reach a forte. The faint echoes of the distant trumpets of the liberal Democratic Joshuas are becoming louder as they reach the approaches and gather strength for an assault on the conservative walls of these communities. Inside the walls of these Jerichos, the ideologically oriented conservative defenders of the citadels are marshaling their forces in preparation for the defense of the established order. Between the ideological zealots stand the mass of the populace— some unknowing, some unseeing, some uninterested, some uncertain of what the controversy is about, and some unsure of which group of ideological activists is right about the need for change in their communities. The spreading malignancy of political and administrative controversy is disturbing the outwardly peaceful suburban body politic. If it continues to grow, a new era of suburban politics may be at hand.

It is clear that, in the near future, the political power centers of our society will be in the suburban areas. In those areas, the political leaders will increasingly have to concentrate their efforts. Since private self-interest is a dominant motivation in the political behavior of the suburban voters, as well as of the politicians, the politicians will have to search out the relevant self-interests of the voters. Their problem will be complicated by the fact that the primary self-interests of the voters will be in a constant state of flux. What they need today, they will not need tomorrow. What satisfied them yesterday will not pacify them today. They are products of a fast-changing society. In contemporary American society, no man is sure of his place and no man need be satisfied with his place.

The primary requisite of successful political leadership in both parties in a rapidly changing society will be, as it always has been, to give service to the current needs of the voters. But the attempt to give that service will be enormously complicated by the constantly changing nature of the demands the voters will make. When they first move out to these suburban areas they need elementary schools, parks, tot lots, and superhighways to get them into the city to their jobs. As the expressways become clogged with traffic, they will blame the politicians in frustration as they creep toward home at night at ten miles per hour. They will need government-subsidized rail transportation to get them to their jobs quickly and safely. As the shopping centers and factories move out to their communities, they demand public bus transportation within their communities. As the children grow up, they will lose interest in parks and tot lots and will need high schools and local recreational facilities to keep the teen-agers out of trouble. As the cost of educating their children at the good private colleges and state universities increases steadily, they will need community junior and four-year commuter colleges. As taxes go up to provide funds for these manifold necessities, they will become increasingly suspicious of and bitter toward the political leadership which they will hold responsible for their troubles. When the children leave, they will resist tax increases for services they no longer need. As the inevitable pattern of slow deterioration of communities sets in, and as the urban problems they fled multiply and begin to plague them in their new communities, they will be ready to vent their ire on those whom they elected to office. Every practicing politician knows how easily the voters forget past services, how quickly their attitude changes from appreciation for services rendered to "what have you done for me lately?" They will be much more difficult to deal with than their fathers and mothers in the city. They will be better educated, more demanding, more expectant of things which they consider a birthright, not a gift, and more capable of exacting retribution from those they hold responsible.

The New Politics of Old Suburbia. For the Democratic party in the establishment suburban communities, the old appeal of Jeffersonian and Jacksonian democracy will not suffice to hold the Brooks Brothers-clothed liberals in line. Like all newly arrived classes in a developing society, they tend to emulate the attitudes, customs, and traditions of the established ruling class. In their attitudes toward the administrative functions of government they are more like Republicans than like their Democratic fathers. They want merit employment and efficiency in public office. They want, above all, to be respectable, to be accepted as equals, to conform to the mores of the old, established middle class. They do not want to be identified with the proletarian Jacksonian heritage of their party. They will resist all attempts to establish party organizations and party principles in their communities based on patronage, political clout, and political expediency.

Nor will they allow themselves to be identified with a party of "Rum, Romanism and Rebellion." They drink scotch, not rum; their Catholicism is the Americanized version; their Judaism is reform, not orthodox; and they are not rebels but are, rather, dissatisfied conformists.

They reject also the Wilsonian brand of idealism as a guide for political action. It is too impractical, not hardheaded enough, and smacks too much of an ancient reformism which is not suitable to their times. Neither will they identify themselves too strongly with the Rooseveltian, New Deal philosophy of their party in the same sense that their fathers did. They do not need welfare. They already have their civil rights. They are successful enough not to require minimum-wage, maximum-hour and social-security legislation for themselves. They still support these things, not as their fathers did, out of elemental self-interest, but out of a sense of *noblesse oblige* for those less fortunate. In this respect, they are like their Anglo-Saxon-Protestant, moderately liberal Republican counterparts—the Percys, Lindsays, Hatfields, Rockefellers, and Brookes. They will cross party lines to vote for these candidates in preference to the traditional, organization-oriented politicians. They will remain Democrats, but they are a new breed. They are not Jeffersonians, Jacksonians, Wilsonians, Rooseveltians, or even Johnsonians.

John F. Kennedy was more their type. Young, handsome, intellectual, successful, tough-minded but moderately liberal, he appealed to them as the prototype of what they would like to be or to have represent and lead them. They will support such men from their own party at the national, state, or local level. But they will also support Republicans of that type at those levels.

To hold these suburban Democratic liberals, the Democratic party in the establishment suburbs will have to become more like the Republican party in the sense of stressing ideology more than materialistic almsgiving. Not the ideology of conservatism, which they reject, but an ideology of moderate liberalism, tempered by fiscally sound and administratively efficient public policies.

The Old Politics of New Suburbia. The problem for both the Republican and the Democratic parties in the development communities is significantly different from that in the establishment communities. It will be a long time before ideological considerations will be very important in the development communities. Ideology is meaningful to upper-middle-class and wealthy people who are no longer concerned with the elemental struggle for survival in society. Since most of the people in the development communities are lower-middle class or working class, their primary political concerns will continue to be property values, zoning, real estate taxes, and similar matters. They are generally opposed to the extension of civil rights. They don't even think about federal-state relationships. They are not on welfare and are suspicious of those who are. They are thankful that there are schools close by for the children, even if the quality isn't the best. In these communities, politics will be geared for a long time to the bread-and-butter issues and to those candidates, regardless of party affiliation, who will do more to care for their needs and alleviate their problems.

In essence, politics in these communities will be similar to politics in the city, where service rendered by the political organization will be the primary criterion for the voters. The services demanded by the voters will differ from those they asked for in the city, but the relationship will be the same. The one

significant difference is that the Democratic party in these communities does not have the built-in organizations and power
structures that it has in the city. Since these communities are so
new, the Republican organizations in these areas do not have the
built-in strength or power to automatically inherit their votes,
either. The political spoils will go to the most efficient, able, and
successful politicians in both parties who can adapt themselves and
their organizations to the current needs and aspirations of the
people in these communities.

City-Suburban Relationships. If the foregoing analysis is valid,
we are entering a new era in American politics. American society
changed from an agricultural-small-town society to an industrial-
big-city society in the hundred years of the last half of the
nineteenth century and the first half of the twentieth century. We
are now in the process of becoming an urban-metropolitan society.
Political institutions, if they are to survive, must reflect the
character of the societies they represent and adapt themselves to
changing conditions in those societies. The task of local political
leadership in changing times is to point the direction and lead the
way in adapting political institutions to changing local conditions.

How have Democratic machine politicians in the city of
Chicago responded to the challenge of the rapidly changing social,
economic, and political conditions of the city's suburban ring?
Hardly at all. The aging leadership of the machine, made up heavily
of ward committeemen from the city, still refer to the suburbs of
Chicago as "the country towns." Encased within the framework of
their parochialism, the machine's governors have little concept
of the revolutionary social and political changes which are taking
place. Few of them ever leave the boundaries of their own ward,
except to journey to the Loop for business at City Hall or to the
party headquarters in the LaSalle hotel. Any hegira across the city's
boundaries to the suburban areas of Cook County is tantamount to
traveling to a foreign land.

As for the up-and-coming younger leadership of the party in
Chicago, they are, as a group, "young fogies," who differ in age but
not in philosophy or orientation from their senior counterparts in
the machine. While they are better educated than their older peers
in the party, and somewhat less parochial in their view of the world,

they are, on the whole, carbon copies of their elders—conservative, machine oriented, and generally incapable of understanding or dealing with the political revolution taking place in the suburbs.

There is little chance, in the foreseeable future, that the older or younger leadership of the party in the city will ever be capable of understanding or dealing with the needs, interests, and political aspirations of the burgeoning suburban area of Cook County. Given the traditional political orientation of that leadership, and the steadily widening social, cultural, economic, and political cleavages which are developing between the city and the suburbs, the people of Chicago and those in the suburbs will have even less in common in the future than they have in the present or have had in the past. The machine's leadership in the city, whatever their age bracket, will have to come to terms with the problems and aspirations of the black and Spanish-speaking population of the city, while the suburban population will become increasingly uninterested in the problems and politics of the city.

In the past, the interests of the suburban population in the Democratic machine's internal dynamics were of little relevance to the machine's programs and planning. The machine's leaders went about the business of choosing candidates, electing them to office, and distributing the rewards and perquisites of office, with little regard for the interests of the people of the suburbs, either Democrats or Republicans. Suburban Democrats were almost never slated for major offices. Since they were hardly ever slated, they were rarely elected to major public office in Cook County. And, since suburbanites traditionally held almost no major public offices, the influence of the suburban population on the machine's leadership and on the public policies which the machine's minions in government pursued was negligible.

However, as the suburban population continues to grow and as the city population continues to decline in relationship to the suburbs, the suburbs will have an increasingly powerful voice in selecting and electing candidates to all major county offices. The machine's practice of slating city politicians for all major county offices will no longer almost automatically insure the election of those candidates to those offices. And, as machine politicians in the city are driven to pacify the interests and aspirations of the black, Spanish-speaking, and other minority groups in the city, the machine's city leadership will be inevitably separated from the interests and needs of the suburban electorate.

In other words, the growing power of the suburban electorate and the machine's built-in incapacity to pacify the interests of the suburban population while trying to maintain its power base in the city will confront the machine with an almost insoluble dilemma. If the machine continues to slate city politicians for the major county offices, they will have little appeal to a suburban population which will become increasingly cognizant of its own interests and of the machine's policy of subordinating suburban interests to those of the machine in the city. If, on the other hand, the machine gives in and turns major county offices over to Democratic suburban political leadership, the power and prestige of the suburban leadership will be increased at the expense of the city politicians who dominate the machine today. In fact, as the suburban population becomes increasingly aware that their county tax dollars are being used for welfare, jails, criminal courts, hospitals, and other government services, which are generally irrelevant to the needs of the suburban population, the demand for suburban influence on, and control of, county public policies will inevitably be strengthened. If the Democratic party of Cook County is unwilling to pacify suburban interests, a coalition of suburban Democrats and Republicans, and city Republicans and Independents, could capture control of major county offices like president of the county board, county assessor, county clerk, county treasurer, and state's attorney.

The loss of patronage jobs, fundraising capabilities, control of the election machinery in suburban areas, and the prosecutive powers of the state's attorney would be a body blow to the machine's power, not only in the county, but also in the city. Many city precinct captains hold patronage jobs in county offices. Control of the county assessor's office is vital to the fund-raising activities of the Democratic party of Cook County. The county clerk's control of the selection and training of election judges, of designating polling places and positions on the ballot, and of the election machinery in the suburban areas is also an integral part of the Democratic party's strategy for electoral victories. The county assessor and the county treasurer, as well as the board of tax appeals, provide links for the party to the business and financial powers in the city. The state's attorney's powers as the chief prosecutive office for violations of state civil and criminal law in the Circuit Court of Cook County always present an inherent threat to the activities and interests of Democratic politicians in the city.

The loss of major county offices to a coalition of Republicans and independent Democrats could stimulate the reform of patronage practices, closer supervision of elections, investigation of property assessment and tax procedures, and a significant growth in the power of suburban banks, businesses, newspapers, and civic organizations. Advertising contracts could go to suburban newspapers, thus increasing their financial profits and their stake in supporting political candidates from the suburbs who represent their interests. County funds could be deposited in suburban banks rather than in city banks, thus increasing the influence and viability of those banks in the Chicago metropolitan area. Young suburban lawyers, whose interests and objectives could differ considerably from those of city Democratic precinct captain lawyers, could staff the state's attorney's office, and could provide the thrust and manpower for on-going investigations of the city's politicians and their activities. A county board president, whose powers are significant, could be elected on a platform of orienting county public policies toward the interests of the suburban areas rather than to the interests of the city. Thus, the future of the machine, as a county machine, is inevitably bound up with its relationship to the suburban population of Cook County at a time when the interests of the population of the city and those of the population of the suburbs are steadily diverging, and the need to recognize suburban interests conflicts with the machine's need to pacify the interests of the blacks, Latins, and ethnic Catholics in Chicago.

The Machine and the Blacks

The survival of the machine in Chicago will depend heavily upon its ability to come to terms with the blacks, Latins, and other minorities in the city, regardless of what happens to the machine in the county. And the future of the machine in the city will be bound up with the developing course of black and Latin politics in Chicago. It is time to turn to an analysis of the most significant political factor in Chicago's politics today—the future of black politics in the city.

The Evolution of Black Politics in Chicago. The role of blacks in the contemporary Chicago Democratic machine is closely tied to the rise to power of one black leader, William L. Dawson. Although several blacks held public office in Chicago, in Cook County, and in Illinois prior to Dawson's arrival on the political scene in 1933, Dawson almost singlehandedly created a powerful black sub-machine in Chicago as an integral part of the Democratic organization.

Before Dawson's rise to political prominence in Chicago, the black vote had traditionally been solidly Republican. Two leading black politicians, both Republicans, Edward H. Wright and Oscar DePriest, had been the leading black political figures in the city. Both Wright and DePriest, who served as aldermen, achieved prominence in Chicago politics through a relationship with Mayor William Hale ("Big Bill the Builder") Thompson, who was mayor of Chicago from 1915 to 1923, and from 1927 to 1931. Thompson effectively organized Chicago's black community politically as an integral component of his personal political organization. Recognizing the traditional affiliation of the immigrant blacks from the South with the Republican party nationally, as a consequence of the freeing of the slaves during the Civil War, Thompson effectively built upon that base by making concessions to the black community in Chicago and by utilizing black leaders like Wright and DePriest for his own political ambitions, as well as for the needs of the growing black community. Black affiliation with the Republican party in Chicago was buttressed by the fact that black political leaders recognized that they could gain more for themselves and for their constituents by tying themselves to the existing power structure in the city, rather than by attempting to challenge it from the outside.

The Great Depression, beginning in 1929, the coming to power of Franklin D. Roosevelt as president of the United States, and the subsequent New Deal welfare programs offered by Roosevelt's administration, helped to break the political stranglehold of the Republican party in Chicago on the black community. A significant defection of black voters to the local, as well as the national, Democratic party began in the early 1930s. However, many of the old ties and loyalties still influenced black voters in cities like Chicago. Black political leaders across the country reserved judgment on Roosevelt's intentions with regard to their constituencies until he demonstrated that he meant the New Deal to be a permanent part of American life, and that the welfare programs offered by the New Deal would benefit the black community. In this period of tentative black defection from the Republican party to the Democratic party, nationally and locally, without a firm commitment on the part of black voters at either level, William Dawson arrived on the political scene in Chicago.

Dawson was elected as a Republican alderman from the 2nd Ward on Chicago's near South Side in 1933. Six years later, in 1939, Dawson was defeated for his aldermanic seat, running third as a Republican in a field of four candidates. The incumbent Democratic mayor of Chicago, Edward H. Kelly, who had succeeded Anton J. Cermak when Cermak was assassinated in Miami Beach in 1933, was casting about for a black political leader who could assist him and the local Democratic party in solidifying their hold on the black community. Kelly, together with Pat Nash, had inherited the Democratic machine which Cermak had created in 1931. Kelly approached Dawson, after Dawson's loss of his aldermanic seat in 1939, and offered him the position of Democratic committeeman in the 2nd Ward. Dawson accepted, switched parties, and began his rise as the most powerful black political leader in Chicago's history. As James Q. Wilson described it in 1960 in his classic study of black politics in Chicago, *Negro Politics*, "The Negro Democratic machine which now exists in Chicago is the product of twenty years of work. Dawson, by virtue of his considerable political skill, the patronage placed at his disposal, and a favorable public opinion, not only secured his own position as committeeman of the second ward, but created a network of obligations and loyalties which brought under his control the organization of five or six Negro wards. . . . Since 1939, Dawson's power on the South Side has grown steadily, with hardly a single important setback. Negroes objectionable to him were removed from their posts as ward committeemen in other Negro wards and replaced by men in whom he had greater confidence. Dawson was seen by his followers as a stern father, quick to punish insubordination or incompetence, but quick to forgive. He made few lasting enemies, although he frequently dealt very harshly with rivals."

Through gradually building his power and gaining control of the black wards on Chicago's South Side, Dawson became one of the most important figures in the Cook County Democratic organization, subordinate in power and influence only to some of the major Irish committeemen. He controlled massive patronage, dictated to half a dozen ward committeemen and aldermen, dominated a bloc of black votes in the Illinois General Assembly, was named secretary of the Democratic Cook County Central Committee, and had himself elected to Congress in 1942, holding the seat until his death in 1970. In 1955, Dawson was instrumental in helping County Chairman Richard J. Daley deny renomination to incumbent Mayor Martin J. Kennelly as the Democratic party's candidate for the mayoralty, a favor which Daley never forgot.

During Dawson's tenure as boss of the black sub-machine in Chicago, the black wards became the bulwark of Democratic strength in city elections. As the black population rapidly increased between 1940 and 1970, and as the white population moved to the suburbs, Dawson's influence as a major party leader within the overall Democratic machine in the city went unchallenged from within the organization. And, while there were occasional challenges to Dawson's authority from dissatisfied or dissident black politicians on Chicago's South Side, none of them ever seriously threatened Dawson's control or influence while he remained in good health.

Since Dawson's death, no single black political leader has been able to achieve the preeminent, almost dictatorial position that Dawson held within the black political community, partly because Mayor Daley has not bestowed the mantle of leadership on any single black political leader in the way that Mayor Kelly did on Dawson in 1939. Daley recognizes that, because the blacks are the largest ethnic group in the city today, making up approximately 40 percent of the city's population, the situation within the Democratic machine is significantly different than it was in 1939. In 1939, there were approximately 250,000 blacks in Chicago out of a total population of approximately 3,400,000. In 1975 there are approximately 1,300,000 blacks in Chicago out of a total population of 3,300,000. In the contemporary milieu of Chicago politics, an ambitious, capable black political leader who unified the black political community under his control, as Dawson did for 30 years, would automatically become the most powerful political figure in the city and would probably lay claim to the nomination for the mayoralty of Chicago at the end of Daley's current reign. It is better for those who control the machine in Chicago today to keep the black political community fragmented, to divide power so that no single black politician can emerge as the dominant figure, and thus to postpone, if not permanently defer, the day when a black mayor of Chicago will be elected.

It is also true, however, that no black politician on the contemporary political scene has demonstrated the ability and political sagacity to take control of the black sub-machine in the overall citywide machine. This situation is partly due, as Wilson pointed out, to the fact that community and civic leaders in the black community do not have the same goals and aspirations as do black politicians generally. Many of the black community and civic leaders are oriented toward what Wilson called "status ends," toward achieving integration in the community-at-large with their white counterparts of a comparable socioeconomic status. They seek, not so much an across-the-board uplift of the black community but, rather, recognition of themselves and their achievements in the community at large. Black politicians, on the other hand, as Wilson pointed out, are more generally oriented toward "welfare ends." They seek a more general uplift of the black community as a whole. They would rather gild the ghetto than break it up. Gilding the ghetto insures their own tenures of office, indebts their constituencies to them, and enables them to advance themselves within the Democratic machine in the city and to garner unto themselves the political and economic perquisites of their positions. Thus, within the black community, a divergence of ambitions and interests exists between black political leaders who are active in the Democratic machine in Chicago, and black community and civic leaders who have made it in Chicago outside the framework of politics, and who are much more numerous and influential in the city than their forebears were in Dawson's day.

There is also a geographic factor which was nonexistent in Dawson's day, when the blacks who came up from the South to Chicago were concentrated almost exclusively on the near South Side of the city. With the massive growth of the black population in Chicago, however, the black community has spread to the southeast, southwest, and far south sides of the city. In the last two

decades, too, there has been a massive black migration to the west
side of the city into the Lawndale, Garfield Park, and Austin
communities, and a substantial subsidiary black migration to the
North Side lakefront wards from the Near North Side to East
Rogers Park.

The South Side black political leadership has little influence in
or control over the black communities on the west side and the
developing black communities on the North Side. On the west side,
in Lawndale, Austin, and Garfield Park, the black political organizations in the wards in those areas developed under the leadership of
white, absentee-landlord political figures like Bernard Neistein in
the 29th Ward and Izie Horwitz in the 24th Ward. In west side
wards like the 1st, 25th, 26th, 27th, and 28th wards, which do not
have a majority of blacks, the existing machine white political
leadership has managed to contain and control any serious challenge to their power from the black communities in those areas. But
where black majorities developed rapidly, in wards like the 24th
and the 29th, a tentative, uneasy partnership developed between
the aging, absentee white leadership of the wards and ambitious
local black political leaders who are content to go along with a
piece of the pie until such time as they can cut up the whole pie for
themselves.

Thus, for a combination of factors, it is unlikely, in the
immediate future, that any black political leader will be able to
achieve the position that Dawson held in the black community.
With Daley unwilling or unready to put the mantle on any single
black leader; with the growing social, cultural, and economic
divisions within the black community between the black middle
class, the working class, and the welfare poor; and with the
geographic fragmentation of the black community between the
South Side, the west side, and parts of the North Side, it will be
difficult, if not impossible, for any black politician to do what
Dawson did thirty-five years ago.

Contemporary Black Politics in Chicago. If social, cultural, and
economic conditions in a community determine the political
patterns and institutions of that community, then the geographic,
social, cultural, and economic fragmentation of Chicago's black
community make it unlikely that any single, powerful black leader,

comparable to Dawson, will emerge in the foreseeable future. What
is more likely is that black coalition politics, rather than the
monolithic authoritarianism which existed under Dawson, will
slowly develop in Chicago.

Politically, Chicago's black community is fragmented between
three leadership groups and three groups of followers. The leadership groups are black machine politicians, black political independents, and black civil rights activists. The mass of the black
community can be divided into the emerging black middle class, the
black working class, and the black welfare poor.

After Dawson's death, his key lieutenants, committeemen
Claude Holman of the 4th Ward, Ralph Metcalfe of the 2nd Ward,
and Kenneth Campbell of the 20th Ward, had neither the ability
nor the power to assume Dawson's mantle. And, of those three key
black committeemen, two—Holman and Campbell—have died, and
Metcalfe, although elected to Congress in Dawson's place by the
machine, has declared his independence of the machine and has
taken an active role in leadership in the black community on the
civil rights issue.

Within the machine, a group of younger black committeemen
are gradually gaining power, not in the black community as a whole
but within their wards, in the hierarchy of the Democratic
organization, and in the city, county, and state governments. Ward
committeemen like State Senator Cecil Partee, Alderman Wilson
Frost, Alderman William Shannon, County Commissioner John
Stroger, Alderman Eugene Sawyer, and City Treasurer Joseph
Bertrand, the first black elected to a citywide office in Chicago's
history, share some of the power and perquisites that Dawson once
controlled monolithically. As a group, these men are well educated,
articulate, ambitious, and capable. They are, to date, cooperative
with Mayor Daley and the ethnic white leadership of the machine,
and are not yet ready to attempt to seize control of the Democratic
organization or of the city.

The black political independents have had little influence on the
course of politics in Chicago. People like Aldermen William Cousins
and Anna Langford, who vote with the liberal white independents
in the city council, make the newspapers and the television news
broadcasts occasionally but have little influence in the council, in
their own wards, or in the black community at large. They do not

control patronage, are limited in the favors and services that they can perform for their constituents, and, although tolerated by their committeemen and the black leadership in the organization, are not consulted or respected. Other black political independents like former Alderman Fred Hubbard, who was elected as a reform alderman from the 2nd Ward but was co-opted by the machine, and was finally sent to federal prison for embezzlement; A. A. Rayner, who was elected to the city council for one term but then gave up his seat and his political ambitions after an abortive try for Congress; and Augustus Savage, a black newspaper publisher, who tried several times for public office without success; all made a brief splash in Chicago's political waters without leaving a lasting impression.

At this stage of black political development in Chicago, the black political independents in the city are clearly little more than a nuisance to the machine at large, and to the black machine politicians in particular. And, while it may be possible for other black political independents to make it to the city council in the future, it is also unlikely that their numbers will increase significantly or their power radically.

As for the black civil rights activists' influence on Chicago's political scene in general, and on the politics of the black community in particular, their role also has been negligible. In 1966, when the Reverend Martin Luther King, Jr., came to Chicago under the auspices of the Southern Christian Leadership Conference to organize the black community politically, his crusade was an abysmal failure. On his arrival in Chicago, Dr. King declared that he "had never been nonpolitical" and told Chicago's blacks, "Our vote can and will be the balance of power" in electing the next mayor of Chicago. He also warned Mayor Daley that he would "fill the jails if necessary" to call attention to the plight of blacks in Chicago. Daley, on his part, made his position clear. "When you take the law into your own hands," he told Dr. King, "we lose orderly government . . . and this will not be tolerated as long as I am mayor of Chicago."

When the results were in after the 1967 mayoral election, it was clear who had been right about Chicago's politics. Daley carried all fifty wards in the city and Dr. King went home to Alabama, having been taught a lesson in politics by a past master at the game,

Richard J. Daley. "When you take on something like the Chicago machine," said the Reverend Andrew Young, Dr. King's top assistant in the campaign, "you have to be good and ready." In 1966 and 1967, the Southern Christian Leadership Conference, in taking on the Chicago machine and its master tactician, was neither good enough nor really ready. Dr. King had been an effective and articulate spokesman for a national movement, but, as a political strategist in the milieu of Chicago politics, he was playing ball in Daley's league and had neither the muscle nor the talent to win the game.

The same thing has been true, to date, of other anti-Daley black politicians. The Reverend Jesse Jackson, the head of Operation PUSH (People United to Save Humanity), has built an economic power base in the city but has been an abysmal failure as a politician. Other black radicals like Lawrence Landry and Robert Lucas, who opposed the Chicago machine, have disappeared from the scene. An outspoken critic, comedian Dick Gregory, has given up the fight and left the city. Would-be mayoral candidates State Senator Richard Newhouse and Duke McNeil have had little impact on the city's body politic. Politically astute and successful one-time black opponents like State Senator Charles Chew, who defeated the organization twice, have been taken into the fold and given recognition and perquisites. And Congressman Ralph Metcalfe, a one-time machine stalwart who broke away in the early 1970s, backed away from an anti-Daley mayoral candidacy in 1975 after surveying his prospects.

The failures of black radicals and civil rights activists can be attributed to several factors: their mistaken reading of the ambitions and interests of their black constituencies; their inability to seize control of any of the levers of power in the city and in the black community; and Daley's successful co-optation, not only of many of the black political leaders in the city, but also of the major black organizations such as the Urban League and the local NAACP. Many of the civic and community leaders who dominate those organizations have different goals than do the black radicals and civil rights activists, have recognized the reality of the power structure in Chicago, and are aware of what Daley has done and can do for the city and its people, including the leadership and much of the rank and file of the black community.

As for the three major black constituencies that follow the three groups of leadership elites, the machine has managed to pacify and control all of them. The growing black middle class, which is gaining an ever-increasing share of the city's economic, cultural, and social perquisites, has been fairly quiescent politically, satisfied to elect a Cousins, a Langford, or a Hubbard occasionally, but unwilling to participate in the kind of political activity necessary to unseat the black machine politicians in their wards or influence the central leadership of the city machine. As the black middle class has gained economic and social status, it has become increasingly disenchanted with the programs of black radicals and civil rights activists. Indeed, one of the major drives of the black middle class has been to separate itself from the black welfare poor, identify itself more by class than by race, and come to terms with its peers in the white community in Chicago. In other words, the growing black middle class in Chicago is becoming a status quo-oriented, conservative entity within the black community.

The black working class in Chicago, like the black middle class, is basically conservative politically as it gains economic stability. Although its social and cultural interests and ambitions differ somewhat from those of the emerging black middle class in the city, its economic interests propel it toward cooperation with the overall city machine, and its local black subdivisions, since the machine holds the keys to unlock the doors to opportunities and services. Since the goals of the black working class are primarily economic rather than political, it is willing to subordinate its political interests to its economic interests.

The machine deals with the welfare poor in the black community by utilizing and administering federal, state, county, and city welfare programs in a manner best calculated to serve the interests of the machine, as well as of the poor. Since the machine controls the city and county governments, and has a powerful voice in the activities of the state and national governments, access to government welfare programs can best be achieved by cooperating with and supporting the machine politically. The black welfare poor are driven, almost by necessity, to support the status quo in the city, as long as that status quo provides adequate sustenance and care. Since the machine, through its precinct organizations in the black community, provides the link for the welfare poor to the agencies of government which allocate benefits, the great mass of the welfare poor are in no condition to support a political challenge to the machine, particularly at the ward level.

Thus, the machine's relationships with the black community in Chicago are an amalgam of reward and the threat of punishment. Reciprocal cooperation between segments of the black community and the city machine result in mutual benefits to both sides. Political support is rewarded, apathy is punished, and hostility is dealt with by the threat of force or the use of countervailing power. However, this short-term stability is threatened by the development of a long-range inherent problem which is built into the machine's relationships with the black community and with the white ethnics in Chicago. It is time to turn to an analysis of that situation.

Ethnics and Blacks. The most significant fact of cultural, social, economic, and political life in Chicago over the past three decades has been the relationship between the black and ethnic white Catholic populations of the city.

Cities like Chicago have always been made up of ethnically segregated neighborhoods. The Protestants were segregated from the Catholics, the Jews from both Protestants and Catholics, the Irish from the Poles, the Poles from the Lithuanians, the Lithuanians from the Bohemians, the Bohemians from the Germans, the Germans from the Italians, and all these groups from each other. The ethnic groups in Chicago have never really wanted integration with each other, and most of them do not want it today, especially with their black and Latin fellow citizens. They wanted equal opportunity in America, and that, at most, is what they are prepared to give to the last of the great immigrant groups, the blacks and Latins in the city.

An important factor that has to be considered in black-ethnic white relationships is the social and economic status of a large part of the ethnic white community in Chicago. Chicago's ethnic whites, who are heavily working class and lower-middle class, are threatened the most by the black drive for equality in the city. Economically and socially, they are the group that the blacks are pushing in on. It is mostly their neighborhoods and places of employment that are threatened with integration. The black ghetto does not move great distances across the city but, rather, creeps from block to block. Blacks seeking equal employment opportunities are not yet ready to move in great numbers into professional fields like law or medicine, which have a high percentage of Jews and upper-middle-class Irish Catholics, or fields like engineering, middle management, and college teaching, which are dominated by white Protestants. Blacks are pushing hardest into steel mills and stockyards, into factories and construction jobs, into local and federal government jobs, into banking and other clerical tasks, into driving CTA buses and taxicabs.

These are the fields which the Poles, Irish, Bohemians, Lithuanians, and Italians are slowly leaving as they move onto the next levels of American economic society. But now the police and fire departments are being threatened, and the skilled trades and the teamsters unions are targets of the rising black working class. For the Polish, Bohemian, German, Irish, Lithuanian, or Italian second- or third-generation American moving up the economic ladder, there seems to be no escape. As he leaves one level of American economic status to ascend to the next level, the black is hot on his heels, pushing to move in, not behind him, but alongside him and, hopefully, in time, in front of him.

The same thing is true of housing. The neighborhoods of these ethnic groups are being invaded by the spreading black ghetto. No sooner do the members of one ethnic group create a new neighborhood, in which they feel secure and safe culturally and socially with people of their own kind, than the strangers appear again, asking for entrance to the community.

To the working-class or lower-middle-class second-generation American of Eastern or Southern European origin, his home is truly his castle and represents the fulfillment of having achieved a worthwhile social status. That home is most meaningful to him within the confines of a neighborhood in which he feels comfortable and safe. He tends to identify himself, not only with his own personal piece of property, but also with that surrounding area which encompasses other people of a similar nationality, race, and religion. A black moving into any house in *his* community represents a direct, personal affront to *his* neighborhood and, ultimately, as far as he is concerned, to his castle. He escapes racial integration by sending his children to the parochial schools, as most Catholic parents do as a matter of religious preference and obligation. But even that is becoming something of a problem since the parochial elementary and high schools are having serious financial difficulties, and since many black parents are beginning to send their own children to the parochial schools in preference to the city's public schools.

In view of these problems, the prospects for eliminating or significantly reducing tensions between the black population and the ethnic whites of Chicago are doubtful in the near future if the black drive for, not just equality of opportunity, but integration were to continue. While there has been a significant change in the attitude of some of the religious hierarchy and most business leaders, and active pressure from some lay Catholic leaders and members of the religious orders in Chicago, that change has not filtered down much to the great majority of the ethnic whites in the city. Changing their attitudes will take time and continuous effort. If intransigent civil rights leaders continue to push hard for integration, and if the equally intransigent majority of Chicago's ethnic white citizens continue to resist housing integration, black-ethnic white tensions will remain at a fairly high level in the city for some time to come.

There is little reason, however, to believe that the great majority of Chicago's blacks are much more interested in integrating neighborhoods than their ethnic white fellow Chicagoans have been. They are more interested in expanding economic opportunities; in improving the quality of schools, housing, and recreational facilities in the ghetto; in safer streets and better police protection in their neighborhoods from muggers, rapists, and street gang terrorists; and in opening up better opportunities in American life for their children. In this way, their aspirations are not significantly different from those of their ethnic white counterparts among the city's citizenry, except that it is significantly more difficult for the blacks to move down the road toward fulfillment of those aspirations.

There are some indications that the resources of the white community are being mobilized to provide maximum equality of opportunity as quickly as possible. In Chicago, the enlightened attitude of the business leadership of the city, which has been pushing hard to open the doors to economic opportunities, and the willingness of some of the Roman Catholic hierarchy to push forward in helping Chicago's blacks integrate into the life of the city, has been opening the doors steadily, if not completely.

Until recently, the Roman Catholic hierarchy in Chicago, like the Catholic hierarchy in America, had an essentially conservative political outlook. Like the Democratic organization, the Catholic hierarchy in Chicago reflected, not only the attitudes of the churchmen themselves, but also the attitudes of the great majority of their parishioners. Since the Catholic hierarchy has always had strong ties to and considerable influence on the Democratic leaders in the city, who are mostly members of the Church of Rome, the conservative character of Democratic politics in Chicago has been further buttressed by that relationship. The more liberal attitude and leadership espoused by some of the Catholic hierarchy have not struck a very responsive chord among many of their parishioners. They are still a considerable distance out in front of most of their flock on the issue of civil rights. Despite the steady development of active, liberal civil rights leadership among the younger laity, clergy, and members of the religious orders, and in some Catholic organizations, the great majority of the ethnic white Catholics in Chicago resent such activity on the part of the clergy and are not sympathetic to the more liberal elements in the Catholic community. The older generation of Catholics will not change much on the racial issue and are generally even more unhappy with the new trend than they are with the modernization of the liturgy. It will be some time before the younger, more liberal elements in the Catholic community are able to exert enough influence to alter basic attitudes among their parishioners, but the more liberal attitude emanating from the Ecumenical Council in Rome and the pressure applied by some of the leadership in the Chicago archdiocese are bound to bring about a more tolerant attitude, especially among younger Catholics.

It may well be true that, while it is of crucial importance to move rapidly and effectively to give Chicago's blacks, not token-isms, but genuine, full-blown equality of opportunity in education, employment, housing, recreational facilities and political participation, it is probably not imperative to bring about integrated neighborhoods today or even tomorrow. If the more important educational and employment opportunities are made available, neighborhood integration can proceed, if it is to come about, as the

Supreme Court put it in the *Brown* school desegregation case, "with all deliberate speed."

The key to the integration of American blacks into sharing equally in the milk and honey of the Promised Land of twentieth-century American life in cities like Chicago is a rapid and total opening of the doors of economic opportunity. On this front, it may well be true that the city of Chicago will serve as a model of judicious balancing of realism on the parts of the black community, the Democratic political organization, and the business and labor leadership in the city.

In Chicago today, as a result of black pressures, political acquiescence, and business needs, there is much less discrimination against blacks in hiring in most commercial businesses and industrial firms than what formerly existed in the city. Most businessmen have accepted the letter, if not the spirit, of the law, have seen the light, need the workers (black and white), and are more interested in keeping their businesses going and their profits up than in keeping black people out of their plants. In fact, the business community in Chicago is probably the most progressive and liberal element in the city's body politic today on this issue, primarily for pragmatic, not philosophical or ideological, reasons. And most of the labor unions have given ground on the issue, some grudgingly, but others willingly, if not enthusiastically.

The New Status of Blacks in Chicago. The new economic status of many of Chicago's blacks has led to major changes in their social status. Blacks who have achieved success in law, medicine, banking, insurance, publishing, and other economic fields have gained recognition as community leaders and representatives; are appearing with increasing frequency on the boards of corporations, banks, and civic organizations; and are being consulted by the city's political and economic leadership on problems arising in the community. Schools, streets and parks are being named after black leaders. The birthday of the martyred Dr. Martin Luther King, Jr. is commemorated as a holiday for city and county employees and public school children.

A noticeable cultural change is taking place, not only in the black neighborhoods, but also in the heart and hub of the city, the Loop. The city's commercial and entertainment center has shifted gears and appeals greatly now to a black clientele. Loop theaters run black movies, downtown legitimate theaters are booking black plays, and cultural centers schedule black dance groups and other entertainment which attract a significant percentage of black patrons. Loop department stores and retail outlets are increasingly directing their merchandising efforts toward the city's black population, which has now become a mainstay of the central district's commercial and entertainment activities.

The most significant change which is taking place in Chicago's black population, however, is the rapid and steady growth of a black middle class. Chicago's black population is no longer so heavily made up of welfare poor, unskilled workers, and the poorly educated. This is not to say that these economic and social categories do not still exist within the black population of Chicago in significant numbers. They do. But the percentage of middle-class blacks in Chicago's population is increasing steadily, and the approximately 1,300,000 blacks living in Chicago cannot be categorized simplistically as they were several decades ago. The black community contains a broad range of economic, social, and cultural entities, in which the basic factor of race is still important but is being modified and diversified as the economic opportunities made available in the city alter the social and cultural status and the perspective of segments of the black community.

The economic, social, and cultural revolutions which are taking place within Chicago's black community are being reflected in changes in the political and governmental systems of the city. Within the structure of the local party organization, no black politician has achieved a status comparable to that held by Dawson. But the number of black committeemen is increasing steadily, their share of the pie is growing larger, and their influence on party policies is being enhanced.

Governmentally, at the city, county, and state levels, the party is slating more blacks for public offices and giving greater power to black public officials. A black man, George Collins, was slated for Congress from Chicago's west side when the long-time white Irish congressman from that district died. Several years ago, when the city's congressional representation was reduced by two, and there was a conflict between the black and ethnic whites on the west side over whether an incumbent black or white congressman should

retain his seat, Mayor Daley opted for slating the black congressman, George Collins, and forced Italian Congressman Frank
Annunzio to move to the northwest side of Chicago to replace
Roman Pucinski, who ran against Charles Percy for the United
States Senate in 1972. In 1973, when Congressman Collins was
killed in an airplane accident, his widow, Cardiss Collins, who had
never been an active member of the local Democratic party or of a
ward organization, was slated in Collins' place, despite considerable
opposition from the white ethnic committeemen in the congressional district, and from many of the active black politicians from
Chicago's west side who felt that they should have been considered
for the seat. On Chicago's southwest side, in a gradually racially
changing area, it is clear that the days of the incumbent white Irish
Congressman Morgan Murphy, the son of an old friend of the
mayor, may be numbered and that a black man will be slated in
Murphy's place in the not too distant future.

At the state level, black representation in both the house and
senate has increased, and State Senator Cecil Partee, the black
committeeman of the 20th Ward, was elected president of the state
senate in 1975, the first time in the history of Illinois that a black
ever achieved that office, making Partee the highest ranking black
public official in the state of Illinois.

Locally, black representation on the Cook County Board of
Commissioners and the Board of Trustees of the Chicago Metropolitan Sanitary District has been increased, and the number of black
judges slated for the Circuit Court of Cook County has been going
up steadily. In the Chicago City Council, the number of black
aldermen has increased since James Q. Wilson wrote *Negro Politics*
in 1960, when there were six black aldermen in the council. In the
1967 aldermanic election, the number of black aldermen increased
to ten, and, after the 1971 aldermanic election, black aldermen in
the council numbered sixteen out of a body of fifty, making up
one-third of the council. Within the council itself, the last three
aldermen who held the position of president pro tem were
black—Ralph Metcalfe, Claude Holman, and Wilson Frost—
despite some opposition from some of the Democratic ethnic white
aldermen. Black aldermen are getting more chairmanships of
important committees. In 1971, Joseph Bertrand, a black graduate

of Notre Dame University, was elected city treasurer of Chicago, thus becoming the first black man to hold a citywide office.

At other levels of the Chicago political and governmental systems, blacks are garnering unto themselves an ever-increasing share of the pie. Black ward organizations are getting a more substantial share of the patronage; black banks are getting more city and county deposits; black lawyers are getting more city and county business; black real estate developers are being cut in on urban renewal projects; and the black community, as a whole, has had its economic, political, and governmental share of Chicago's good things increased substantially.

The machine's policy of sharing the wealth and power has kept most of the black population quiescent, the political leadership cooperative, the civic and community leadership content, and the civil rights activists and radicals fairly well ostracized for the short-term future. Coming, however, is an almost certain long-term change. What Sidney and Beatrice Webb, the British socialists, once called "the inevitability of gradualness" may well become the overriding factor in black-ethnic white political and governmental relationships in Chicago in the foreseeable future.

As long as blacks are a minority in the city, as long as black political leadership in the machine is kept divided and subordinate to white ethnic politicians, as long as black civic and community leaders are still appreciative of their newly acquired social and economic status, and as long as black civil rights activists pursue goals which are antithetical to the ambitions of the black politicians, the white ethnic leadership of the machine can maintain its control of the key levers of Chicago's political and governmental systems.

But the prospects that any of these conditions will obtain for an indefinite future are dim. What is more likely in Chicago, in the foreseeable future, is that all these conditions will change and that a new era in Chicago's politics will be ushered in. Blacks will become a majority of the population. Black politicians will not always be content to be second best, in a subordinate position in the party hierarchy. Black civic and community leaders will seek enhanced status and recognition. And black civil rights activists will become more politically oriented and attempt to ally with black politicians in pursuit of their own ambitions, and of the interests of the black community-at-large.

The Future of Black Politics in Chicago. According to James Q. Wilson, in *Negro Politics*, two major developments characterize black politics in northern cities like Chicago. First, black politics normally reflect the politics of the community in which blacks become active politically. Second, as black political leaders gain power, they become less and less interested in race issues and more and more interested in personal power and economic gain. They must use race issues to gain power, but, once power is gained, they pursue personal privilege rather than general race goals. Black politics in Chicago has, to date, fairly accurately reflected Wilson's analysis.

Beginning with the creation of Dawson's black sub-machine as an integral part of the citywide Democratic machine in 1939, politics in the black community has fairly consistently reflected the machine politics of the city as a whole. Since Dawson's death, despite the fragmentation of political power among a group of Dawson's potential heirs apparent, there has been no serious challenge to the machine politics practiced by the black politicians who inherited Dawson's political estate. While there have been attempts by black civil rights activists, black political reformers, and some black civic leaders to alter the pattern of black politics in Chicago, those challenges have been either failures at worst or transitory at best.

What of the future course of black politics in Chicago after Daley leaves office? While no one can predict the future with certainty, one can prognosticate the probable future course of politics in Chicago, using Wilson's model as a starting point. According to Wilson, "Three different sets of relationships between Negro political and civic elites can be distinguished. In one sense, they may represent three stages in a single pattern of development. . . . The first pattern we may call the period of *compatible elites*. . . . In Chicago . . . a second stage inevitably seems to emerge out of this early period of overlapping or coinciding elites. This we may call the pattern of *diverging elites*. . . . A third pattern can be detected in one or two cities. . . . This is the period in which Negro politics become 'reformed' in the eyes of the civic leaders. . . . This we can call the *new merger*." According to Wilson, while the first two stages of this kind of black political evolution were likely in Chicago, the third was not.

Wilson's first stage of *compatible elites* accurately described the evolution of black politics in Chicago in the early days of Dawson's power. According to Wilson, at that stage, blacks were first trying to "break into" the white political organization. In order to accomplish that end, they utilized race issues and welfare ends. At that stage, the interests of black politicians coincided with the interests of black civic leaders, whose objectives were essentially the same— "prestige, access, and limited influence." For both the political and civic black leaders at this stage, race was a lever which could be used to pry open the doors of the white power elites in both the political and civic spheres.

In Chicago, Wilson's second stage of black politics, of *diverging elites*, has also occurred. At this stage, black politicians have achieved their goals by gaining power and prestige in both the political and economic spheres and by becoming an integral part of the citywide machine. They tend then to become conservative, status quo-oriented, and disinterested in race issues. But then the interests of black civic leaders begin to diverge from those of black political leaders. As black political leaders gain power, the role of black civic leaders, both in the black community and in the city at large, is diminished and denigrated. Consequently, they are more inclined to continue to use race issues as a tool for increasing their power and status, both in the black community and in the city at large.

But Wilson's third stage, the *new merger*, has not yet emerged in Chicago. At that stage, according to Wilson, in cities like Los Angeles and Detroit, the interests of black politicians and black civic leaders coincided in a new situation in which both elites gained mutual benefits by forming a coalition and winning political, economic, and social power in the city at large. Also, in those kinds of cities, the black political and civic leadership finds basic common interests with white reform political and civic groups. Eventually, black and white reform groups join together to challenge and conquer the entrenched status quo elites in their communities.

Wilson's prognosis of the efficacy of the three stages in Chicago has been borne out in the fifteen years since he published *Negro Politics*. The black community of Chicago has passed through the first two stages but has not yet achieved the third stage of the *new merger*. Nor is it likely that that stage will be achieved in the foreseeable future. Wilson argued that a prerequisite for the third stage was the emergence of successful white reform politics in the city. That has not occurred in Chicago, except on a limited scale. Since the city machine has demonstrated its ability to fend off and contain the white reform political movement in Chicago, that movement has not gained the mass support and elite participation needed to make a significant impact on the city's politics.

The failure of a citywide white reform movement in Chicago has had a deleterious effect on the creation of a black political reform movement within the black community. Without substantial political, economic, and social support from a powerful white reform movement in Chicago, the black political reform movement has been severely limited in its drive for power, and contained within a fairly small segment of the black community. Thus, unless a white political reform movement makes headway in the city, the prospects for a successful black political reform movement in the black community, and in the city at large, are dim for the foreseeable future.

What is more likely in the future, in Chicago's politics, is the continuation of the black-ethnic white political coalition which exists in the city today. However, the influence, power, and perquisites of black politicians in the coalition will steadily increase. As black political power increases in the city at large, and as the influence of white ethnic politicians decreases, it is likely that black politicians will remain in a modified *compatible elite* relationship, not with black civic leaders but, rather, with white ethnic politicians. Black and white ethnic politicians will have a stake in the maintenance of a status quo different from the one which existed in the first stage of black politics, when black politicians were attempting to break into the white political organization. In that first stage of *compatible elites*, black politicians and civic leaders were driven into an alliance with each other on the basis of a common interest—achieving for themselves a fair share of the city's political and economic power, using race issues as a tool. Since the constituency that they represented, the black community, constituted a minority element in the city's body politic, black political and civic leaders were limited in their aspirations and in the demands they could make on the white political and civic leadership of the city.

However, in a new situation in which the black population is by far the largest segment of the city's population, black political leaders can and will demand and get a much bigger piece of the pie. Black civic and community leaders, however, will probably not achieve the same status and make the same gains as their black political counterparts. It is unlikely, for the foreseeable future, that black businessmen, bankers, and lawyers, can make the same inroads into the economic and civic power structure of the city that black politicians can make into the city's political system. Since their goals are essentially, in Wilson's terms, "status ends," they will have little support in the great mass of the black community, which is heavily welfare poor and working class, and oriented toward "welfare ends."

Black politicians, who can continue to use "welfare ends" in pursuit of their own political and economic ambitions, can remain close to, and representative of, the great mass of the black population of the city. Since the black vote has become the major source of the machine's strength in the city, the new breed of black politicians can utilize the power of their black constituency to become the dominant figures and power bloc in the citywide machine. If that happens, the white economic elite which controls the city will, in all likelihood, come to terms with the black politicians, and ally with them to maintain a stable city and an economic climate in which their economic interests and the political interests of the black politicians can be served.

In other words, what is likely in Chicago, in the years ahead, is that black politicians will assume the role that Irish politicians have played in the city for the past forty years, and that an alliance can be formed between *compatible elites* made up of the white economic power structure in the city and the black political leadership of the machine. In such a milieu, the old cliché can be amended to take into account the new realities of life in Chicago to read, "White Protestants own it, black politicians run it, and blacks and Latins live in it."

The power of black politicians vis-à-vis black civic and community leaders will be enhanced by the nature of the constituencies which these two elites represent, and by the future interests and aspirations of those constituencies. The natural constituencies of the black politicians are the black welfare poor and the black working class. The alliance between black politicians, the black welfare poor, and the black working class is based on a common interest, their espousal of "welfare ends." Black politicians, like white politicians in cities like Chicago, gain and retain political power by performing a myriad of functions and services for those in need of those functions and services. The welfare poor and the working class in Chicago, black or white, are cognizant of their own needs and interests, and recognize the value of the political machine and its minions as agents for satisfying their needs and aspirations.

There is no reason to believe, given the massive black welfare poor and working class population of the city, that the relationship of that population to the black politicians will change, or that the machine politics which has characterized Chicago's political system will disappear. If Wilson is right, in his thesis that black politics in American cities reflect communitywide politics of those cities, it is also true that the politics of a community are rooted in and reflect the cultural, economic, and social realities of the community. As long as Chicago's population is heavily made up of the poor and the working class, whose interests and aspirations can best be satisfied and realized through the processes of machine politics, it is unlikely that the political patterns will change.

The natural constituency of black civic and community leaders is the emerging black middle class in the city. Theoretically, the black middle class, as it gains economic power and social status, will turn to politics as the process through which it can best achieve its goals. The great hope of the urban reformers is that the black middle class in cities like Chicago will recognize a common interest with the white Protestant-Jewish-led reform movement in the city, and create a political coalition capable of overthrowing the machine and instituting a new political era in the city's history. It is this third stage of Wilson's trilogy, the *new merger* stage of black politics, which reformers, black and white, are hoping to realize in Chicago.

It is unlikely, however, if Chicago's past history has any relevance, that the hopes of the city's reformers can be realized in the foreseeable future. Just as the urban reformers who anticipated and projected the reform of machine politics in the city when the ethnic poor and working class achieved middle-class status were wrong in the 1930s and '40s, so are their heirs apparent likely to be wrong in the '70s and '80s. The belief that the welfare state, a rise in the educational level of the working class, and a new middle class would transform the urban population into a politically involved, reform-minded constituency was never realized. As the working class achieved middle-class status, they fled the city for the greener pastures of suburban life, for what they believed would be better homes for their wives, better schools for their children, and fewer problems for themselves.

There is little reason to believe that the black middle class will be different from their white ethnic predecessors. As Chicago's blacks achieve middle-class status, they too will seek better homes for their wives, better schools for their children, safer streets and neighborhoods for their families, and fewer problems for themselves. They, too, will head for the suburbs through doors opened by pressure from white middle-class city and suburban liberals. Black politicians in Chicago, recognizing their own interests, will probably also push to open suburban doors to the exiting black middle class, thus getting rid of the major source of potential political opposition in the black community, and depriving black civic and community leaders, whose natural constituency is the black middle class, of any solid base of support in the city's body politic.

The future of the machine in Chicago is inextricably bound up with the economic, social, and cultural evolution of Chicago's black community. Given the future prospects of those economic, social, and cultural conditions in Chicago's black community, the chances of wiping out the machine in Chicago are dim. It is more likely that the machine will continue to exist, changing in its internal makeup from white ethnic to black, but pursuing the same policies and utilizing the same tactics that the machine has employed in the past to retain its power in the city.

Where will white ethnic politicians fit into this picture? An inevitable concomitant of the growth of black political power in the machine will be a diminution of the power of the white ethnic politicians. Young married whites with children will continue to leave the city for the suburbs. White ethnics will retreat to the fringes of the city or to the suburbs. Those who leave for the suburbs will never return. Those who move to the fringes of the city will lose contact with much of what the city has had to offer and will lose interest in the city's problems, as long as they can remain fairly safe and sequestered in their neighborhoods. The days of white absentee political bosses who govern inner city wards from afar (or even from near) are coming to an end. And the days in which white ethnic politicians, in control of the party's hierarchy, can racially gerrymander districts, select black political leaders and candidates responsive to white ethnic control, and reserve unto themselves the choice fruits of political life in Chicago are numbered.

Race issues and welfare ends will become the dominant themes in Chicago's politics. In such a milieu, black politicians will have significant built-in advantages over their white counterparts in the city. They can identify racially with their constituencies. They can reflect and represent the aspirations of the black community without fear of retribution from the white ethnic population of the city. And, as they gain citywide power and control of the political and governmental machinery of the city, they will control and dispense the perquisites of politics, and benefit from the gratitude of their black constituents.

For white ethnic politicians in Chicago, however, the future alternatives may well be between the Scylla of attempting to pacify blacks and other minorities in the city at the expense of white constituencies, and the Charybdis of supporting the aspirations and interests of their white constituents, thus insuring their alienation from blacks and other minorities who will constitute a majority in Chicago. White ethnic politicians who seek citywide power and influence will discover that access to those prerogatives can best be achieved by appealing to the interests of blacks and other minorities in the city. If they cannot or will not do that, they may find the doors closed to them in the party hierarchy and in the city government, thus depriving their constituencies in their wards of ready access to the centers of power and jeopardizing their own political situations in their wards.

However, white ethnic politicians in the city who try to retain power and perquisites by pacifying the interests and aspirations of blacks and other minority groups will almost certainly find themselves in conflict with the interests and aspirations of their white ethnic constituencies. Those white ethnic constituencies either could retaliate by withholding support for white ethnic politicians who travel the route of minority-group pacification, or could respond by leaving the city for the suburbs, thus further reducing the natural constituency of the white ethnic politicians. Caught on the horns of a dilemma, white ethnic politicians in Chicago can oppose the aspirations of blacks and other minority groups of the city in an attempt to pacify the interests of their white ethnic constituencies and, by so doing, alienate the majority of the city's population. Or they can attempt to come to terms with blacks and other minorities and run the risk of alienating their diminishing white ethnic constituencies. Whichever of the two alternatives they choose, however, their power and influence in the machine will be diminished vis-à-vis their black political counterparts in the foreseeable future.

The Future of the Machine

The Chicago machine was created by Mayor Anton J. Cermak in 1931 and was nurtured by Mayor Edward J. Kelly and Patrick Nash from 1933 to 1947. It survived under Mayor Martin Kennelly's interregnum reform administration from 1947 to 1955 and achieved its greatest successes under Mayor Richard J. Daley's leadership and control during the past twenty years. For almost four decades, pundits have predicted the machine's downfall, reformers have tried to force it to alter its course, opponents have tried to destroy its power, and scholars have analyzed its dynamics. What does the future hold in store for the Chicago machine when Mayor Daley, by personal choice, the action of the sovereign voters, or an act of God, is removed from the Chicago political scene?

It is my conviction that the machine will survive, changed internally by the developing political patterns in Chicago and Cook County but unaltered in its basic dynamics, tactics, and objectives. The machine will gradually lose influence and power at the county level in Cook County. The continued growth of the suburban population of Cook County, the decline of the city of Chicago's population vis-à-vis the suburbs, and the realities of suburban interests and political power will gradually erode one of the machine's bases—its control of the county government and the prerogatives which flow from that control. A suburban electorate, hostile to the machine's practices, apathetic toward Chicago's problems, and involved in its own new-found way of life, will not much longer tolerate or support the machine's domination of the government of Cook County.

When that time comes, in the not-too-distant future, and the machine's control of the government of Cook County is loosened, the machine, in accord with its traditional basic strategy, will turn inward to solidify its hold on the city of Chicago. In the city, the machine should be able to survive and prosper without serious challenge to its existence or erosion of its power base for the foreseeable future. It will change in the makeup of its basic constituency and leadership but not in its tactics and objectives.

In Chicago, the machine will go black, both in its mass base in the city's electorate and in the Democratic party hierarchy, reflecting the reality of the interests and aspirations of the heavily black population of the city. But the black politicians who will take over the machine and the control of the city's government will not be reformers and liberals. They will be, as they are today, hardheaded, pragmatic power seekers and manipulators, who will play the game and operate the levers of power in accordance with the rules they learned from their white ethnic predecessors. They will pursue their own political and economic self-interests primarily, the interests of the white economic overlords of the city secondarily, and attempt to pacify the aspirations of their black constituency last, as a necessary concomitant of gaining and maintaining their own power. They will not attempt to reform radically either the city's political system or its government, since such reform would threaten their own power and prerogatives, and probably the interests and aspirations of the majority of their constituents. Further, a black-controlled machine in Chicago will have to deal, for some time to come, with two other constituencies in the city outside of the black community—the white ethnics who are left in the city and the rapidly growing Latin population of Chicago.

Until then, a black-ethnic white alliance between politicians representative of the two constituencies will control the city, after Richard J. Daley leaves office as mayor and party chairman. No white ethnic politician can hope to take Daley's place with comparable political and governmental power. Nor could any black politician move easily into Daley's two chairs as mayor and party leader. For some time to come, a collective leadership, made up of white ethnic and black politicians, will have to share power in order to retain the prerogatives they cherish. They will have more in common with each other than with any other element of Chicago's body politic, including their own white ethnic and black constituencies. In that period, Chicago's political scene should strongly resemble the early 1950s in Soviet Russia after Stalin's death, when the collective leadership of the Communist Party Politburo assumed power. So it will probably be in Chicago, after Daley's passing, among the leading members of his Democratic Party Politburo.

In time, as more white ethnics and middle-class blacks leave the city and as those constituencies decline in size and influence, the role of white ethnic politicians in the alliance will be diminished, and the status of black politicians will be enhanced. Black Richard Daleys, Tom Keanes, Vito Marzullos, Marshall Korshaks, and Matthew Biesczats will take over the party leadership and the city government. The white ethnic politicians who are left in the city will have to assume the role that black politicians in the machine— the William Dawsons, Claude Holmans, Ralph Metcalfes, and Kenneth Campbells—had to assume in the past, that of taking crumbs from the table and being grateful for having been given power and prerogatives in their wards and neighborhoods, but not in City Hall or in the party's headquarters in the Sherman House. The roles of white ethnic and black politicians will be reversed. But there will be no need for black politicians to try to exclude white ethnic politicians from a role in the machine they control. Black politicians will need white ethnic politicians to buttress their citywide aspirations and interests, and to help fend off black and white reformers.

As for the Latins in the city, their day will come, too, as soon as they can organize effectively, build electoral constituencies, and develop political leadership. It will take time to accomplish these goals. The Latins have only recently arrived in the city in significant numbers, are handicapped by English-language deficiencies and lack of American citizenship, and are just beginning to understand the political game as it is practiced in Chicago. But all these conditions can be overcome. According to the 1970 census, Chicago had 247,343 Spanish-speaking persons. But knowledgeable observers are convinced that the number of Spanish-speaking persons far exceeds that figure and is probably over 500,000. Many are

Mexicans who migrated illegally to Chicago. Most of these Mexicans, as well as a substantial number of Puerto Ricans, are well settled in the city. They will not leave voluntarily and will almost certainly not be deported. While it is difficult, at this writing, to prognosticate the political future of the Latins in the city, it is certain that they will play an increasingly important role in Chicago's politics. The time will come when Latin politicians of demonstrated political acumen will be taken into the party leadership, granted power and prerogatives, and utilized to advance the interests of a black-Latin, white-ethnic machine, as well as their own aspirations and interests.

In such a milieu, there is no reason to suspect that the twin maxims which have guided the machine throughout its past history and contemporary status will not also guide its future practices. "Don't make no waves" and "Don't back no losers" will still be the watchwords for some time to come in Chicago's political future.

Bibliography

✻

Books

Asbury, Herbert. *Gem of the Prairie*. Garden City, New York: Garden City Publishing Company, 1942.

Banfield, Edward C., and Wilson, James Q. *City Politics*. Cambridge: Harvard University Press, 1963.

Banfield, Edward C. *Political Influence*. Glencoe, Illinois: The Free Press, 1961.

Chicago Home Rule Commission. *Report and Recommendations*. Chicago: University of Illinois at Chicago Circle, 1972.

Demaris, Ovid. *Captive City*. New York: Lyle Stuart, Inc., 1969.

Dobyns, Fletcher. *The Underworld of American Politics*. New York: F. Dobyns, 1932.

Drake, St. Clair, and Cayton, Horace R. *Black Metropolis: A Study of Negro Life in a Northern City*. New York: Harcourt, Brace and Company, 1945.

Ellis, William Whit. *White Ethics and Black Power*. Chicago: Aldine Publishing Company, 1969.

Gleason, Bill. *Daley of Chicago*. New York: Simon and Schuster, 1970.

Gosnell, Harold Foote. *Machine Politics: Chicago Model*. Chicago: University of Chicago Press, 1937.

————. *Negro Politicians: The Rise of Negro Politicians in Chicago*. Chicago: University of Chicago Press, 1967.

Gottfried, Alex. *Boss Cermak of Chicago.* Seattle: University of Washington Press, 1962.

Hodge, Patricia Leavey, and Kitagawa, Evelyn. *Population Projections for the City of Chicago and the Chicago Standard Metropolitan Statistical Area 1970 and 1980.* Chicago: Population Research and Training Center and Chicago Community Inventory, University of Chicago, 1964.

Knatzelson, Ira. *Black Men, White Cities.* London and New York: Oxford University Press, 1973.

Knauss, Peter R. *Chicago: A One Party State.* Champaign, Illinois: Stipes Publishing Company, 1972.

Kupcinet, Irv. *Kup's Chicago.* Cleveland: World Publishing Company, 1962.

Levine, Edward M. *The Irish and Irish Politicians.* Notre Dame, Indiana: University of Notre Dame Press, 1966.

Liebling, A. J. *Chicago: The Second City.* New York: Alfred A. Knopf, 1952.

Mathewson, Joe. *Up Against Daley.* LaSalle, Illinois: Open Court Publishing Company, 1974.

Merriam, Charles Edward. *Chicago: A More Intimate View of Urban Politics.* New York: The Macmillan Company, 1929.

Meyerson, Martin, and Banfield, Edward C. *Politics, Planning and the Public Interest.* Glencoe, Illinois: The Free Press, 1955.

O'Connor, Len. *Clout: Mayor Daley and His City.* Chicago: Henry Regnery Company, 1975.

Royko, Mike. *Boss: Richard J. Daley of Chicago.* New York: Dutton, 1971.

Simpson, Dick W. *Winning Elections.* Chicago: Swallow Press, Inc., 1972.

Spear, Allan H. *Black Chicago: The Making of a Negro Ghetto, 1890–1920.* Chicago: University of Chicago Press, 1967.

Stead, William Thomas. *If Christ Came to Chicago.* Chicago: Laird and Lee, 1894.

Stuart, William Hervey. *The Twenty Incredible Years.* Chicago and New York: M. A. Donohue and Company, 1935.

Wendt, Lloyd, and Kogan, Herman. *Big Bill of Chicago.* Indianapolis: Bobbs-Merrill, 1953.

———. *Bosses in Lusty Chicago.* Bloomington: Indiana University Press, 1962.

Wilson, James Q. *Negro Politics.* Glencoe, Illinois: The Free Press, 1960.

———. *The Amateur Democrat.* Chicago: University of Chicago Press, 1962.

Yehzne, Peter. *Quotations from Mayor Daley.* New York: Putnam, 1969.

Monographs

Mayer, Harold M. *Chicago: City of Decisions.* Chicago: The Geographic Society of Chicago, 1955.

Rakove, Milton L. *The Changing Patterns of Suburban Politics in Cook County, Illinois.* Chicago: Loyola University Press, 1965.

Small, Joseph F. *Governmental Alternatives Facing the Chicago Metropolitan Area.* Chicago: Loyola University Press, 1966.

Steiner, Gilbert Y. *Metropolitan Government and the Real World,* Chicago: Loyola University Press, 1966.

Chapters

Rakove, Milton L. "Chicago." In *Great Cities of the World, Their Government, Politics, and Planning,* ed. William A. Robson and D. E. Regan. London: Allen and Unwin, 1972.

———. "Government Operation and Structure." In The Chicago Home Rule Commission, Report and Recommendations. Chicago: University of Illinois at Chicago Circle, 1972.

Magazine and Journal Articles

Baron, Harold M. "Black Powerlessness in Chicago." *Trans-action,* November 1968.

Bowen, William. "Chicago: They Didn't Have to Burn It Down After All." *Fortune,* January 1965.

Bruno, Hal. "Chicago Ain't Ready for Reform." *The Reporter,* March 28, 1963.

Corditz, Don. "Mayor Daley Battles a New Fire." *Fortune,* July 1968.

Despres, Leon M. "The Chicago the Delegates Won't See." *The Progressive,* August, 1968.

Dyer, K. J. "The Mob and Mayor Daley." *Chicagoland,* August 1969.

Gilbreth, Edward S. "Making Book on Mr. Daley." *The Nation,* March 27, 1967.

Greeley, Andrew M. "Take Heart from the Heartland." *The New Republic,* December 12, 1970.

Halberstam, David. "Daley of Chicago." *Harper's Magazine,* August 1968.

Kelly, Tom. "Mayor Daley's Smart, but What Else?" *The New Republic,* December 26, 1970.

Lens, Sidney. "Daley of Chicago." *The Progressive*, March 1966.

Pekannen, John. "Lincoln Park 1969: Love and Music." *Life*, September 12, 1969.

Rakove, Milton L. "The People Win with Second Best." *New City*, August 1, 1965.

———. "State Action in Illinois: Some Political Considerations." *The State and Its Cities, University of Illinois Bulletin*, April 28, 1967.

———. "Chronic Togetherness." *National Civic Review*, May, 1968.

———. "The Suburbs, the City, and the State: New Trends in the '70's." *The States and the Urban Crisis, University of Illinois Bulletin*, July 6, 1971.

———. "Breaking Bread with the Pols." *Chicago Guide*, August, 1974.

———. "The Old Politics—the Ward as Fief: A Chicago Alderman at Work." *Harper's Weekly*, December 20, 1974.

Rose, Don, and Canter, David S. "Mayor Daley: Solvent but Worried." *The Nation*, September 1, 1969.

Viorst, Milton. "Mayor Daley's Convention: Can the Ringmaster Keep the Show Going?" *Saturday Evening Post*, August 24, 1968.

Wheeler, Keith. "Last Big Boss on U.S. Scene." *Life*, February 8, 1960.

Zimmerman, Gereon. "Chicago's Mayor: Durable Dick Daley." *Look*, September 3, 1968.

Newspaper Articles

Bruckner, D. J. R. "Richard J. Daley Is: A. Powerful, B. Ruthless, C. Decent, D. None of These, E. All of These." *Los Angeles Times*, August 18, 1968.

Golden, Harry Jr. "Fifteen Years of Mayor Daley: A Sure Hand, a Hard Hat." *Chicago Sun-Times*, April 19, 1970.

Higdon, Hal. "A Minority Objects, but Daley Is Chicago." *New York Times Magazine*, September 11, 1966.

Karaganis, Joseph. "Who's on the Bench? In Cook County, It's Usually a Politician." *Chicago Sun-Times*, September 7, 1969.

Lahey, Edwin A. "King Richard of Chicago." *Chicago Daily News*, July 11–16, 1966.

Rakove, Milton L. "Daley's Balance of Power." *Chicago Sun-Times*, April 9, 1967.

———. "Suburbia's New Politics." *Chicago Sun-Times*, May 21, 1967.

———. "They Flee Chicago—But To What?" *Chicago Daily News*, June 26, 1971.

Wille, Lois. "Patronage and Power." *Chicago Daily News*, February 6–9, 1967.

Zekman, Pamela; Crawford, William; Egler, Daniel; and Gaines, William. "Task Force Report." *Chicago Tribune*, November 24–30, 1974.

Newspapers

Chicago Daily News
Chicago Defender
Chicago Sun-Times
Chicago Tribune
Christian Science Monitor
New York Times
Polish American
Wall Street Journal

Index

※

Accardo, Tony ("Big Tuna"), 25

Adamowski, Benjamin, 47, 150–51, 158, 229–30

Adesko, Thaddeus V., 118

Altgeld, Peter, 143

Annunzio, Frank, 118, 123, 272

Arvey, Jacob M., 113, 145

Austin, Richard, 147, 202–3

Bailey, Steve, 47, 50

Bakalis, Michael, 142

Barrett, Edward J., 108–9

Bauler, Mathias ("Paddy"), 24, 103, 116, 190, 215–16

Bentham, Jeremy, 156

Berg, Raymond K., 230

Bertrand, Joseph, 262, 272–73

Bieszczat, Matthew, 94, 109, 115, 283

Bilandic, Michael, 94, 215

black politics in Chicago: effect of New Deal, 257–58; William L. Dawson's rise to power, 257–59; machine control of leaders since Dawson, 259–60; contrasting aspirations of black civic leaders and politicians, 260; geographic fragmentation of black community, 260–61; black machine politicians, 262; black political independents, 262–63; black civil rights activists, 263–64; anti-Daley black politicians, 264; reasons for failure of black radicals and civil rights activists, 264; black middle class, 265; black working class, 265; black welfare poor, 265–66; relationship with Chicago machine, 265–66; black-ethnic white relationship, 266–68; integration issue, 267–68; support of Roman Catholic hierarchy in Chicago, 268–69; broadening economic opportunity, 270; cultural changes in the Loop, 270–71; growth of black middle class, 271; slating for Congress, 271–72; increased representation in state house and senate, 272; increased power on local level, 272–73; prospects for the future, 273, 276–79, 282–83; Wilson's analysis of black politics ("Wilson's trilogy"), 274–76; place of white ethnics in future of black politics, 279–81

Bonk, Charles S., 118, 122–23

Boss (Royko), 17

Bowen, William, 45

Bowler, James, 216

Bridgeport, community of: citizenry, 54–55; racial discrimination, 55–57; "mother of mayors," 56

Brown, Madison, 118

Bruckner, D. J. R., 47–48

Bundensen, Herman, 144

Burke, Edmund, 74, 82

Bush, Earl, 50

Butler, Michael, 182

Cafferty, Pastora San Juan, 59

Cain, Richard, 25

Campbell, Kenneth, 262

Capone, Al, 25

Carey, Archibald J., Jr., 221

Carey, Bernard, 230

Catholic Church, the. *See* Roman Catholic church

Cerda, David, 228

Cermak, Anton J., 147, 258, 281

Chesser, Al, 125, 128

Chew, Charles, 264

Chicago, city of: citizenry, 14–15, 18, 23–24, 26–27, 133; physical characteristics, 21–22; climate, 22–23; crime and corruption, 23–26; Mafia, 24–25; population statistics, 27, 234; geographic location, 28; Roman Catholic strength, 31–32; Irish dominance, 32–42, 57; Bridgeport mayors, 56; architectural accomplishments under Daley, 77; cultural advancements under Daley, 77–78; suburbanites, 132–33; racial tensions, 134; statistics comparing Chicago mayoral and national elections, 180; first-wave migration of middle- and working-class Democrats to new suburban communities, 234–35; first-wave migration of upper-middle-class Democrats to older suburban communities, 235–36; suburbs in the 70s, 236–38; second-wave migration of young marrieds and diehards to suburbs, 239–40; role of parochial schools in migration to suburbs, 240; projected migration continuation, 241; new suburban politics, 241–42; ideological trend in Democratic party in older suburban communities, 243–44; ideological trend in Republican party in older suburban communities, 244–49; new political philosophy of old-suburbia Democrats, 251–52; bread-and-butter politics of new suburban communities, 252–53

Chicago machine: model of successful politics, 1–3; characteristics, 3–4; leaders, 4–12; objectives, 5, 17–18; parochialism, 6–7, 10–11, 105, 135, 138–39, 155–56, 161–62; political philosophy, 11–12, 156; services, 14; integration policy, 16; future of, 19; motives of its politicians, 129; city-suburban relationship on community level, 133; city-suburban relationship on governmental level, 134–35, 137–38; city-suburban relationship on political level, 135–37, 140–41; dominance of city Democrats in county offices, 135–40; relationship to state and national Democratic party, 141; relationship to Cook County Republican party, 141–42; backing of gubernatorial candidates, 143–49; Republican mayoral candidates, 149–51; relationship with downstate politics, 152–55; backing of presidential candidates, 157–60; backing of Hubert Humphrey in presidential campaign, 159–60; refusal to back Eugene McCarthy in presidential campaign, 159–60; backing of U.S. congressional and senatorial candidates, 160–61; backing of candidates for state senate and house of representatives, 161; status of Republican committeemen, 166–74; collaboration of Republicans with Democrats, 174–77; advantageous scheduling of election dates, 178–81; tactics used by Democratic organization in elections, 181–82; problems of Republican party, 182–84, 186–87; contrast of Democratic and Republican constituency, 183–84; sources of workers for Republican organization, 184–87; financial backing of Republican party, 186, 188; financial advantage of Democratic party, 186–87; relationship of Republican economic aristocracy and Democratic machine, 188–90; members of independent political organizations, 191–92; political philosophy of independents, 192–93; limited success of independents, 193–95; future of independent political organizations, 195–97; dealing with Congress, 199; dealing with Democratic presidents, 200–2; dealing with Republican presidents, 200–2; threat from state government, 203–5; patronage system, 205–6; professional politics in Illinois, 208–11; dealing with city council, 212; control of city council, 213–21; control of county judiciary, 223–32; control of state's attorney's office, 229–30; shift in political power due to suburban migration, 241; consequences of ideological trends in Democratic party in older suburban communities, 244; increasing importance of city-suburban relationships to future of machine power, 253–56; relationship with black community, 265–66, 272–73; future erosion of control over Cook County, 281–82; role of blacks in future of machine, 282–83; role of Latins in future of machine, 283–84

Churchill, Winston, 233

Clark, William, 99–101, 117, 148, 161, 197

Collins, Cardiss, 272

Collins, George, 109, 271–72

Cook County: Irish dominance, 33–42; population statistics, 92; power distribution in Republican Central Committee, 93–94; framework of judicial system, 222–23

Cook County Democratic Central Committee: headquarters, 90–92; political functions, 92; legal structure, 92–93; power distribution, 93; informal politburo, 94; committeemen, 94–95; slating of candidates for public office on county level, 95–100; dealing with dissidents, 100–5; parochialism, 105, 116–17; election of committeemen, 107; authority of committeemen in ward organizations, 107–8; responsibilities of committeemen, 108, 111; elective, appointed, and private positions held by committeemen, 109–10; black committeemen, 110–11; patronage statistics, 112–13; patronage system, 113–16; responsibilities of precinct captains, 115–16; precinct work, 117–27; motives of committeemen and precinct captains, 128–29; role of precinct captains, 129–31; dominance of city committeemen in county offices, 135–40; problems of suburban committeemen, 138

Coughlin, "Bathhouse" John, 214

Cousins, William, 217, 262, 265

Cowan, Arthur ("Boodie"), 24

Cronkite, Walter, 59

Cullerton, P. J., 99, 109

Curry, Richard, 52

Daley, Eleanor ("Sis") Guilfoyle (Mrs. Richard J. Daley), 51

Daley, John M., 52

Daley, Martin, 52

Daley, Richard J.: character, 16–17, 48; patronage, 34–41, 111; biographical information, 44–45; political philosophy, 44–45, 62–75, 81–82; physical appearance, 45–47; oratory style (malapropisms), 45–46; personal finances, 49–50; physical stamina, 50; family life, 50–51; parents, 51; children, 51; nepotism, 51–53; Bridgeport community, 54–57; Irish heritage, 57–58; political career, 61–62; relationship to Democratic party, 69–73; political philosophy applied to Chicago, 82–89; chairman, Cook County Democratic Central Committee, 92, 106; as ward committeeman, 128; speaks on role of precinct captains, 129–30; mayoral race against John Hoellen, 150; mayoral race against Robert Merriam, 151; mayoral race against Benjamin Adamowski, 151; relationship with Dan Walker, 155; backing of John F. Kennedy in presidential campaign, 158–59; relationship to black political leaders, 259–60

Daley, Richard Michael, 52–53

D'Amico, John, 130–31

Danaher, Matt, 124, 148

D'Andrea, Mike, 216

D'Arco, John, 10

Dawson, William L., 103, 110–11, 128, 157, 168, 258–62, 274–75

Democracy in America (Tocqueville), 80

Democratic party (national): statistics showing dominance, 164

DePriest, Oscar, 157

DeSimone, Charles J., 167

Despres, Leon, 78–79, 104–5, 176, 197, 216–19

Dewey, Thomas E., 145, 176

Dirksen, Everett McKinley, 101, 117, 148, 161, 199, 202

Dixon, Sherwood, 146

Domagala, John, 122, 128

Douglas, Paul, 105, 145, 160, 197, 202

Dunne, Edward, 143

Dunne, George, 46–47, 94, 109, 123, 128, 149, 167

Eisenhower, Dwight D., 146–47, 155, 177, 229

Epstein, Joseph, 17

Faherty, Roger, 149

Federalist Papers, The (Madison), 11, 87, 206

Fitzpatrick, Tom, 118, 123, 125, 131

Flynn, Fahey, 59
Foran, Thomas, 201
Freeman, Allen, 173
Friedman, Richard, 150
Frost, Wilson, 94, 220, 262, 272
Funkhouser, Major M. C. L., 26

Geocaris, John, 101
Giancana, Sam ("Momo"), 25
Goldwater, Barry, 181
Graver, Clem, 176–78
Green, Dwight, 144, 146–47
Green, George A., 52
Green, Larry, 227
Gregory, Dick, 55, 264
Gross, Charles, 173
Guilfoyle, Tom, 52

Halberstam, David, 45, 50
Hanrahan, Edward, 124, 148, 201, 230
Harrison, Carter H., 25
Hartigan, Neil, 50, 94
Hatcher, Richard, 19
Herberg, Will, 236
Hobbes, Thomas, 74
Hodge, Orville, 146
Hoellen, John, 150, 173, 217–18
Holman, Claude, 262, 272
Horner, Henry, 143–44
Horwitz, Izzie, 100, 261
Houlihan, John J., 52
Hubbard, Fred, 104, 263, 265
Humphrey, Hubert, 73, 117, 124–25, 157, 159–60
Huppert, Jerome, 109

immigrants: ethnic, 15; black and Spanish-speaking, 15–19, 31; ethnic settlement patterns, 29–31
Irish: dominance in Cook County, 32–42; "Irish Mafia," 34, 40, 57, 148; political style, 60–61; dominance in Chicago machine, 110–11

Jackson, Jesse, 19, 264
Jacksonian democracy, 251
Jarett, Vernon, 197
Jeffersonian democracy, 151–52
Johnson, Lyndon B., 156–57, 181
Junquera, Mrs. Al (Mary Mullen), 91, 99

Karaganis, Joseph, 225–26
Keane, Tom, 34–35, 49, 94, 100, 109, 123, 128, 167, 172–73, 215, 217, 219–20, 283
Kelly, Edmund, 94
Kelly, Edward J., 34, 49, 56, 258–59, 281
Kempton, Murray, 154
Kenna, Hinky Dink, 214
Kennedy, Edward, 160
Kennedy, John F., 71, 156–60, 230, 252
Kennedy, Robert F., 200
Kennelly, Martin, 56, 151, 259, 281
Kent, Frank, 11
Kerner, Otto, 101, 105, 142–44, 147–48, 181–82, 201
King, Martin Luther, Jr., 263–64, 270
Kipling, Rudyard, 22
Kogan, Herman, 26–27, 214
Kogut, Anthony, 118
Korshak, Marshall, 94, 283
Krska, Alderman, 215
Kucharski, Edmund, 174
Kusper, Stanley, 109

Landon, Alfred E., 125
Landry, Lawrence, 264
Langford, Anna, 217, 262, 265
Laurino, Anthony, 101, 130
Lens, Sidney, 79
Levine, Edward M., 60, 64
Lewis, Ben, 23, 216
Liebling, A. J., 22–23
Lincoln, Abraham, 131,
Lohman, Joseph, 142–43, 146
Lucas, Robert, 264
Lynch, William, 49

McCarthy, Eugene, 159–60
McCutcheon, Barr, 103–4
McGovern, George, 73
McKibben, George B., 149
McMullen, Jay, 126–27, 190
McNeil, Duke, 264
Madison, James, 11, 87, 206
Mailer, Norman, 21
Mankowski, Steve, 167
Mann, Robert, 105, 197
Marcin, John C., 109, 128
Martin, John Bartlow, 176–77
Marzullo, Vito, 94, 109, 111–12, 115, 117–25, 128, 131, 171, 174, 187, 205, 215–17, 220, 283

Mason, Roswell B., 25
Mehler, Neil, 129
Mencken, Henry L., 210
Merriam, Charles E., 26, 214
Merriam, Robert, 149–51
Metcalfe, Ralph, 109, 262, 264, 272
Mikva, Abner, 105, 160, 197
Mill, John Stuart, 156
Mitchell, Steven, 143, 146–47
Morgenthau, Hans J., 129
Moynihan, Daniel Patrick, 61
Mullen, Mary, 91, 99
Murphy, Morgan, 47, 272
Murphy, William, 169
Muskie, Edmund, 124

Nash, Patrick, 258, 281
Neistein, Bernard, 10–11, 114–15, 126, 171, 261
New Deal, 15, 144, 155–56, 235, 243, 251, 257–58
Newhouse, Richard, 161, 264
Nihill, Edward, 53
Nixon, Richard M., 117, 125, 147, 177, 200–2

O'Donohue, James, 52
Ogilvie, Richard B., 101–2, 117, 148, 155, 174

Partee, Cecil, 94, 161, 262, 272
Paschen, Herbert, 46, 146
patronage system, 34–41, 112–16, 205–6
Pekkanen, John, 42
Percy, Charles, 147, 174, 182, 202, 272
Powers, Johnny, 216
Prince, Donald, 142
Pucinski, Roman, 109, 272

Quinn, Robert, 36, 47
Quigley, Edward, 122

Rayburn, Sam, 100
Rayner, A. A., 263
Redmond Plan, 67
Reichley, James, 99–100
Republican party (Illinois): fragmentation, 165
Ringer, Jack, 103
Robertson, Hayes, 174

Roman Catholic church: strength of, in Chicago, 31–32; support of black politicians, 268–69
Romano, Sam, 118, 120
Rooney, Edmund J., 24
Roosevelt, Franklin Delano, 125, 144, 151–52, 156, 176, 257–58
Root, Russell W., 149
Ropa, Matt, 118
Rosewell, Edward, 109
Rostenkowski, Dan, 94, 97, 109, 111, 161
Royko, Mike, 17, 45–46, 53, 77–78, 167, 216
Ryan, Dan, 46

Sandburg, Carl, 21
Savage, Augustus, 263
Sawyer, Eugene, 262
Scariano, Anthony, 105, 197
Scott, William, 174
Shannon, William, 262
Shapiro, Sam, 101, 105, 117, 124, 143, 148
Sheehan, Timothy P., 149, 173
Shriver, R. Sargent, 102–3, 143, 147
Simon, Paul, 102, 148–49, 154–55, 197
Simon, Ray, 50
Simon, Seymour, 100–1, 217–18
Simpson, Dick, 194, 197, 217
Singer, William, 151, 194, 197, 217
Smith, Adam, 84
Smith, Ralph, 126
Stead, William, 24, 214
Steffens, Lincoln, 22
Steinman, Sidney, 128
Stelle, John, 143
Stevenson, Adlai, 142–46, 157–58
Stevenson, Adlai III, 101–2, 105, 126, 143, 148, 160, 197
Stokes, Carl, 19
Stone, W. Clement, 188
Stratton, William G., 146–47, 154
Strauss, Robert, 73
Stroger, John, 109, 262
Sumner, William Graham, 63
Sutton, Percy, 19

Terkel, Studs, 16–17
Thompson, James R., 202
Thompson, William Hale ("Big Bill the Builder"), 25, 48–49, 257
Tocqueville, Alexis de, 80
Torrio, Johnny, 25

Touhy, John, 94
Truman, Harry, 144, 156

Udall, Morris K., 73
urban crisis: roots, 13
Utley, T. E., 74–75

Varchmin, Arthur W., 126–28
Viorst, Milton, 76
Vrdolyak, Edward, 94, 215

Walker, Dan, 102, 143–44, 154–55, 197
Waner, John, 149, 173

Ward, Daniel, 229–30
Washington, Harold, 197
Wendt, Lloyd, 26–27, 214
Wetten, Emil, 149
Wille, Lois, 187
Wilson, James Q., 192–93, 258, 260, 272,
   274–78
Wilsonian idealism, 151–52
Winkler, George, 128
Woods, L. C., 103–4
Wright, Edward H., 157

Yates, Sidney, 160–61
Young, Andrew, 264